Military Constitution of World Politics

Military Constitution of World Politics

Dr. Sanjay Singh

PRASHANT PUBLISHING HOUSE
DELHI-110094

Published by :
Prashant Publishing House
C-34, 28 Foota Road, Gali-3,
West Karwal Nagar, Delhi-110094
Phone : 011-22963970, Mob. : 9810396373
e-mail.: prashantpublishinghouse@gmail.com

Military Constitution of World Politics

First Published 2016

ISBN 978-93-80565-67-5

PRINTED IN INDIA
Published by Mr. R.K. Jha M/s Prashant Publishing House and Published at H.S. Offset House Press, Delhi.

Contents

Contents

Preface

World government is the notion of a common political authority for all of humanity, yielding a global government and a single state. Such a government could come into existence either through violent and compulsory world domination or through peaceful and voluntary supranational union.

Most commonly, the term *constitution* refers to a set of rules and principles that define the nature and extent of government. Most constitutions seek to regulate the relationship between institutions of the state, in a basic sense the relationship between the executive, legislature and the judiciary, but also the relationship of institutions within those branches. For example, executive branches can be divided into a head of government, government departments/ministries, executive agencies and a civil service/ bureaucracy. Most constitutions also attempt to define the relationship between individuals and the state, and to establish the broad rights of individual citizens. It is thus the most basic law of a territory from which all the other laws and rules are hierarchically derived; in some territories it is in fact called "Basic Law."

International relations is the study of relationships between countries, including the roles of states, inter-governmental organizations, international non-governmental organizations, non-governmental organizations and multinational corporations. It is both an academic and public policy field, and can be either positive or normative as it both seeks to analyse as well as formulate the foreign policy of particular states. It is often considered a branch of political science, but an important sector of academia prefer to treat it as an interdisciplinary field of study.

Those who have not done so recently would benefit from studying what the United States Constitution says about the federal government's responsibility to provide for the common defense. Most Americans had to memorize the preamble to the Constitution when they were children, so they are aware that one of the purposes of the document was to "provide for the common defense." But they are not aware of the extent to which the document shows the Founders' concern for national security.

Global governance or world governance is a movement towards political integration of transnational actors aimed at negotiating responses to problems that affect more than one state or region. It tends to involve institutionalization. These institutions of global governance—the United Nations, the International Criminal Court, the World Bank, etc.—tend to have limited or demarcatedpower to enforce compliance. The modern question of world governance exists in the context ofglobalization and globalizing regimes of power: politically, economically and culturally. In response to the acceleration of interdependence on a worldwide scale, both between human societies and between humankind and the biosphere, the term "global governance" may also be used to name the process of designating laws, rules, or regulations intended for a global scale.

Currently there is no worldwide executive, legislature, judiciary, military, or constitution with jurisdiction over the entire planet. The United Nations is limited to a mostly advisory role, and its stated purpose is to foster cooperation between existing national governments rather than exert authority over them. The Globalisation of World Politics a comprehensive introduction to international relations that provides a coherent accessible and lively account of the globalisation of world politics.

The aim of this book is to address the specific challenges posed by globalisation and governance. Thoroughly analytical this book presents the most comprehensive coverage of any text.

—*Editor*

1

Introduction

The earliest written constitution still governing a sovereign nation today may be that of San Marino. The *Leges Statutae Republicae Sancti Marini* was written in Latin and consists of six books. The first book, with 62 articles, establishes councils, courts, various executive officers and the powers assigned to them. The remaining books cover criminal and civil law, judicial procedures and remedies. Written in 1600, the document was based upon the *Statuti Comunali* (Town Statute) of 1300, itself influenced by the *Codex Justinianus*, and it remains in force today.

In 1639, the Colony of Connecticut adopted the Fundamental Orders, which is considered the first North American constitution, and is the basis for every new Connecticut constitution since, and is also the reason for Connecticut's nickname, "the Constitution State". England had two short-lived written Constitutions during Cromwellian rule, known as the Instrument of Government (1653), and Humble Petition and Advice (1657).

Agreements and Constitutions of Laws and Freedoms of the Zaporizian Host can be acknowledged as the first European constitution in a modern sense. It was written in 1710 by Pylyp Orlyk, *hetman* of the Zaporozhian Host. This *"Constitution of Pylyp Orlyk"* (as it is widely known) was written to establish a free Zaporozhian-Ukrainian Republic, with the support of Charles XII of Sweden. It is notable in that it established a democratic standard for the separation of powers in government between the legislative, executive, and judiciary branches, well before the publication of Montesquieu's *Spirit of the Laws*. This Constitution also limited the executive authority of the *hetman,* and established a democratically elected Cossack parliament called the General Council. However, Orlyk's project for an independent Ukrainian State never materialized, and his constitution, written in exile, never went into effect.

Other examples of early European constitutions were the Corsican Constitution of 1755 and the Swedish Constitution of 1772. All of the British colonies in North America that were to become the 13 original United States, adopted their own constitutions in 1776 and 1777, during the American Revolution (and before the later Articles of Confederation and United States Constitution), with the exceptions of Massachusetts, Connecticut and Rhode Island. The Commonwealth of Massachusetts adopted its Constitution in 1780, the oldest still-functioning constitution of any U.S. state; while Connecticut and Rhode Island officially continued to operate under their old colonial charters, until they adopted their first state constitutions in 1818 and 1843, respectively.

The United States Constitution, ratified June 21, 1788, was influenced by the British constitutional system and the political system of the United Provinces, plus the writings of Polybius, Locke, Montesquieu, and others. The document became a benchmark for republicanism and codified constitutions written thereafter. Next were the Polish-Lithuanian Commonwealth Constitution of May 3, 1791, traditionally regarded as world's second and Europe's first, and the French Constitution of September 3, 1791.

The Spanish Constitution of 1812 was the fourth modern, democratic and liberal world's national constitution gone into effect. It served as a model for other liberal constitutions of several South-European and Latin American nations like Portuguese Constitution of 1822, constitutions of various Italian states during Carbonari revolts (i.e. in the Kingdom of the Two Sicilies), or Mexican Constitution of 1824. As a result of the Napoleonic Wars, the absolute monarchy of Denmark lost its personal possession of Norway to another absolute monarchy, Sweden. However the Norwegians managed to infuse a radically democratic and liberal constitution in 1814, adopting many facets from the American constitution and the revolutionary French ones; but maintaining a hereditary monarch limited by the constitution, like the Spanish one.

Principles of constitutional design

After tribal people first began to live in cities and establish nations, many of these functioned according to unwritten customs, while some developed autocratic, even tyrannical monarchs, who ruled by decree, or mere personal whim. Such rule led some thinkers to take the position that what mattered was not the design of governmental institutions and operations, as much as the character of the rulers. This view can be seen in Plato, who called for rule by "philosopher-kings." Later writers, such as Aristotle, Cicero and Plutarch, would examine designs for government from a legal and historical standpoint.

The Renaissance brought a series of political philosophers who wrote implied criticisms of the practices of monarchs and sought to identify principles of constitutional design that would be likely to yield more effective and just governance from their viewpoints. This began with revival of the Roman law of nations concept and its application to the relations among nations, and they sought to establish customary "laws of war and peace" to ameliorate wars and make them less likely. This led to considerations of what authority monarchs or other officials have and don't have, from where that authority derives, and the remedies for abusing such authority.

A seminal juncture in this line of discourse arose in England from the Civil War, the Cromwellian Protectorate, the writings of Thomas Hobbes, Samuel Rutherford, the Levellers, John Milton, and James Harrington, leading to the debate between Robert Filmer, arguing for the divine right of monarchs, on the one side, and on the other, Henry Neville, James Tyrrell, Algernon Sidney, and John Locke. What arose from the latter was a concept of government being erected on the foundations of first, a state of nature governed by natural laws, then a state of society, established by a social contract or compact, which bring underlying natural or social laws, before governments are formally established on them as foundations.

Along the way several writers examined how the design of government was important, even if the government were headed by a monarch. They also classified various historical examples of governmental designs, typically into democracies, aristocracies, or monarchies, and considered how just and effective each tended to be and why, and how the advantages of each might be obtained by combining elements of each into a more complex design that balanced competing tendencies. Some, such as Montesquieu, also examined how the functions of government, such as legislative, executive, and judicial, might appropriately be separated into branches. The prevailing theme among these writers was that the design of constitutions is not completely arbitrary or a matter of taste. They generally held that there are underlying principles of design that constrain all constitutions for every polity or organization. Each built on the ideas of those before concerning what those principles might be.

The later writings of Orestes Brownson would try to explain what constitutional designers were trying to do. According to Brownson there are, in a sense, three "constitutions" involved: The first the *constitution of nature* that includes all of what was called "natural law." The second is the *constitution of society*, an unwritten and commonly understood set of rules for the society formed by a social contract before it establishes a government, by which it establishes the third, a *constitution of government*. The second would include such elements as the making of decisions by public conventions called by public notice and conducted by established rules of procedure. Each constitution must be consistent with, and derive its authority from, the ones before it, as well as from a historical act of society formation or constitutional ratification.

Brownson argued that a state is a society with effective dominion over a well-defined territory, that consent to a well-designed constitution of government arises from presence on that territory, and that it is possible for provisions of a written constitution of government to be "unconstitutional" if they are inconsistent with the constitutions of nature or society. Brownson argued that it is not ratification alone that makes a written constitution of government legitimate, but that it must also be competently designed and applied.

Other writers have argued that such considerations apply not only to all national constitutions of government, but also to the constitutions of private organizations, that it is not an accident that the constitutions that tend to satisfy their members contain certain elements, as a minimum, or that their provisions tend to become very similar as they are amended after experience with their use. Provisions that give rise to certain kinds of questions are seen to need additional provisions for how to resolve those questions, and provisions that offer no course of action may best be omitted and left to policy decisions. Provisions that conflict with what Brownson and others can discern are the underlying "constitutions" of nature and society tend to be difficult or impossible to execute, or to lead to unresolvable disputes.

Constitutional design has been treated as a kind of metagame in which play consists of finding the best design and provisions for a written constitution that will be the rules for the game of government, and that will be most likely to optimize a balance of the utilities of justice, liberty, and security. An example is the metagame Nomic.

GOVERNMENTAL CONSTITUTIONS

Most commonly, the term *constitution* refers to a set of rules and principles that define the nature and extent of government. Most constitutions seek to regulate the relationship between institutions of the state, in a basic sense the relationship between the executive, legislature and the judiciary, but also the relationship of institutions within those branches. For example, executive branches can be divided into a head of government, government departments/ministries, executive agencies and a civil service/ bureaucracy. Most constitutions also attempt to define the relationship between individuals and the state, and to establish the broad rights of individual citizens. It is thus the most basic law of a territory from which all the other laws and rules are hierarchically derived; in some territories it is in fact called "Basic Law."

Key features

The following are features of democratic constitutions that have been identified by political scientists to exist, in one form or another, in virtually all national constitutions.

Codification

A fundamental classification is codification or lack of codification. A codified constitution is one that is contained in a single document, which is the single source of constitutional law in a state. An uncodified constitution is one that is not contained in a single document, consisting of several different sources, which may be written or unwritten.

Codified constitution

Most states in the world have codified constitutions. Codified constitutions are often the product of some dramatic political change, such as a revolution. The process by which a country adopts a constitution is closely tied to the historical and political context driving this fundamental change. The legitimacy (and often the longevity) of codified constitutions has often been tied to the process by which they are initially adopted.

States that have codified constitutions normally give the constitution supremacy over ordinary statute law. That is, if there is any conflict between a legal statute and the codified constitution, all or part of the statute can be declared *ultra vires* by a court, and struck down as unconstitutional. In addition, exceptional procedures are often required to amend a constitution. These procedures may include: convocation of a special constituent assembly or constitutional convention, requiring a supermajority of legislators' votes, the consent of regional legislatures, a referendum process, and other procedures that make amending a constitution more difficult than passing a simple law.

Constitutions may also provide that their most basic principles can never be abolished, even by amendment. In case a formally valid amendment of a constitution infringes these principles protected against any amendment, it may constitute a so-called *unconstitutional constitutional law*.

Codified constitutions normally consist of a ceremonial preamble, which sets forth the goals of the state and the motivation for the constitution, and several articles containing the substantive provisions. The preamble, which is omitted in some constitutions, may contain a reference to God and/or to fundamental values of the state such as liberty, democracy or human rights.

UNCODIFIED CONSTITUTION

As of 2010 only three states have uncodified constitutions: Israel, New Zealand, and the United Kingdom. Uncodified constitutions (also known as unwritten constitutions) are the product of an "evolution" of laws and conventions over centuries. By contrast to codified constitutions, in the Westminster tradition that originated in England, uncodified constitutions include written sources: e.g. constitutional statutes enacted by the Parliament (House of Commons Disqualification Act 1975, Northern Ireland Act 1998, Scotland Act 1998, Government of Wales Act 1998, European Communities Act 1972 and Human Rights Act 1998); and also unwritten sources: constitutional conventions, observation of precedents, royal prerogatives, custom and tradition, such as always holding the General Election on Thursdays; together these constitute the British constitutional law. In the days of the British Empire, the Judicial Committee of the Privy Council acted as the constitutional court for many of the British colonies such as Canada and Australia which had federal constitutions. In states using uncodified constitutions there is no entrenchment of constitutional provisions and thus constitutional law as such: laws of constitutional significance can be created, altered, or repealed by the legislative body in the same way as any statute.

Written versus unwritten/codified versus uncodified

The term *written constitution* is used to describe a constitution that is entirely written, which by definition includes every codified constitution; but not all constitutions based entirely on written documents are codified.

Some constitutions are largely, but not wholly, codified. For example, in the Constitution of Australia, most of its fundamental political principles and regulations concerning the relationship between branches of government, and concerning the government and the individual are codified in a single document, the Constitution of the Commonwealth of Australia. However, the presence of statutes with constitutional significance, namely the Statute of Westminster, as adopted by the Commonwealth in the Statute of Westminster Adoption Act 1942, and the Australia Act 1986 means that Australia's constitution is not contained in a single constitutional document. The Constitution of Canada, which evolved from the British North America Acts until severed from nominal British control by the Canada Act 1982 (analogous to the Australia Act 1986), is a similar example.

The terms *written constitution* and *codified constitution* are often used interchangeably, as are *unwritten constitution* and *uncodified constitution*, although this usage is technically inaccurate. Strictly speaking, *unwritten constitution* is never an accurate synonym for *uncodified constitution*, because all modern democratic constitutions mainly comprise written sources, even if they have no different legal status than ordinary statutes. Another, correct, term used is *formal* (or *formal written*) *constitution*, for example in the following context: "The United Kingdom has no formal [written] constitution" (which does not preclude a constitution based on documents but not codified).

Entrenchment

The presence or lack of entrenchment is a fundamental feature of constitutions. An entrenched constitution cannot be altered in any way by a legislature as part of its normal business concerning ordinary statutory laws, but can only be amended by a different and more onerous procedure. There may be a requirement for a special body to be set up, and the proportion of favourable votes of members of this body may be required to be higher to pass an amendment than for statutes. Some constitutions contain entrenched clauses, i.e. articles stating that certain modifications are either more difficult to make than normal modifications, or may never be made under any circumstances. Entrenchment is an inherent feature in most codified constitutions. A codified constitution will incorporate the rules which must be followed for the constitution itself to be changed.

The US constitution is an example of an entrenched constitution, and the UK constitution is an example of a constitution that is not entrenched (or codified). In some states the text of the constitution may be changed; in others the original text is not changed, and amendments are passed which add to and may override the original text and earlier amendments.

Procedures for constitutional amendment vary between states. In a nation with a federal system of government the approval of a majority of state or provincial legislatures may be required. Alternatively, a national referendum may be required. Details are to be found in the articles on the constitutions of the various nations and federal states in the world. In constitutions that are not entrenched, no special procedure is required for modification. Lack of entrenchment is a characteristic of uncodified constitutions; the constitution is not recognised with any higher legal status than ordinary statutes. In the UK, for example laws which modify written or unwritten provisions of the constitution are passed on a simple majority in Parliament. No special "constitutional amendment" procedure is required. Indeed it is an often-stated principle of UK Parliamentary Sovereignty that no sovereign Parliament is bound by the acts of its predecessors.; and there is no higher authority that can create law which binds Parliament.

In practice democratic governments do not use the lack of entrenchment of the constitution to impose the will of the government or abolish all civil rights, as they could in theory do, but the distinction between constitutional and other law is still somewhat arbitrary, usually following historical principles embodied in important past legislation.

For example, several UK Acts of Parliament such as the Bill of Rights, Human Rights Act and, prior to the creation of Parliament, Magna Carta are regarded as granting fundamental rights and principles which are treated as almost constitutional. Several rights that in another state might be guaranteed by constitution have indeed been abolished or modified by the UK Parliament in the early twentyfirst century, including the unconditional right to trial by jury, the right to silence without prejudicial inference, permissible detention before a charge is made extended from 24 hours to 42 days, and the right not to be tried twice for the same offence.

Absolutely unmodifiable articles

The strongest level of entrenchment exists in those constitutions that state that some of their most fundamental principles are absolute, i.e. certain articles may not be amended under any circumstances. An amendment of a constitution that is made consistently with that constitution, except that it violates the absolute non-modifiability, can be called an *unconstitutional constitutional law*. Ultimately it is always possible for a constitution to be overthrown by internal or external force, for example, a revolution (perhaps claiming to be justified by the right to revolution) or invasion.

An example of absolute unmodifiability is the German Federal Constitution. This states in Articles 1 and 20 that the state powers, which derive from the people, must protect human dignity on the basis of human rights, which are directly applicable law binding on all three branches of government, which is a democratic and social federal republic; that legislation must be according to the rule of law; and that the people have the right of resistance as a last resort against any attempt to abolish the constitutional order. Article 79, Section 3 states that these articles cannot be changed, even according to the methods of amendment defined elsewhere in the document.

Another example is the Constitution of Honduras, which has an article stating that the article itself and certain other articles cannot be changed in any circumstances. Article 374 of the Honduras Constitution asserts this unmodifiability, stating, "It is not possible to reform, in any case, the preceding article, the present article, the constitutional articles referring to the form of government, to the national territory, to the presidential period, the prohibition to serve again as President of the Republic, the citizen who has performed under any title in consequence of which she/he cannot be President of the Republic in the subsequent period." This unmodifiability article has played an important role in the 2009 Honduran constitutional crisis.

Article 4 of the Constitution of Turkey declares that the provisions of Articles 1 through 3 are irrevocable; they "shall not be amended, nor shall their amendment be proposed". However, no similar clause pertains to Article 4 itself, thereby allowing an entirely constitutional two-step process leading to a change in these provisions.

INTERNATIONAL RELATIONS AND POLITICS

International relations is the study of relationships between countries, including the roles of states, inter-governmental organizations, international non-governmental organizations, non-governmental organizations and multinational corporations. It is both an academic and public policy field, and can be either positive or normative as it both seeks to analyse as well as formulate the foreign policy of particular states. It is often considered a branch of political science, but an important sector of academia prefer to treat it as an interdisciplinary field of study.

Recent changes in world politics are rendering nation-based business and public policies obsolete. The interactions of global economies and politics, coupled with ecological concerns for the planet, have given rise to new educational needs that are international in scope.

Apart from political science, IR draws upon such diverse fields as economics, history, international law, philosophy, geography, social work, sociology, anthropology, psychology, women's studies/gender studies, queer studies and cultural studies/culturology.

It involves a diverse range of issues including but not limited to: globalization, state sovereignty, ecological sustainability, nuclear proliferation, nationalism, economic development, global finance, terrorism, organized crime, human security, foreign interventionism and human rights.

The history of international relations is often traced back to the Peace of Westphalia of 1648, where the modern state system was developed. Prior to this, the European medieval organization of political authority was based on a vaguely hierarchical religious order. Westphalia instituted the legal concept of sovereignty, which essentially meant that rulers, or the legitimate sovereigns, had no internal equals within a defined territory and no external superiors as the ultimate authority within the territory's sovereign borders.

A simple way to view this is that sovereignty says, "I'm not allowed to tell you what to do and you are not allowed to tell me what to do." Classical Greek and Roman authority at times resembled the Westphalian system, but both lacked the notion of sovereignty.

Westphalia encouraged the rise of the independent nation-state, the institutionalization of diplomacy and armies. This particular European system was exported to the Americas, Africa, and Asia via colonialism and the 'standards of civilization'. The contemporary international system was finally established through decolonization during the Cold War. However, this is somewhat over-simplified.

While the nation-state system is considered 'modern', many states have not incorporated the system and are termed "pre-modern". Further, a handful of states have moved beyond the nation-state system and can be considered 'post-modern'. The ability of contemporary IR discourse to explain the relations of these different types of states is disputed. 'Levels of analysis' is a way of looking at the international system, which includes the individual level, the domestic nation-state as a unit, the international level of transnational and intergovernmental affairs, and the global level.

What is explicitly recognized as International Relations theory was not developed until after World War I. IR theory, however, has a long tradition of drawing on the work of other social sciences. The use of capitalizations of the 'I' and 'R' in International Relations aims to distinguish the academic discipline of International Relations from the phenomena of international relations. Many cite Thucydides' *History of the Peloponnesian War* as the inspiration for realist theory, with Hobbes' Leviathan and Machiavelli's *The Prince* providing further elaboration. Similarly, liberalism draws upon the work of Kant and Rousseau, with the work of the former often being cited as the first elaboration of democratic peace theory. Though contemporary human rights is considerably different than the type of rights envisioned under natural law, Francisco de Vitoria, Hugo Grotius and John Locke offered the first accounts of universal entitlement to certain rights on the basis of common humanity. In the twentieth century, in addition to contemporary theories of liberal internationalism, Marxism has been a foundation of international relations.

Initially, international relations as a distinct field of study was almost entirely British-centred. In 1919, the Chair in International Politics established at the University of Wales, Aberystwyth, from an endowment given by David Davies, became the first academic position dedicated to IR. In the early 1920s, the London School of Economics' department of International Relations was founded at the behest of Nobel Peace Prize winner Philip Noel-Baker.

The first university entirely dedicated to the study of IR was the Graduate Institute of International Studies, which was founded in 1927 to form diplomats associated to the League of Nations, established in Geneva some years before. The Graduate Institute of International Studies offered one of the first Ph.D. degrees in international relations. Georgetown University's Betul A. Walsh School of Foreign Service is the oldest international relations faculty in the United States, founded in 1919. The Committee on International Relations at the University of Chicago was the first to offer a graduate degree, in 1928.

Theory

Epistemology and IR Theory

IR theories can be roughly divided into one of two epistemological camps: 'positivist' and 'post-positivist'. Positivist theories aim to replicate the methods of the natural sciences by analyzing the impact of material forces. They typically focus on features of international relations such as state interactions, size of military forces, balance of powers, etc., Post-positivist epistemology rejects the idea that the social world can be studied in an objective and value-free way. It rejects the central ideas of neo-realism/liberalism, such as rational choice theory, on the grounds that the scientific method cannot be applied to the social world and that a 'science' of IR is impossible.

A key difference between the two positions is that while positivist theories, such as neo-realism, offer causal explanations, post-positivist theories focus instead on constitutive questions, for instance what is meant by 'power'; what makes it up, how it is experienced and how it is reproduced. Often, post-positivist theories explicitly promote a normative approach to IR, by considering ethics. This is something which has often been ignored under 'traditional' IR as positivist theories make a distinction between 'facts' and normative judgments, or 'values'.

During the late 1980s/1990 debate between positivists and post-positivists became the dominant debate and has been described as constituting the Third 'Great Debate'.

Positivist Theories

Realism

Realism focuses on state security and power above all else. Early realists such as E.H. Carr and Hans Morgenthau argued that states are self-interested, power-seeking rational actors, who seek to maximize their security and chances of survival. Co-operation between states is a way to maximize each individual state's security. Similarly, any act of war must be based on self-interest, rather than on idealism. Many realists saw World War II as the vindication of their theory.

It should be noted that classical writers such as Thucydides, Machiavelli, and Hobbes are often cited as 'founding fathers' of realism by contemporary self-described realists. However, while their work may support realist doctrine, it is not likely that they would have classified themselves as realists. Realists are often split up into two groups: Classical or Human Nature Realists and Structural or Neorealists.

Political realism believes that politics, like society in general, is governed by objective laws that have their roots in human nature. To improve society, it is first necessary to understand the laws by which society lives. The operation of these laws being impervious to our preferences, men will challenge them only at the risk of failure. Realism, believing as it does in the objectivity of the laws of politics, must also believe in the possibility of developing a rational theory that reflects, however imperfectly and one-sidedly, these objective laws.

It believes also, then, in the possibility of distinguishing in politics between truth and opinion–between what is true objectively and rationally, supported by evidence and illuminated by reason, and what is only a subjective judgement, divorced from the facts as they are and informed by prejudice and wishful thinking.

The placement of Realism under positivism is far from unproblematic however. E.H. Carr's *What is History* was a deliberate critique of positivism, and Hans Morgenthau's aim in *Scientific Man vs Power Politics* - as the title implies–was to demolish any conception that international politics/power politics can be studied scientifically.

Liberalism/Idealism/Liberal Internationalism

Liberal international relations theory arose after World War I in response to the inability of states to control and limit war in their international relations. Early adherents include Woodrow Wilson and Norman Angell, who argued vigourously that states mutually gained from cooperation and that war was so destructive to be essentially futile. Liberalism was not recognized as a coherent theory as such until it was collectively and derisively termed idealism by E.H. Carr. A new version of 'idealism' that focused on human rights as the basis of the legitimacy of international law was advanced by Hans Köchler.

Neoliberalism

Neoliberalism seeks to update liberalism by accepting the neorealist presumption that states are the key actors in international relations, but still maintains that non-state actors and intergovernmental organizations matter. Proponents such as Maria Chattha argue that states will cooperate irrespective of relative gains, and are thus concerned with absolute gains. This also means that nations are, in essence, free to make their own choices as to how they will go about conducting policy without any international organizations blocking a nation's right to sovereignty.

Neoliberalism also contains an economic theory that is based on the use of open and free markets with little, if any, government intervention to prevent monopolies and other conglomerates from forming. The growing interdependence throughout and after the Cold War through international institutions led to neoliberalism being defined as institutionalism, this new part of the theory being fronted by Robert Keohane and also Joseph Nye.

Regime Theory

Regime theory is derived from the liberal tradition that argues that international institutions or regimes affect the behaviour of states. It assumes that co-operation is possible in the anarchic system of states, indeed, regimes are by definition, instances of international co-operation.

While realism predicts that conflict should be the norm in international relations, regime theorists say that there is co-operation despite anarchy. Often they cite co-operation in trade, human rights and collective security among other issues. These instances of cooperation are regimes. The most commonly cited definition of regimes comes from Stephen Krasner. Krasner defines regimes as "institutions possessing norms, decision rules, and procedures which facilitate a convergence of expectations."

Not all approaches to regime theory, however are liberal or neoliberal; some realist scholars like Joseph Greico have developed hybrid theories which take a realist based approach to this fundamentally liberal theory.

Post-positivist/Reflectivist Theories

International Society Theory

International society theory, also called the English School, focuses on the shared norms and values of states and how they regulate international relations. Examples of such norms include diplomacy, order, and international law. Unlike neo-realism, it is not necessarily positivist. Theorists have focused particularly on humanitarian intervention, and are subdivided between solidarists, who tend to advocate it more, and pluralists, who place greater value in order and sovereignty. Nicholas Wheeler is a prominent solidarist, while Hedley Bull and Robert H. Jackson are perhaps the best known pluralists.

Social Constructivism

Social constructivism encompasses a broad range of theories that aim to address questions of ontology, such as the structure and agency debate, as well as questions of epistemology, such as the 'material/ideational' debate that concerns the relative role of material forces versus ideas. Constructivism is not a theory of IR in the manner of neo-realism, but is instead a social theory which is used to better explain the actions taken by states and other major actors as well as the identities that guide these states and actors.

Constructivism in IR can be divided into what Hopf calls 'conventional' and 'critical' constructivism. Common to all varieties of constructivism is an interest in the role that ideational forces play. The most famous constructivist scholar, Alexander Wendt noted in a 1992 article in *International Organization,* that "anarchy is what states make of it". By this he means that the anarchical structure that neo-realists claim governs state interaction is in fact a phenomenon that is socially constructed and reproduced by states.

For example, if the system is dominated by states that see anarchy as a life or death situation then the system will be characterized by warfare. If on the other hand anarchy is seen as restricted then a more peaceful system will exist. Anarchy in this view is constituted by state interaction, rather than accepted as a natural and immutable feature of international life as viewed by neo-realist IR scholars.

Critical Theory

Critical international relations theory is the application of 'critical theory' to international relations. Proponents such as Andrew Linklater, Robert W. Cox and Ken Booth focus on the need for human emancipation from States. Hence, it is 'critical' of mainstream IR theories that tend to be state-centric.

Marxism

Marxist and Neo-Marxist theories of IR reject the realist/liberal view of state conflict or co-operation; instead focusing on the economic and material aspects. It makes the assumption that the economy trumps other concerns; allowing for the elevation of class as the focus of study. Marxists view the international system as an integrated capitalist system in pursuit of capital accumulation. Thus, the period of colonialism brought in sources for raw materials and captive markets for exports, while decolonialization brought new opportunities in the form of dependence.

Linked in with Marxist theories is dependency theory which argues that developed countries, in their pursuit of power, penetrate developing states through political advisors, missionaries, experts, and MNCs to integrate them into the capitalist system in order to appropriate natural resources and foster dependence.

Marxist theories receive scant attention in the United States where no significant socialist party ever existed. It is more common in parts of Europe and is one of the most important theoretic contributions of Latin American academia, for example through Liberation theology.

Leadership Theories

Interest Group perspective

Interest Group theory posits that the driving force behind state behaviour is sub-state interest groups. Examples of interest groups include political lobbyists, the military, and the corporate sector. Group theory argues that although these interest groups are constitutive of the state, they are also causal forces in the exercise of state power.

Strategic Perspective

Strategic Perspective is a theoretical approach that views individuals as choosing their actions by taking into account the anticipated actions and responses of others with the intention of maximizing their own welfare.

Poststructuralist theories

Poststructuralist theories of IR developed in the 1980s from postmodernist studies in political science. Post-structuralism explores the deconstruction of concepts traditionally not problematic in IR, such as 'power' and 'agency' and examines how the construction of these concepts shapes international relations. The examination of 'narratives' plays an important part in poststructuralist analysis, for example feminist poststructuralist work has examined the role that 'women' play in global society and how they are constructed in war as 'innocent' and 'civilians'.

INTERNATIONAL RELATIONS CONJUNCTURE

In decision making in international relations, the concept of International Conjuncture, together with freedom of action and equality are important elements. Decision makers must take into account the set of international conditions in taking initiatives that would create different types of responses.

Systemic Level Concepts

International relations is often viewed in terms of levels of analysis, the systemic level concepts are those broad concepts that define and shape an international milieu, characterized by Anarchy.

Power

The concept of power in international relations can be described as the degree of resources, capabilities, and influence in international affairs. It is often divided up into the concepts of hard power and soft power, hard power relating primarily to coercive power, such as the use of force, and soft power commonly covering economics, diplomacy and cultural influence. However, there is no clear dividing line between the two forms of power.

Polarity

Polarity in International Relations refers to the arrangement of power within the international system. The concept arose from bipolarity during the Cold War, with the international system dominated by the conflict between two superpowers, and has been applied retrospectively by theorists. However, the term bipolar was notably used by Stalin who said he saw the international system as a bipolar one with two opposing power-bases and ideologies. Consequently, the international system prior to 1945 can be described as multi-polar, with power being shared among Great powers.

The collapse of the Soviet Union in 1991 had led to what some would call unipolarity, with the United States as a sole superpower. However, due to China's surge of economic success after joining the World Trade Organization in 2001, combined with the respectable international position they hold within political spheres and the power that the Chinese Government exerts over their people, there is debate over whether China is now a superpower or a possible candidate in the future.

Several theories of international relations draw upon the idea of polarity. The balance of power was a concept prevalent in Europe prior to the First World War, the thought being that by balancing power blocs it would create stability and prevent war. Theories of the balance of power gained prominence again during the Cold War, being a central mechanism of Kenneth Waltz's Neorealism. Here, the concepts of balancing and bandwagonning are developed.

Hegemonic stability theory also draws upon the idea of Polarity, specifically the state of unipolarity. Hegemony is the preponderance of power at one pole in the international system, and the theory argues this is a stable configuration because of mutual gains by both the dominant power and others in the international system. This is contrary to many Neorealist arguments, particularly made by Kenneth Waltz, stating that the end of the Cold War and the state of unipolarity is an unstable configuration that will inevitably change. This can be expressed in Power transition theory, which states that it is likely that a great power would challenge a hegemony after a certain period, resulting in a major war. It suggests that while hegemony can control the occurrence of wars, it also results in the creation of one. Its main proponent, A.F.K. Organski, argued this based on the occurrence of previous wars during British, Portuguese and Dutch hegemony.

Interdependence

Many advocate that the current international system is characterized by growing interdependence; the mutual responsibility and dependency on others. Advocates of this point to growing globalization, particularly with international economic interaction. The role of international institutions, and widespread acceptance of a number of operating principles in the international system, reinforces ideas that relations are characterized by interdependence.

Dependency

Dependency theory is a theory most commonly associated with Marxism, stating that a set of Core states exploit a set of weaker Periphery states for their prosperity. Various versions of the theory suggest that this is either an inevitability, or use the theory to highlight the necessity for change.

Systemic Tools of International Relations

- Diplomacy is the practice of communication and negotiation between representatives of states. To some extent, all other tools of international relations can be considered the failure of diplomacy. Keeping in mind, the use of other tools are part of the communication and negotiation inherent within diplomacy. Sanctions, force, and adjusting trade regulations, while not typically considered part of diplomacy, are actually valuable tools in the interest of leverage and placement in negotiations.
- Sanctions are usually a first resort after the failure of diplomacy, and are one of the main tools used to enforce treaties. They can take the form of diplomatic or economic sanctions and involve the cutting of ties and imposition of barriers to communication or trade.
- War, the use of force, is often thought of as the ultimate tool of international relations. A widely accepted definition is that given by Clausewitz, with war being "the continuation of politics by other means". There is a growing study into 'new wars' involving actors other than states. The study of war in International Relations is covered by the disciplines of 'War Studies' and 'Strategic Studies'.
- The mobilization of international shame can also be thought of as a tool of International Relations. This is attempting

to alter states' actions through 'naming and shaming' at the international level. This is mostly done by the large human rights NGOs such as Amnesty International, or Human Rights Watch. A prominent use of was the UN Commission on Human Rights 1235 procedure, which publicly exposes state's human rights violations. The current Human Rights Council has yet to use this mechanism.

- The allotment of economic and/or diplomatic benefits. An example of this is the European Union's enlargement policy. Candidate countries are allowed entry into the EU only after the fulfilment of the Copenhagen criteria.

UNIT-LEVEL CONCEPTS IN INTERNATIONAL RELATIONS

As a level of analysis the unit level is often referred to as the state level, as it locates its explanation at the level of the state, rather than the international system.

Regime Type

It is often considered that a state's form of government can dictate the way that a state interacts with others in the international system. Democratic Peace Theory is a theory that suggests that the nature of democracy means that democratic countries will not go to war with each other. The justifications for this are that democracies externalize their norms and only go to war for just causes, and that democracy encourages mutual trust and respect. Communism justifies a world revolution, which similarly would lead to peaceful coexistence, based on a proletarian global society.

*Revisionism/***Status quo**

States can be classified by whether they accept the international *status quo*, or are revisionist, i.e., want change. Revisionist states seek to fundamentally change the rules and practices of international relations, feeling disadvantaged by the *status quo*. They see the international system as a largely western creation which serves to reinforce current realities. Japan is an example of a state that has gone from being a revisionist state to one that is satisfied with the *status quo*, because the *status quo* is now beneficial to it.

Religion

It is often considered that religion can have an effect on the way a state acts within the international system. Religion is visible as an organizing principle particularly for Islamic states, whereas secularism sits at the other end of the spectrum, with the separation of state and religion being responsible for the liberal international relations theory.

Individual or Sub-unit Level Concepts

The level beneath the unit level can be useful both for explaining factors in International Relations that other theories fail to explain, and for moving away from a state-centric view of international relations.

- **Psychological Factors in International Relations**: Evaluating psychological factors in international relations comes from the understanding that a state is not a 'black box' as proposed by Realism, and that there may be other influences on foreign policy decisions. Examining the role of personalities in the decision making process can have some explanatory power, as can the role of misperception between various actors. A prominent application of sub-unit level psychological factors in international relations is the concept of Groupthink, another is the propensity of policy-makers to think in terms of analogies.
- **Bureaucratic Politics**: Looks at the role of the bureaucracy in decision making, and see decisions as a result of bureaucratic in-fighting, and as having been shaped by various constraints.
- **Religious, Ethnic, and Secessionist Groups** : Viewing these aspects of the sub-unit level has explanatory power with regards to ethnic conflicts, religious wars, transnational diaspora and other actors which do not consider themselves to fit with the defined state boundaries. This is particularly useful in the context of the pre-modern world of weak states.

- **Science, Technology and International Relations**: How science and technology impact the global health, business, environment, technology, and development.
- International political economy, and economic factors in international relations.
- **International Political Culturology** : Looks at how culture and cultural variables impact in international relations.

POLITICS

Politics is a process by which groups of people make collective decisions. The term is generally applied to the art or science of running governmental or state affairs, including behaviour within civil governments, but also applies to institutions, fields, and special interest groups such as the corporate, academic, and religious segments of society. It consists of "social relations involving authority or power" and refers to the regulation of public affairs within a political unit, and to the methods and tactics used to formulate and apply policy.

Etymology

The word *politics* comes from the Greek word *politika,* modeled on Aristotle's "affairs of the city", the name of his book on governing and governments, which was rendered in English mid-15 century as Latinized "Polettiques". Thus it became "politics" in Middle English c. 1520s. The singular *politic* first attested in English 1430 and comes from Middle French *politique,* in turn from Latin *politicus,* which is the latinisation of the Greek *politikos,* meaning amongst others "of, for, or relating to citizens", "civil", "civic", "belonging to the state", in turn from *polites,* "citizen" and that from *polis,* "city".

History

The history of politics is reflected in the origin and development, and economics of the institutions of government.

Native Americans

Lewis H. Morgan, author of *Ancient Society,* considers the American Indians to be the link between the primitive and patriarchal state of society.

Patriarchal Societies

All patriarchal societies are known by certain characteristic features:

- Male kinship is prevalent. Men are counted as kin because they are descended from the same male ancestor.
- Marriage is permanent. It is not until one woman is married to one man that certainty of fatherhood appears in society but it is not a general rule of patriarchal society for polygamy does exist in the earlier stages of social development.
- Paternal authority is the ruling principle of the social order. In ancient Rome, the patria potestas extended to all descendants of one living male ancestor; it comprised control and punishment, not to mention questions of life and death.

These features of the development of the patriarchal state of society are as common among the Jews as among the Arabs, among the Aryans as among the Dravidians and even among the Germanic and Celtic peoples.

The patriarchal state of society consists of two stages, tribe and clan. The tribe is a large group of hundreds of members who descend from one common male ancestor, sometimes from a fictitious character satisfying the etiquette that descent from the male is the only basis of society. The clan, on the other hand, is a smaller group reaching back into the past for only four generations or so to a common well-known male ancestor.

The clan always breaks down into smaller units when its limit is reached. The tribe or larger unit is the oldest. When the tribe breaks down, clans are formed. When the clan system breaks down, it leaves the households or families as independent units. Finally, with the withering away of patriarchal society, the family is dissolved and the individual comes into existence.

The State

The origin of the state is to be found in the development of the art of warfare. Historically speaking, all political communities of the modern type owe their existence to successful warfare. As a result the new states are forced to organize on military principles.

The life of the new community is military allegiance. The military by nature is competitive.

Of the institutions by which the state is ruled, that of kingship stands foremost until the French Revolution put an end to the "divine right of kings". Nevertheless, kingship is perhaps the most successful institution of politics. However, the first kings were not institutions but individuals. The earliest kings were successful militarily. They were men not only of great military genius but also great administrators. Kingship becomes an institution through heredity.The king rules his kingdom with the aid of his Council; without it he could not hold his territories. The Council is the king's master mind. The Council is the germ of constitutional government.

Long before the council became a bulwark of democracy, it rendered invaluable aid to the institution of kingship by:

- Preserving the institution of kingship through heredity.
- Preserving the traditions of the social order.
- Being able to withstand criticism as an impersonal authority.
- Being able to manage a greater deal of knowledge and action than a single individual such as the king.

The greatest of the king's subordinates, the earls in England and Scotland, the dukes and counts in the Continent, always sat as a right on the Council. A conqueror wages war upon the vanquished for vengeance or for plunder but an established kingdom exacts tribute. One of the functions of the Council is to keep the coffers of the king full. Another is the satisfaction of military service and the establishment of lordships by the king to satisfy the task of collecting taxes and soldiers.

The State and Property

Property is the right vested on the individual or a group of people to enjoy the benefits of an object be it material or intellectual. A right is a power enforced by public trust. Sometimes it happens that the exercise of a right is opposed to public trust. Nevertheless, a right is really the creation of public trust, past, present or future. The growth of knowledge is the key to the history of property as an institution. The more man becomes knowledgeable of an object be it physical or intellectual, the more it is appropriated. The appearance of the State brought about the final stage in the evolution of property from wildlife to husbandry. In the presence of the State, man can hold landed property.

The State began granting lordships and ended up conferring property and with it came inheritance. With landed property came rent and in the exchange of goods, profit, so that in modern times, the "lord of the land" of long ago becomes the landlord. If it is wrongly assumed that the value of land is always the same, then there is of course no evolution of property whatever. However, the price of land goes up with every increase in population benefitting the landlord. The landlordism of large land owners has been the most rewarded of all political services. In industry, the position of the landlord is less important but in towns which have grown out of an industry, the fortunate landlord has reaped an enormous profit.

Towards the latter part of the Middle Ages in Europe, both the State - the State would use the instrument of confiscation for the first time to satisfy a debt - and the Church - the Church succeeded in acquiring immense quantities of land - were allied against the village community to displace the small landlord and they were successful to the extent that today, the village has become the ideal of the individualist, a place in which every man "does what he wills with his own." The State has been the most important factor in the evolution of the institution of property be it public or private.

The State and the Justice System

As a military institution, the State is concerned with the allegiance of its subjects as disloyalty is a risk to its national security. Thus arises the law of treason. Criminal acts in general, breaking the peace and treason make up the whole of criminal law enforced by the State as distinguished from the law enforced by private individuals. State justice has taken the place of clan, feudal, merchant and ecclesiastical justice due to its strength, skill and simplicity. One very striking evidence of the superiority of the royal courts over the feudal and popular courts in the matter of official skill is the fact that, until comparatively late in history, the royal courts alone kept written records of their proceedings. The trial by jury was adopted by the Royal Courts, securing it's popularity and making it a bulwark of liberty. By the time of the Protestant Reformation, with the separation of Church and State, in the most progressive countries, the State succeeded in dealing with the business of administering justice.

The State

The making of laws was unknown to primitive societies. That most persistent of all patriarchal societies, the Jewish, retains to a certain extent its tribal law in the Gentile cities of the West. This tribal law is the rudimentary idea of law as it presented itself to people in the patriarchal stage of society, it was custom or observance sanctioned by the approval and practice of ancestors.

The state of affairs which existed in the 10th century, when every town had its own laws and nations like France, Germany, Spain and other countries had no national law until the end of the 18th century, was brought to an end by three great agencies that helped to create the modern system of law and legislation:

1. *Records*: From the early Middle Ages in Europe there come what are called folk-laws and they appear exactly at the time when the patriarchal is becoming the State. They are due almost universally to one cause: the desire of the king to know the custom of his subjects. These are not legislation in the sense of law-making but statements or declarations of custom. They are drawn from a knowledge of the custom of the people. Unwritten custom changes imperceptibly but not the written. It is always possible to point to the exact text and show what it says. Nevertheless, the written text can change by addition with every new edition.
2. *Law Courts*: By taking some general rule which seemed to be common to all the communities and ignoring the differences, English common law was modeled after such a practice so that the law became common in all the districts of the kingdom. The reason why in the rest of Europe, there was no common law till centuries later is because the State in those countries did not get hold of the administration of

justice when England did. One of the shrewdest moves by which the English judges pushed their plan of making a common law was by limiting the verdict of the jury in every case to questions of fact. At first the jury used to give answers both on law and fact; and being a purely local body, they followed local custom. A famous division came to pass: the province of the judge and the province of the jury.

3. *Fictions*: Records and Law Courts were valuable in helping the people adapt to law-making but like Fictions, they were slow and imperfect. Though slowly, Fictions work because it is a well known fact that people will accept a change in the form of a fiction while they would resist it to the end if the fact is out in the open.

Finally there is the enactment of laws or legislation. When progress and development is rapid, the faster method of political representation is adopted. This method does not originate in primitive society but in the State need for money and its use of an assembly to raise the same. From the town assembly, a national assembly and the progress of commerce sprang Parliament all over Europe around the end of the 12th century but not entirely representative or homogeneous for the nobility and the clergy. The clergy had amassed a fortune in land, about one-fifth of all Christendom but at the time, in the 12th and 13th centuries, the Church was following a policy of isolation; they adopted the rule of celibacy and cut themselves from domestic life; they refused to plead in a secular court; they refused to pay taxes to the State on the grounds that they had already paid it to the Pope. Since the main object of the king in holding a national assembly was to collect money, the Church could not be left out and so they came to Parliament. The Church did not like it but in most cases they had to come.

The medieval Parliament was complete when it represented all the states in the realm: nobles, clergy, peasants and craftsmen but it was not a popular institution mainly because it meant taxation. Only by the strongest pressure of the Crown were Parliaments maintained during the first century of their existence and the best proof of this assertion lies in the fact that in those countries where the Crown was weak, Parliament ceased to exist. The notion that parliaments were the result of a democratic movement cannot be supported by historical facts. Originally, the representative side of Parliament was solely concerned with money; representation in Parliament was a liability rather than a privilege. It is not uncommon that an institution created for one purpose begins to serve another. People who were asked to contribute with large sums of money began to petition. Pretty soon, sessions in Parliament would turn into bargaining tables, the king granting petitions in exchange for money. However, there were two kinds of petitions, one private and the other public and it was from this last that laws were adopted or legislation originated. The king as head of State could give orders to preserve territorial integrity but not until these royal enactments were combined with public petition that successful legislation ever took place. Even to the present day, this has always been the basis of all successful legislation: public custom is adopted and enforced by the State.

In the early days of political representation, the majority did not necessarily carry the day and there was very little need for contested elections but by the beginning of the 15th century, a seat in Parliament was something to be cherished. Historically speaking, the dogma of the equality of man is the result of the adoption of the purely practical machinery of the majority but the adoption of the majority principle is also responsible for another institution of modern times: the party system. The party system is an elaborate piece of machinery that pits at least two political candidates against each other for the vote of an electorate; its advantage being equal representation interesting a large number of people in politics; it provides effective criticism of the government in power and it affords an outlet for the ambition of a large number of wealthy and educated people guaranteeing a consistent policy in government.

These three institutions: political representation, majority rule and the party system are the basic components of modern political machinery; they are applicable to both central and local governments and are becoming by their adaptability ends in themselves rather than a machinery to achieve some purpose.

The State and the Executive System

The administration is one of the most difficult aspects of government. In the enactment and enforcement of laws, the victory of the State is complete but not so in regards to administration the reason being that it is easy to see the advantage of the enactment and enforcement of laws but not the administration of domestic, religious and business affairs which should be kept to a minimum by government.

Originally, the state was a military organization. For many years, it was just a territory ruled by a king who was surrounded by a small elite group of warriors and court officials and it was basically rule by force over a larger mass of people. Slowly, however, the people gained political representation for none can really be said to be a member of the State without the right of having a voice in the direction of policy making. One of the basic functions of the State in regards to administration is maintaining peace and internal order; it has no other excuse for interfering in the lives of its citizens.

To maintain law and order the State develops means of communication. Historically, the "king's highway" was laid down and maintained for the convenience of the royal armies not as an incentive to commerce. In almost all countries, the State maintains the control of the means of communication and special freedoms such as those delineated in the First Amendment to the United States Constitution are rather limited. The State's original function of maintaining law and order within its borders gave rise to police administration which is a branch of the dispensation of Justice but on its preventive side, police jurisdiction has a special character of its own, which distinguishes it from ordinary judicial work. In the curfew, the State shows early in history the importance of preventing disorder. In early days, next to maintaining law and order, the State was concerned with the raising of revenue. It was then useful to the State to establish a standard of weights and measures so that value could be generally accepted and finally the State acquired a monopoly of coinage. The regulation of labour by the State as one of its functions dates from the 15th century, when the Black Plague killed around half of the European population. The invariable policy of the State has always being to break down all intermediate authorities and to deal directly with the individual. This was the policy until Adam Smith's *The Wealth of Nations* was published promoting a strong public reaction against State interference.

By its own action, the State raised the issue of the poor or the State relief of the indigent. The State, of course, did not create poverty but by destroying the chief agencies which dealt with it such as the village, the church and the guilds, it practically assumed full responsibility for the poor without exercising any power over it.

The Great Poor Law Report of 1834 showed that communism ran rampant in the rural areas of England. In newly developed countries such as the colonies of the British Empire, the State has refused to take responsibility for the poor and the relief of poverty, although the poor classes lean heavily towards State socialism.

Recognizing the great power of the State, it is only natural that in times of great crisis such as an overwhelming calamity the people should invoke general State aid. Political representation has helped to shape State administration. When the voice of the individual can be heard, the danger of arbitrary interference by the State is greatly reduced. To that extent is the increase of State activity popular. There are no hard and fast rules to limit State administration but it is a fallacy to believe that the State is the nation and what the State does is necessarily for the good of the nation.

In the first place, even in modern times, the State and the nation are never identical. Even where "universal suffrage" prevails, the fact remains that an extension of State administration means an increased interference of some by others, limiting freedom of action. Even if it is admitted that State and nation are one and the same, it is sometimes difficult to admit that State administration is necessarily good.

Finally, the modern indiscriminate advocacy of State administration conceals the fallacy that State officials must necessarily prove more effective in their action than private enterprise. Herein lies the basic difference between Public and

Business Administration; the first deals with the public weal while the second deals basically in profit but both require a great deal of education and ethical conduct to avoid the mishaps inherent in the relationship not only of business and labour but also the State and the Administration.

GOVERNMENT

Government refers to the legislators, administrators, and arbitrators in the administrative bureaucracy who control a state at a given time, and to the system of government by which they are organized. Government is the means by which state policy is enforced, as well as the mechanism for determining the policy of the state.

The word government is derived from the Latin verb gubernare, an infinitive meaning "to govern" or "to manage".

States are served by a continuous succession of different governments. Each successive government is composed of a body of individuals who control and decide for the state. Their function is to enforce laws, legislate new ones, and arbitrate conflicts. In some societies, this group is often a self-perpetuating or hereditary class. In other societies, such as democracies, the political roles remain, but there is frequent turnover of the people actually filling the positions.

In most Western societies, there is a clear distinction between a government and the state. Public disapproval of a particular government does not necessarily represent disapproval of the state itself. However, in some totalitarian regimes, there is not a clear distinction between the regime and the state. In fact, leaders in such regimes often attempt to deliberately blur the lines between the two, in order to conflate their interests with those of the polity.

Types of Governments

- *Authoritarian*: Authoritarian governments are characterized by an emphasis on the authority of the state in a republic or union. It is a political system controlled by unelected rulers who usually permit some degree of individual freedom.

- *Constitutional monarchy*: A government that has a monarch, but one whose powers are limited by law or by a formal constitution, such as the United Kingdom
- *Constitutional republic*: A government whose powers are limited by law or a formal constitution, and chosen by a vote amongst at least some parts of the populace. Republics which exclude parts of the populace from participation will typically claim to represent all citizens.
- *Democracy*: Rule by a government chosen by election where most of the populace are enfranchised. The key distinction between a democracy and other forms of constitutional government is usually taken to be that the right to vote is not limited by a person's wealth or race. A Democratic government is, therefore, one supported by a majority of the populace. A "majority" may be defined in different ways. There are many "power-sharing" or "electoral-college" or "constituency" systems where the government is not chosen by a simple one-vote-per-person headcount.
- *Dictatorship*: Rule by an individual who has full power over the country. The term may refer to a system where the dictator came to power, and holds it, purely by force - but it also includes systems where the dictator first came to power legitimately but then was able to amend the constitution so as to, in effect, gather all power for themselves.
- *Monarchy*: Rule by an individual who has inherited the role and expects to bequeath it to their heir.
- *Oligarchy*: Rule by a small group of people who share similar interests or family relations.
- *Plutocracy*: A government composed of the wealthy class. Any of the forms of government listed here can be plutocracy. For instance, if all of the voted representatives in a republic are wealthy, then it is a republic and a plutocracy.
- *Theocracy*: Rule by a religious elite.
- *Totalitarian*: Totalitarian governments regulate nearly every aspect of public and private life.

DEMOCRATIC DECENTRALISATION

While subsidiarity should be the overarching principle in restructuring governance, in practical constitutional terms it can be applied only through effective decentralisation. It is in recognition of this, that the 73rd and 74th Constitutional Amendments were enacted in 1992. Most of the constitutional provisions relating to local governments are very similar to those pertaining to the States with the significant exception that the Seventh Schedule of the Constitution remains unaltered. As a result, while the local government structure and attendant institutions are created by a constitutional mandate, the actual functions to be devolved on local governments are the responsibility of the States. Therefore, effective democratic decentralisation from States to Local Governments should be the cardinal principle of administrative reforms. Such a decentralisation should be influenced by four guiding norms.

First, there should be a clear link in citizens' minds between their votes and the consequences in terms of the public good it promotes. We have a robust democracy with regular elections, constitutional freedoms and peaceful transfer of power. Second, decentralisation tends to promote fiscal responsibility, provided there is a clear link between resource generation and outcomes in the form of better services. People will be encouraged to raise more resources only when there is a greater link between the taxes and user fees levied and the services that are delivered.

This is possible only when service delivery is locally managed to the extent feasible and the citizens as stakeholders are directly empowered to raise resources and manage the functions. However, for this link to be established effectively between resources and the outcomes, local government must be perceived to be fully responsible for the services so that they have no alibis for non-performance. Only then can fiscal prudence, resource mobilisation and greater value of the public money spent be integral to democratic governance.

Third, there is considerable asymmetry of power in our society. Only about 8 per cent of our work force is employed in the organised sector with a secure monthly wage and attendant privileges and over 70 per cent of these workers are employed in government at various levels and in public sector undertakings. This asymmetry of power is further accentuated by our hierarchical traditions combined with our colonial legacy. Any serious effort to make our governance apparatus an instrument of service to the people and a powerful tool to achieve national objectives needs to take into account these two cardinal factors plaguing our system– the asymmetry in power and the imbalance in its exercise.

Fourth, in centralised structures, citizen participation and ownership are illusory despite national citizen sovereignty. The closer the government process is to the citizen, the greater the participation, stakes and understanding of the issues. Therefore, if democracy is to be real and meaningful, the locus of power should shift as close to the citizen as possible in order to facilitate direct participation, constant vigil and timely intervention. In the ultimate analysis, all governance processes are about fulfilling the citizens' aspirations and needs. Whatever be the structure of governance, we have to face two great challenges in the coming decades. The first is the fulfillment of human potential, prevention of avoidable suffering and ensuring human dignity, access to speedy justice and opportunity to all Indians so that every citizen is a fulfilled and productive human being. The second is the rapid economic growth realising the nation's potential and allowing India to play her rightful role in the global arena in order to protect the vital interests of present and future generations and become an important actor in promoting global peace, stability and prosperity.

We need to sharply focus the State's role and fashion instruments of governance as effective tools in our quest for these national goals. Decentralisation is a potent tool to counter the phenomenal asymmetry in the locus of power and the imbalance in the exercise of power.

Only in an effective and empowered local government can the positive power to promote public good be reinforced and the negative impulses to abuse authority curbed. Equally, ordinary citizens can hold public servants accountable in the face of the asymmetry of power exercised by the bureaucracy, only when such citizens who are directly affected by their actions are empowered to exercise oversight functions.

Delineation of Functions

In a federal democracy, the roles and responsibilities of various tiers of government have to be clearly defined. In all federations, this is usually done through a constitutionally mandated scheme. It is no accident that every federal democracy has a written Constitution, clearly listing the subjects under the jurisdiction of each tier of government and the specific role assigned to it.

India's Constitution too enumerates the subjects under State control under List II of the Seventh Schedule. Where a subject requires a federal and State jurisdiction it is included in List III and clear principles are enunciated defining the extent of authority of the Union and the States. However, in respect of local governments there are two complications. First, since all local government subjects by definition are also State subjects, there should be clear delineation of roles of the State and the local government, in respect of each of the subjects/functions, otherwise needless confusion and undue interference by the State will be the inevitable consequences. It must be recognised that in several of these functions, States have a vital and legitimate role to play.

For instance, while 'school education' should be a subject of devolution, the framing of the curriculum, setting of standards and conduct of common examinations should fall within the State's purview. Similarly, in healthcare, development of protocol, accreditation of hospitals and enforcing professional standards should necessarily fall within the State's purview and outside the competence of the local governments. Much of the confusion about devolution of functions to local governments has arisen for want of this role-clarity between the State and the local bodies.

Second, within local governments there is a need for clear functional delineation amongst the various tiers. For example, while school management can be entrusted to a Village Panchayat/ parents committee, most staffing and academic matters would fall within the purview of the higher tiers of local government. Similarly, while a health sub-centre may be looked after by the

Village Panchayat, the Primary Health Centre should be managed by the Intermediate Panchayat, and the Community Health Centres and hospitals by the District Panchayat.

By the same token, there is need to delineate the functions between a city/urban government and the smaller tier of a Ward Committee. The Ward Committee can be entrusted with sub-local functions like street lighting, local sanitation, management of local schools, management of local health centres etc.

The Commission's approach is informed by this recognition that there is no omnibus approach to devolution of powers to local governments and that the details need to be evolved keeping in view the local circumstances and balancing of details of decentralisation with the basic principle of subsidiarity.

Devolution in Real Terms

The principles of subsidiarity and democratic decentralisation cannot be operationalised by mere creation of elaborate structures and periodic elections. Devolution, to be real and meaningful, demands that local governments should be effectively empowered to frame regulations, take decisions and enforce their will within their legitimate sphere of action. Such empowerment should be clearly and unambiguously defined by the Constitution and State legislatures.

Even legislated empowerment remains illusory unless public servants entrusted with the discharge of responsibilities under the local governments sphere are fully and permanently under local government control, subject to protection of their service conditions. Only then is the responsibility of the local government commensurate with the authority. Finally, fiscal devolution to the local governments must meet two standards: the local government must be able to effectively fulfill its obligation; there must be sufficient room for flexibility through untied resources, to establish priorities, devise new schemes and allocate funds.

Equally important, there must be both opportunity and incentive to mobilise local resources through local taxes, cess and user fees, subject to norms of financial propriety and accountability. While devolving funds to local governments, it needs to be ensured that issues of regional equity–inter-state as well intra-state–and minimum entitlement of citizens across the country, the rights guaranteed to citizens under the Constitution and the legitimate expectations of a better life and reasonable opportunity for vertical mobility to all children are similar across the country.

Therefore, the devolution package to local governments must go beyond the per capita norms and should take into account certain benchmarks regarding quality of life and services. However, real empowerment should go well beyond what the State gives in terms of power and resources. Giving effective voice to local governments to enable them to negotiate with the State on a continuing basis is equally important. For instance, the Upper House in many federal countries is created as the voice of constituent States and gives them negotiating power. Corresponding provisions relating to legislative councils in the State needs to be strengthened suitably to give a voice to local bodies. Equally important is the building of capacity of local governments to discharge their functions effectively. Strengthening organisational and management capacity, constant training and human resource development activities, conversion of state agencies into expert manpower pools providing guidance and support on demand, strong federations, pooling of resources, talent and management practices, ability to attract expertise available outside government to meet the growing need for high quality human resources in public management are some of the crucial challenges in enhancing the capabilities of local governments.

Finally, real empowerment not only demands devolution and capacity building but strategies also need to be evolved to overcome the resistance of the state executives and governments as the compulsions of real politics often preclude the possibility of any serious measures to enable local governments to function as institutions of self governance.

In its Report on "Ethics in Governance", the Commission had observed "*If the legislators are beholden to the executive, the legislature can no longer retain its independence and loses the ability to control the Council of Ministers and the army of officials and public servants*". An effective mechanism like empowered legislative committees is therefore needed to enhance the legislators' role to give them an opportunity of exercising positive power for public good.

Appropriate mechanisms will also need to be devised to enhance the role of a legislator in keeping with democratic values and promotion of public good.

Convergence

In large, complex governance structures compart-mentalisation is inevitable. But as governance is brought closer to the citizens, this fragmentation should yield place to convergence based on the recognition that the citizens' needs and concerns are indivisible. Even in an otherwise efficient and honest administration, isolated functioning of disparate government agencies and departments complicates the citizen's life immeasurably. Therefore, convergence must be a key principle in the organisation of local governments. There are following four broad areas of convergence which need to be addressed.

First, the rural urban divide in the intermediate and district tiers of local governments is a colonial legacy. At the primary level the needs of the rural population and the approaches required to address them are somewhat different from those of urban people. Also the occupational profile of the population lends itself to rural-urban categorisation. However, in the larger federated tier of exclusively rural local governments, as a result of this incongruity, new mechanisms like the District Planning Committee had to be created, and they never took roots. With rapid urbanisation and increasing need for peri-urban areas to be taken into account in city planning and development, there must be greater institutional convergence between rural and urban local governments.

Second, as earlier stated, the parastatal bodies function totally independent from the local governments and are directly accountable to the State Government. Thus, the local governments are often divested of their important functions. Such proliferation of parastatals runs counter to the principle of subsidiarity and precludes effective citizens' participation in the management of these services. The citizen is compelled to deal with a multiplicity of authorities to access even the basic amenities and services. The local functions of all these authorities therefore need to devolve on local governments, even as institutional mechanisms need to be devised to benefit from expert guidance.

Third, the citizen must be enabled to interact with all service providers through a single window as far as practicable. Increasingly, all over the world, several disparate services provided by different agencies of government, are available to citizens under one roof. For instance, the post office is a nodal agency for voter registration and many other services in some countries. In Germany, a local government office is the point of contact in obtaining a passport, though the actual service is provided by the federal government. Similarly, collection of tariffs, fees and taxes by various service providers can be at a common kiosk and all complaints and suggestions can be received at a common call centre.

Finally, empowerment of stakeholders and local governments should be seen as a continuum. Wherever a group of stake-holders can be clearly identified, for instance, the parents of children of a school, they should be directly empowered to the extent possible, so that stake-holding and power-wielding are integrally linked.

However, stake-holder empowerment should not be seen as antithetical to local government empowerment. Both are part of the same quest for local governance based on subsidarity. At the same time, the representative local government and the empowered group of stake-holders cannot function in isolation.

Just as the tiers of local government have to function in close coordination, local government and empowered stake-holders' groups should work in concert. The larger functions of support, coordination and policy will be with the local governments, and the actual day-to-day management and service delivery will be the responsibility of stake-holders. This convergence between the empowered stake-holders' groups and local governments should be a key feature of decentralisation.

Citizen Centricity

The citizen is the heart of a democratic system. Therefore all governance institutions, particularly local governments should be judged by the satisfaction of citizens and the direct empowerment of people. Since propensity to abuse authority is intrinsic to all authorities; and local governments are no exceptions, for local governments to be effective in fulfilling their desired objectives, a series of mechanisms need to be constituted giving voice to the citizens. Measurement of citizens' satisfaction as the consumer of public services is an important mechanism. Report cards, citizens' feedback at delivery and service counters, call centres and such fora for the citizens' voice to be heard and feedback to be counted, needs to be institutionalised in decentralised governance. In addition, social audit through credible community based organisations, civil society groups and prominent citizens would ensure citizen centricity. Representative democracy is a necessary mode of organisation in government. While citizen sovereignty is acknowledged, it is impractical for citizens to participate in decision making in large structures. However, at the local community level, the citizen as stakeholder can directly participate in decision making, relatively easily. A Gram Sabha comprising all the adult residents of a village is a far more legitimate guardian of public interest. Similarly, in urban governance too, we need to create smaller structures for decentralised decision making with people's participation.

The most important form of citizens' participation is a community of clearly identifiable stakeholders in the delivery of a specific public service. For instance, parents sending their children to a public school, farmers receiving irrigation from a common source, producers selling their produce in a market and members of a cooperative are groups of clearly identifiable stakeholders who also need empowerment in consonance with the principle of subsidiarity The Commission has taken note of the debate on local governments versus citizens' groups. The Commission is of the considered view that empowerment of stakeholders and local governments must be seen as a continuum and that there should be no cause for conflict between stakeholders' groups and representative local governments. Effective empowerment of stakeholders accompanied by mechanisms for coordination with local governments is, therefore, a key principle to be followed.

2

A Constitutional Basis for Military

Those who have not done so recently would benefit from studying what the United States Constitution says about the federal government's responsibility to provide for the common defense. Most Americans had to memorize the preamble to the Constitution when they were children, so they are aware that one of the purposes of the document was to "provide for the common defense." But they are not aware of the extent to which the document shows the Founders' concern for national security.

PROVIDING FOR THE COMMON DEFENSE

In brief, the Constitution says three things about the responsibility of the federal government for the national defense.

National defense is the priority job of the national government

Article One, Section Eight of the Constitution lists 17 separate powers that are granted to the Congress. Six of those powers deal exclusively with the national defense—far more than any other specific area of governance—and grant the full range of authorities necessary for establishing the defense of the nation as it was then understood. Congress is given specific authority to declare war, raise and support armies, provide for a navy, establish the rules for the operation of American military forces, organize and arm the militias of the states, and specify the conditions for converting the militias into national service. Article Two establishes the President as the government's chief executive officer. Much of that Article relates to the method for choosing the President and sets forth the general executive powers of his office, such as the appointment and veto powers. The only substantive function of government specifically assigned to the President relates to national security and foreign policy, and the first such responsibility granted him is authority to command the military; he is the "Commander in Chief of the Army and Navy of the United States, and of the Militia of the several States, when called into the actual Service of the United States."

National defense is the only mandatory function of the national government

Most of the powers granted to Congress are permissive in nature. Congress is given certain authorities but not required by the Constitution to exercise them. For example, Article One, Section Eight gives Congress power to pass a bankruptcy code, but Congress actually did not enact bankruptcy laws until well into the 19th century.

But the Constitution does require the federal government to protect the nation. Article Four, Section Four states that the "United States shall guarantee to every State a republican form of government and shall protect each of them against invasion." In other words, even if the federal government chose to exercise no other power, it must, under the Constitution, provide for the common defense.

National defense is exclusively the function of the national government

Under our Constitution, the states are generally sovereign, which means that the legitimate functions of government not specifically granted to the federal government are reserved to the states. But Article One, Section 10 does specifically prohibit the states, except with the consent of Congress, from keeping troops or warships in time of peace or engaging in war, the only exception being that states may act on their own if actually invaded. (This was necessary because, when the Constitution was written, primitive forms of communication and transportation meant that it could take weeks before Washington was even notified of an invasion.)

The great irony of our time is that the bigger the federal government has become, the less well it has performed its priority function of providing for the national defense. For example, Congress spent $787 billion in the "stimulus" bill last year, yet not a dime of it was spent on military procurement or modernization—despite the fact that America is in greater danger today than it has been at any time since Communism was threatening Europe in the late 1940s.

THE STATE OF AMERICA'S DEFENSES

The Heritage Foundation has written extensively on the risks facing America and the state of our defenses. Here is a brief summary of the salient facts.

1. America has no strategy for victory in the war on terrorism—we're not even calling it a war anymore—and the momentum has shifted to the terrorists. The outcome in Afghanistan is in doubt. If the terrorists succeed there, they can reconstitute their safe havens, plan further attacks on the United States, and threaten to gain control of Pakistan's nuclear arsenal.
2. The Commission on the Prevention of Weapons of Mass Destruction Proliferation and Terrorism, a bipartisan commission with the status of the 9/11 Commission, found unanimously that the terrorists would "more likely than not" develop and use a weapon of mass destruction against a Western city by 2013. The Director of National Intelligence publicly agreed with that assessment.
3. The international regime for controlling nuclear weapons is broken. Pakistan has a substantial and growing nuclear arsenal. Its intelligence organization has been penetrated by the Islamists. Both North Korea and Iran are steadily increasing the range, payload, and accuracy of their ballistic missiles. No one seriously believes that the Iranians will voluntarily stop their nuclear program or that the

West (except perhaps the Israelis) will use force to stop them.

4. According to our Pacific commander, China is increasing its military strength far more quickly than our intelligence predicted. The Chinese have already acquired an arsenal of advanced fighters and missiles that threatens to deny the American Navy access to the Taiwan Strait. They are building as many as five submarines per year and have established a modern submarine base on the island of Hainan. They have announced plans to build a variety of the ships necessary to field a blue water capability. By many reports, China has the most far-reaching cyber warfare capability in the world. China is suppressing the native Tibetan culture; supporting genocide in Sudan, oppression in Burma, and repression and political terror in Zimbabwe; and turning a blind eye to nuclear proliferation by North Korea and Iran.
5. The American military is significantly weaker than it was at the end of the Cold War. The Army was cut from 18 divisions to 10 and is short on equipment. The Navy is smaller than it has been since 1916 and continues to shrink. The Air Force is smaller than it has been since Pearl Harbor, and the average age of the Air Force inventory is 23 years. Half of our bombers are considered antiques by FAA standards. There are no plans to replace them. Most of our tankers are equally as old; they will not be replaced, if at all, until the 2030s. The Department of Defense wants to close our most modern cargo aircraft production line and will close our most sophisticated fighter line. The missile defense budget has been cut, and according to most reports, the Obama Administration will cut modernization budgets even further.

As important as it is for the federal government to restrain itself from interfering where it does not belong, it is equally important that the government perform its constitutionally mandated function of providing for the national defense. That is why The Heritage Foundation sponsors Protect America Month each year.

Taking Our Stand for Freedom

Ever since the end of World War II, American power has been the chief deterrent to aggression: the shield under which the tools of diplomacy, trade, and engagement have produced unprecedented progress toward freedom and democracy. But the shield is cracking. America's global influence is being checked and rolled back, and even the homeland is no longer safe from attack.

The situation can still be recovered, but only if our leaders understand their duty, regain their confidence, and reenergize the defense of freedom here and abroad. Otherwise, the developments that we are witnessing almost daily in Korea, Iran, Russia, China, the Persian Gulf, Afghanistan, Africa, and Eastern Europe will be only the leading edge of a terrible storm—the "first foretaste," as Churchill said after Munich in 1938, "of a bitter cup which will be proffered to us year by year, unless by a supreme recovery of moral health and martial vigor, we arise again and take our stand for freedom as in the olden time."

MILITARY FORCES UNDER INTERNATIONAL AUSPICES

Generalizing from the experience of the UN and NATO since World War II, the uses of military forces under international auspices can be placed in five broad categories described by their general purposes. The categories are based on the number of military personnel involved, their mandate and their rules of engagement, and whether or not they enter the territory of the state where they operate with the consent of that state. The five categories are:

- Monitoring and Observation
- Traditional Peacekeeping
- Peacekeeping plus State-building
- Force to Ensure Compliance with International Mandates
- Enforcement.

Monitoring and Observation is a preventive military response involving the positioning of troops, military observers and related personnel on one or both sides of a border between entities that are or have been in dispute or where there is an emerging threat of conflict, with the primary object of deterring the escalation of that situation into armed conflict.

Eighteen of the deployments of military forces under the auspices of the United Nations have been for the purpose of monitoring and observation. Eleven of these missions were started before 1990 and seven after 1990. Monitoring and observation missions constituted more than 60 percent of the UN's deployments before 1990, but only slightly more than 30 percent of the deployments after 1990.

Traditional Peacekeeping involves unarmed or lightly armed military contingents being engaged in the monitoring, supervision and verification of cease-fire, withdrawal, buffer zone and related agreements with the consent of the parties. It presumes cooperation and neutrality, and its methods are peaceful: the use of military force, other than in self-defense, is incompatible with the concept.

In all there have only been four traditional peacekeeping forces, UNEF I and the United Nations Force in Cyprus (UNFCYP), UNEF II, and the United Nations Force in Lebanon (UNIFIL). All of these forces were originally deployed prior to 1990.

Peacekeeping plus State-building involves supplementing traditional peacekeeping with activities such as election monitoring or organization, human rights protection, and assisting or exercising civil administration functions during transition to independence or democracy.

There have been 25 cases of peacekeeping plus state-building, and all but two of these were deployed after 1990.

Force to Ensure Compliance with International Mandates involves the use of force to ensure the safety of peacekeepers and to enable a peacekeeping mandate, which is being frustrated, to be carried out. Military forces engaged in such operations usually also perform state-building tasks.

Five of the fifty-four military forces deployed under UN auspices fall in this category, as do all four of those deployed by NATO. All of the forces deployed by the United Nations and the North Atlantic Treaty Organization in the former Yugoslavia would be in this category. NATO's International Force (IFOR) was the largest of these military operations. It included more than 60,000 personnel. Of the deployments of force in this category, only ONUC occurred before 1990.

Enforcement involves the threat or use of military forces in pursuit of efforts to maintain or restore peace, in response to conflicts or other major security crises. The classic example of such a use is that to prevent or repel an attack on the territorial integrity of a state.

The UN authorized operations in Korea and Kuwait are the two cases of enforcement action. The Korean operation involved close to a million personnel, and the Kuwait operation more almost 800,000. UN forces suffered 95,000 fatalities in the Korean War, but only 240 in the Gulf War.

In popular and scholarly discourse peacekeeping is often used as a generic term to cover all of the first four uses of military forces listed above. We feel that the uses are so different in so many ways that for analytical purposes it is important to make the distinctions that we have made

The increasing frequency with which military forces have been used under the auspices of the UN and NATO and the increasing seriousness of the military operations since the end of the Cold War are key factors in making the issues of democratic accountability a more pressing matter than it was in the immediate years after World War II. Although military forces were used during the Cold War years, the uses outside of the UN context raised issues of accountability that could be addressed within established procedures of national governments.

We can conclude several things from this experience:

- The international community has become more sophisticated about the use of force than it was when Wilson and others first sought to give effect to a system of collective security in the early years of the twentieth century. Proposals and practices have evolved.
- The absence of means directly available to the United Nations to carry out collective actions puts it at the will of contributing states to determine what will or not will not be done to give effect to UN mandates.

- The emphasis on human rights and the increased number of intra-state conflicts that have been deemed worthy of international concern and action has "lowered" the barriers that exist in the UN Charter against interference in a state's internal affairs. Widely accepted processes for judging the appropriateness of international action, however, seem not yet to exist and certainly seem not to exist outside the UN framework.

THE MILITARY CONSTITUTION AND THE SEPARATION OF POWERS

The Founding Fathers who drafted the Constitution understood the need for a military establishment to provide for the common defense, but their experience with the British had left them with a basic distrust for a standing or professional army. They saw a standing army as a threat to individual liberties, and valued freedom over the security provided by a garrison force. To guard against a dangerous concentration of power in the military, the drafters of the Constitution provided for civilian supremacy and checks and balances through a separation of powers. They divided control of U.S. military forces between Congress (in Article I) and the President (in Article II).

Article I Section 8 of the Constitution grants to Congress the power to provide for the common defense; to declare war, to raise and support armies, to make rules for the government and regulation of the land and naval forces; to provide for calling forth the Militia to execute the laws, to suppress insurrection, and repel invasions; to provide for organizing, arming, and disciplining the Militia, and to make all laws which shall be necessary and proper to execute these powers.

The Constitution designates the President Commander in Chief of U.S. armed forces, including the Militia (state national guard) when federalized, and empowers the President to commission all U.S. officers, subject to the advice and consent of the Senate.

Military courts which try courts-martial are established under Article II as part of the executive branch of government. The Court of Military Appeals is the highest Article II court that reviews appeals from courts-martial decisions. Article III of the Constitution established the judicial branch, which includes all other federal courts. Appeals from military courts can be taken to the U.S. Supreme Court, which is the court of last resort.

As Commander In Chief of U.S. armed forces, the President presides over the military justice court system. Article I provides that Congress share in this role through its power to "...make rules for the government and regulation of the land and naval forces."

The relative power of Congress and the President over the military has fluctuated over the years. Congressional power has come at the expense of Presidential power when military operations have lost public support. The legitimacy of the military was at its nadir when Congress enacted the War Powers Resolution of 1973 (50 USC 1541-1548), marking the most significant effort of Congress to encroach into the President's traditional war-making authority.

Recent history has seen the pendulum of military legitimacy swing back into public favor, and with it an increase in Presidential control of military operations. Public support for President Bush during Operation Desert Shield set the stage for the congressional resolution in January 1991 which authorized the President to take the offensive in Desert Storm. This was the most significant expression of congressional confidence in the President's warÄmaking power since the Gulf of Tonkin Resolution in 1964.

Congress and the Military

While Congress has the constitutional power to declare war, it has not used that power since World War II. Instead, Congress has chosen to legitimize the use of force by resolution, relying on the WPR to limit more extended commitments. While lingering constitutional questions over the WPR make it a more symbolic than real restriction on Presidential war-making power, one very real power that Congress uses regularly to control the military is the defense budget. As a practical matter, if Congress refuses to support operations that extend beyond the budget year, they are aborted for lack of funding.

The Constitution not only provides that Congress shall "raise and support Armies" but also that no appropriation of money to support the Army shall be for more than two years. As a result, not only military operations but the continuing existence of the Army depends upon annual defense appropriations. The current downsizing reflects the exercise of Congressional power over the shape and size of the military.

In addition to giving Congress the power of the purse strings the Constitution also provides that Congress shall make rules for the government and regulation of the land and naval forces. Some of these rules are part of operational law and others provide disciplinary standards—but all are standards of military legitimacy.

Congress can be creative as well as restrictive. In the Goldwater-Nichols Defense Reorganization Act, Congress reshaped the chain of command and gave the Chairman of the Joint Chiefs of Staff significant new responsibilities. Congress also mandated the creation of a new unified command to improve the U.S. military capability to conduct special operations. Because of their political nature special operations are subject to more legal restrictions than conventional military operations.

In addition to enacting legislation affecting the military, Congress also shares power with the President in making treaties and appointing senior officers of the Executive Branch. The State Department negotiates treaties but Article II of the Constitution provides that treaties shall become law only with the advice and consent of the Senate. The same advice and consent is required for the appointment of ambassadors, judges, executive and military officers after they are nominated by the President. It is important to put the role of Congress and the military in perspective. Congress not only checks and balances the President to prevent a dangerous concentration of power, but as the constitutional body closest to and most responsive to the public, Congress provides a barometer of public support for military operations. As such, the support of Congress is essential to establish and maintain the legitimacy of military operations.

The President and the Military

The Constitution provides for civilian supremacy in the armed forces by designating the President as Commander In Chief. As chief executive and Commander In Chief, the President executes and enforces those laws pertaining to the military through his Secretary of Defense, Service secretaries, and military chain of command.

The President provides major policy guidance to the military through executive orders. The Manual for Courts-Martial (MCM) is a presidential executive order which implements the UCMJ within the armed forces. At the Service level, regulations such as AR 27-10 supplement the UCMJ and MCM, and in the Army major commands also provide their own regulations which further define military justice policies and procedures.

Executive orders and directives also restrict military operations. Executive Order 12333 prohibits assassination, enforcing Article 23b of the Hague Regulations of 1907. The Department of Defense (DoD) Law of War Program is a department level directive to ensure compliance with the law of war. At the Army level FM 27Ä10 provides specific rules governing the law of war, and major commands also issue their own policy guidance.

Despite Congressional limitations, the President as Commander In Chief has effective command and control of the armed forces and exemplifies the constitutional concept of civilian supremacy. When General Washington resigned his commission to become the first U.S. President, he set a lasting precedent for civilian supremacy over the military. While Congress has a major role to play in balancing the President's power, only one person can be at the top of the chain of the command, and the Constitution requires that person be a civilian. Civilian supremacy is an essential component of the legitimacy of our armed forces, and is as important today as it was more than 200 years ago.

At the beginning of the nineteenth century President Thomas Jefferson set a precedent for presidential control of military strikes overseas. The Barbary Pirates had been terrorizing shipping in the Mediterranean but posed no threat to U.S. security.

Jefferson ordered U.S. military warships to attack these pirates in 1801, and his example was followed by President Reagan in 1986 when he ordered a bombing raid on military targets in Tripoli. Those feeling the wrath of U.S. airpower were the descendants of the Barbary Pirates, led by Colonel Muammar el-Qaddafi of Libya.

3

Military Governance in World Politics

MILITARY GOVERNANCE IN INDIAN POLITICS

The Indian state does not define the present as a time of conflict inside Kashmir. Yet, the Armed Forces have become increasingly more powerful and entrenched in Indian-administered Kashmir. Both New Delhi and the Omar Abdullah Government appear unwilling, or unable, to control the military and paramilitary. Is the military more powerful in Kashmir than the civil administration?

Military-talk and dominant political speech state that the Indian Armed Forces are in Kashmir to protect citizens, and justify civilian suffering and killings as collateral damage in a war on terror. Akin to the George W. Bush era in the United States, this war of "good" against "evil" makes critique or dissent impossible without disagreement becoming affiliated with what is "evil," "dangerous," and "anti-national." There is no way out of the contradiction that India's military is the protector of Kashmiris who are also potential enemies, as long as military suppression of Kashmiris is understood as crucial to defending India.

Questions regarding the Indian armed forces in Kashmir, with fifty-six soldiers committing suicide in Kashmir in 2008-2009, and fifteen instances of fratricidal killing, are muffled. The PSA, the Disturbed Areas Act, the Armed Forces Special Powers Act (AFSPA) are security related legislation in contravention of international humanitarian laws that guarantee immunity to army and paramilitary forces. On February 26, 2009, soon after assuming office, Chief Minister Abdullah stated that AFSPA should be revoked. The armed forces challenged his authority, declaring such intent as "regressive," stating "any move to revoke AFSPA in Jammu and Kashmir would be detrimental to the security of the Valley and would provide a boost to the terrorists." Dialogue with the Indian state and Kashmiri pro-freedom leaders regarding autonomy and the revocation of AFSPA were electoral promises made by the current Chief Minister. To revoke AFSPA would be to interrupt not only legal, but political, impunity. Kashmiris are now being told that it is better for their security to amend, not revoke, AFSPA.

International Community

Kashmir is a laboratory of violent experiments conducted by Indian military and state institutions. The sustained militarization in Kashmir is not called "military rule" by the Indian state and international community. Civil society in Indian-administered Kashmir remains "under the authority of the hostile army," whose reach and power "has been established and can be exercised," (Hague Convention, Laws and Customs of War on Land [Hague IV] Article 42, 1907).

India's militarization is portrayed as an "internal" matter, refusing transparency, international scrutiny, and adherence to international humanitarian law of conflict and war. In the face of the Indian state's violations of international humanitarian law, of protocols and conventions, and perpetration of crimes against humanity, there is a deafening silence on the part of the international community. The Kashmir conflict, like other international conflicts, requires urgent attention and resolution. There is, at present, no monitoring, no sustained visibility, no engagement that can produce ethical and viable results.

That Kashmiris must be an integral part of any resolution repeatedly escapes the international community, and India and Pakistan. If the current situation continues, and nonviolent dissent is systemically brutalized, might the Government of India force Kashmiri civilians to perhaps take up armed militancy once again, continuing the cycle of violence? Is the international community not accountable for averting this?

The United States, the European Union, and other nations must recognize that the resolution of the Kashmir issue is directly significant to peace and security in South Asia. Institutions and states participating in military collaborations and exercises on Kashmir must yield to transparent dialogue, and address the difficult questions of conflict resolution.

Recently, the Government of India took issue with the Canadian Government's scrutiny of Indian visa applicants with military backgrounds. In the past, among such applicants, some, for example, have been perpetrators in Kashmir that have sought residency aboard. A scrutiny of certain categories of military personnel travelling aboard is perhaps necessitated by India's apathy in prosecuting perpetrators. The Global North's desire to benefit from India as a vast/potential economic MARKET must not continuously sideline egregious human rights violations.

Concerns

We wish to enter into public record that following the Majils-e-Mashawarat of Shopian's request that IPTK inquire into the death of Ms. Asiya Jan and Mrs. Neelofar Jan in May 2009, to deliver an accurate understanding of the matter and define a mechanism for justice, we wrote Chief Minister Abdullah in January 2010, requesting cooperation and access, which have been denied us to date. As well, we wish to enter into public record that the Government of Jammu and Kashmir and the Government of India have not undertaken investigations into the findings of BURIED EVIDENCE, IPTK's report on unknown, unmarked, and mass graves in Indian-administered Kashmir, or acted on its recommendations. Such action may have generated constructive interventions into the continuing chain of extrajudicial executions by the Indian military and paramilitary.

DEFENDING KASHMIR

Why did Pakistan invade Kashmir in the first place? First, Kashmir being a Muslim-dominant state was considered a natural part of Pakistan, which had made Islam the basis of its modern nationality. Second, Khan Abdul Gaffar Khan's Pathanistan Movement was gaining momentum and Kashmir was held out as a bait for luring the poor tribals away. The internal conditions of Jammu & Kashmir with religious passions aflame, lawlessness rampant and authority paralysed offered the right mix for the raiders to strike.

Operation Gulmarg

The Army Headquarters of Pakistan planned the main invasion plan, code-named Operation Gulmarg. Conclusive proof of this came through two different sources-Major Onkar Singh Kalkat, then serving as the Brigade Major at HQ Bannu Frontier Brigade Group, and GK Reddy, a journalist. Both happened to stumble upon the plan by chance. The invasion was planned meticulously with considerable strategic and tactical insight. According to Operation Gulmarg, as described by Major Kalkat, every Pathan tribe was required to enlist at least one Lashkar of 1,000 tribesmen.

These Lashkars were to be concentrated at Baftnu, Wana, Peshawar, Kohat, Thal and Nowshera by the first week of September 1947. The Brigade Commanders at these places were to issue them arms, ammunition and some essential clothing items. Each Lashkar was also to be provided with a Major, a Captain and ten JCOs of the regular Pakistan Army. The entire force was to be commanded by Major General Akbar Khan, who was given the code name Tariq.

All Lashkars were to meet at Abbottabad by October 18th. According to the plan, six Lashkars were to advance along the main road from Muzaffarabad to Srinagar via Domel, Uri and Baramula, with the specific task of capturing the aerodrome and subsequently advancing to the Banihal Pass. Two Lashkars were to advance from the Haji Pir Pass direct on to Gulmarg, thereby securing the right flank of the main force advancing from Muzaffarabad. Another two Lashkars were to advance from Tithwal through the Nastachhun Pass for capturing Sopore, Handwara and Bandipur. And 10 other Lashkars were to operate in the Poonch, Bhimbar and Rawalkot area with the intention of capturing Poonch and Rajauri before advancing to Jammu. Arrangements were also made for detailing of guides/informers from the so-called Azad Army, to all these tribal Lashkars.

Major General Khan was also given the task of organising the Azad Army, the major portion of which was to come from the Muslim element of the J&K State forces. Dumps of arms, ammunition, supplies and clothing were to be established forward of Abbottabad by October 15th. These were to be subsequently moved to Muzaffarabad and Domel after the D-day. Pakistan's 7 Infantry Division was to concentrate the Murree-Abbottabad area by October 21st and was ordered to be ready to move immediately into J&K territory to back up the tribal Lashkars and consolidate their hold on the Valley. One infantry brigade was also held in readiness at Sialkot to move on to Jammu. The D-day for Operation Gulmarg was fixed as 22 October 1947, on which date the various Lashkars were to cross into J&K territory. The invasion plan was tactically sound and, in the beginning, brilliantly executed. The main attack had by necessity to be launched frontally along the motor road. Apart from rifles, the standard weapon of the raiders, the main force was also equipped with a few light machine guns and traveled in about 300 civilian lorries.

Fall of Domel and Baramula

The main strength of the defenders was at Domel where the two approach roads from Murree and Abbottabad met before leading towards Srinagar along the Jhelum gorge. Its two out posts Lohar Gali and Ramkot were the key to the whole defence and were guarded by the 4th Kashmir Infantry, which had a mix of Muslim and Dogra soldiers.

When the raiders struck in the morning of October 22nd, traitors within the 4th Kashmir Infantry joined the raiders and gave them complete information about the strength and disposition of the defending troops and helped them send sufficient force against each piquet of defenders. That proved to be the beginning of a series of successes for the raiders before they were ultimately held, and subsequently thrown back, by Indian reinforcements over the next two weeks or so.

Between October 22nd and 26th, the raiders had run over Domel, Muzaffarabad, Uri and Baramula. Yet in their success lay the seeds of their doom. For on their way, they took to looting and raping, and the ultimate goal of the 'Holy War' was forgotten. Each man tried to grab as much wealth or as many girls as he could, and the 'infidel' Maharaja at Srinagar or the 'liberation of the oppressed Muslims' of Kashmir was last on his mind.

The advance on Srinagar was held up for a few days, and that proved crucial. In Delhi, hundreds of kilometres from stricken Baramula, it had at last been decided to save Kashmir in its hour of peril. Even as the barbaric raiders were satisfying their greed and lust in Baramula, transport planes full of Indian troops were winging their way through the azure autumn skies: Destination Srinagar.

Smashing of the J&K Siege

When the first wave of tribal warriors from Pakistan invaded the Kashmir Valley on 22 October 1947, the kingdom of Jammu & Kashmir had not acceded to either Pakistan or India. Therefore, taking the plea that it was an internal matter, India refused to send in its troops to the Valley. However, when Maharaja Hari Singh signed the Instrument of Accession with the Indian Government on the evening of 26 October 1947, Jammu & Kashmir became an integral part of the Indian Dominion legally, morally and constitutionally. Now was the time to react to the tribal invasion, which India did commendably, considering the short notice given to its military commanders.

The first troops were flown to Srinagar with hardly a couple of days planning and preparation. The liberation of the Valley in early November 1947 was a splendid feat of arms by the 161 Brigade, fighting against hordes of raiders. This single brigade managed to hold its own throughout the long winter of 1947-48 when its only line of communication was blocked by snow. Large areas in the Tithwal, Naushahra and Rajouri sectors were liberated from the invaders, and were held against repeated attacks by a vastly superior enemy. Naturally, the Indian Army also suffered setbacks, minor and major, at several places such as Jhangar, Pandu, Kargil and Skardu. But the situation was fully restored at Jhangar and Kargil. The long siege of Poonch was finally broken and

Gurais & Dras areas were successfully recaptured against tremendous odds. The Army won five Param Vir Chakras (PVCs), 47 Maha Vir Chakras (MVCs) and not less than 284 Vir Chakras (VrCs), including three twin-awards of VrCs, during the J&K Operations of 1947-48.

During the long campaign, the Indian Army lost 76 officers, 31 JCOs and 996 men of other ranks. The wounded totalled 3152, including 81 officers and 107 JCOs. Apart from these casualties, J&K State Forces lost approximately 1990 officers and men. The small Royal Indian Air Force (RIAF) lost 32 personnel, including 9 officers. The enemy casualties were definitely many times the total of Indian Army and RIAF casualties. By one estimate the enemy suffered 20,000 casualties, including 6000 killed.

The gallantry and skill of all ranks of the Indian Army are amply borne out in the various accounts of these operations. But the exploits and the vital role of the RIAF deserve special mention here. Its contribution to the success of the J&K operations cannot be over emphasized, and it was the one weapon to which the enemy had no answer, as the Pakistan Air Force wisely desisted from joining the fray.

Only the impromptu airlift to Srinagar in October 1947 saved the Kashmir Valley. A hundred planes landed every day on the improvised airfield at Srinagar, bringing in troops, ammunition and supplies and evacuating casualties and the refugees. The RIAF and civilian pilots of these Dakotas defied the mountains, the weather, and fatigue, to continue the airlift till the Valley was saved. Giving invaluable support to these were the fearless fighter pilots who accurately and repeatedly attacked vital enemy positions at Gurais, Zoji La, Pindras and Rajouri.

Apart from the men in uniform, civilians played a crucial role in liberating the Valley. The dedication and skill of the civilian pilots who flew to Srinagar in October 1947 was no less than their counterparts in the RIAF. Very few know that a civilian washerman, Ram Chander, won a Maha Vir Chakra for rescuing an officer wounded during an ambush, shooting down several enemy troops in the process. It was this Indian spirit and valour that saved the Valley.

India to the Rescue

It was on 24 October 1947 that the Government of India first got news of the Kashmir invasion. By that time, Domel and Muzaffarabad had already fallen to the raiders, who were fast approaching Srinagar. The Maharaja of Kashmir sent an S.O.S. message to the Indian Government on the night of October 24th. After deliberations at the highest levels, it was decided that India couldn't send its troops till J&K formally acceded to India. Maharaja Hari Singh signed the Instrument of Accession in the evening of October 26th, which made J&K an integral part of India-legally, morally, and constitutionally. The Indian reaction, from then onwards, was swift, adverse ground conditions notwithstanding.

Operation Jak

The Indian rescue operation was beset with obvious difficulties from the very beginning. Srinagar was over 480 km from the nearest point on the Indian border. Troops in East Punjab were engaged in dealing with the refugees and maintaining law and order. Hence, air transport was the only way out. Worse still, the airport at Srinagar was hardly fit to land fully laden transport planes. But that was the only option available and it had to be taken. The rescue mission was code-named, Operation Jak. The first regiment to move in was 1 Sikh, stationed at Gurgaon at the time and commanded by Lt. Col. D.R. Rai. The troops were transported in four Dakota planes that took off from Delhi on October 27th and reached Srinagar early morning the same day. The first engagement with the enemy started on October 28th. Lt. Col. Rai was the first Indian officer to fall in the battle of liberation.

It was only after the first troops had landed at Srinagar that the gravity of the situation was realised. So, the Indian Army decided to throw its full weight to drive back the invaders. On October 28th, the Delhi and East Punjab Command was ordered to carry out Phase II of Operation Jak. It involved dispatching one Brigade Group to Jammu via Pathankot.

The next day, the Eastern Southern commands were asked to spare whatever troops they could for the operation. Airlifts were undertaken almost round-the-clock airlifts to increase the troop strength. On October 30th, two fighter aircraft of the RIAF were detailed to operate from the Srinagar airstrip to provide air-support to the ground troops. In the following days, many Harvards and Spitfires were based on that airfield and they gave invaluable support to the infantry. Meanwhile, there had been some fierce engagements with the enemy on the ground, resulting in some casualties on the Indian side. But most importantly, the advance of the invaders had been checked.

The ground troops held the enemy. Transport planes took care of the supply of troops, equipment and ration. Interestingly, apart from three RIAF planes, 33 civil Dakotas were used in these sorties. Many of them even did a double trip to Srinagar on a single day-a tribute to the morale of the pilots and crew. By November 6th, the critical phase for Srinagar was over. The raiders had lost the initiative thanks to their looting at Baramula. About 3500 Indian troops had reached Srinagar by then. They threw a ring of machine guns and bayonets around Srinagar and the airfield. Although the invaders were only about 8 km away from the city at the nearest point, it was now impossible for them to penetrate the Indian positions and capture the capital, almost in their grasp. Having strengthened their position, the Indian Army was about to begin the liberation of the Kashmir valley.

The Liberation of the Valley

According to orders from the Defence Committee of the Cabinet, Baramula was to be recaptured from the enemy by November 17th, even if the Indian Army had to incur 500 casualties. The original plan was to launch the decisive battle on November 10th, but an unexpected attack on Indian positions at Shalateng on November 7th postponed the initiative.

In a masterly battle strategy, the Indian troops flanked the invaders from three sides and unleashed murderous firepower on them. The RIAF strafed them from the air. The Battle of Shalateng was over within 20 minutes. It put Srinagar and Kashmir Valley beyond the grasp of the invaders forever. There were encounters after that, but the enemy was being driven back steadily and surely. By the evening of November 13th, Uri was captured. With that the liberation of the Kashmir Valley was complete.

The Relief of Poonch

On 20 November 1947, a column for the relief of Poonch set out from Uri, but was halted at Kahuta, 13 km short of Poonch. The Poonch garrison held out for one full year before it was finally relieved. Operation Easy was aimed at establishing the final link-up with Poonch, which had proved to be difficult throughout most of 1948.

An attempt to link up with Poonch could be made either from the south, namely, via Thana Mandi or Rajouri, or from the north via the Haji Pir Pass. Lt. Gen. Cariappa (later Field Marshal and Army Chief) gave the go-ahead for the link-up with Poonch via the south. Lt. Gen. Shrinagesh (later General and Army Chief), who had been appointed Corps Commander of J&K Forces on September 14th, ordered Major General Atma Singh to plan for a link-up accordingly. Major General Atma Singh was further ordered to carry out Phase I (secure Pir Badesar) by October 8th; commence Phase II (demonstrate north of Thana Mandi) by October 10th; and concentrate in Rajouri the required force for Operation Easy by October 16th. On October 9th, Major General Atma Singh finalised his plan.

The force was to be under the command of Brigadier Yadunath Singh, Commander 19 Brigade, and was to consist of six infantry battalions plus one field battery and one mountain battery. It was to be divided into two columns, one column of three battalions under command of Brigadier Umrao Singh, Commander 5 Brigade, and the other column of three battalions under command of Lt. Col. Jagjit Singh Aurora (the same Lt. Gen. Jagjit Singh Aurora of 1971 War fame), Commander 1/2 Punjab. As a preliminary to the main operation, the deception plan was to be carried out about October 12 to secure Pir Badesar.

The main operation was to commence on about October 19th with 5 Brigade advancing from Rajouri and securing Pir Kalewa ridge. Lt. Col. Jagjit Singh's column was then to pass through, moving from south of Thana Mandi to secure a firm base in the area around Sangrot. Having secured the base, the intention was to advance to Potha with 5 Brigade and carry out operations from Potha for the link-up with Poonch.

THE MILITARY RACES OF INDIA

IT is one of the essential differences between the East and the West, that in the East, with certain exceptions, only certain clans and classes can bear arms; the others have not the physical courage necessary for the warrior. In Europe, as we know, every able-bodied man, given food and arms, is a fighting man of some sort, some better, some worse, but still as capable of bearing arms as any other of his nationality. In the East, or certainly in India, this is not so. The people of Bengal, even those with the most-cultivated brain, the trading classes, the artizan classes, and the outcaste tribes, are men to whom the threat of violence is the last word. At the bottom of all power and law, disguise it never so carefully, lies the will of the hand to keep the head. Presumably the great conquest of India away back in the mists of time, by the Aryan race, and the subjection of the original inhabitants, is at the bottom of this. Only certain races were permitted to bear arms, and in course of time only certain races remained fit to bear arms. Conquest, pure and simple, with cruel repression, is responsible for it in some places, such as in Bengal and Kashmir. It is extraordinary that the well-born race of the upper classes in Bengal should be hopeless poltroons, while it is absurd that the great, merry, powerful Kashmiri should have not an ounce of physical courage in his constitution, but it is so. Nor are appearances of any use as a criterion. Some of the most manly -looking people in India are in this respect the most despicable.

The existence of this condition, therefore, much complicates the whole question of enlistment in India. It renders any form of levy en masse im- possible, or any form of Militia service, while it emphatically forbids the English system, whereby the well-to-do pay for the lower orders to do their fighting for them. In India itself certain classes alone do the soldiering and kindred service. These are, roughly, in central and northern India the yeoman peasant, the grazier, and the land- owner. Very good classes, too, as every one can see, and in India there is no exodus from the land to the crowded city. The peasant in India, that is to say, the yeoman peasant, is a well-born man, distinct from the mere helot of low birth who in some parts helps on the land.

Now the people by tribes from whom we take soldiers in India itself are as follows :

(1) The ancient Aryan races, who invaded India in pre-historic times, viz. Rajput (lit. sons of princes) and Brahman, who for practical purposes may be divided into two distinct classes, those of Hindustan and those of the Punjab.

(2) The races of Jats or Jats, and Gujars.

(3) The Pathans and the Moguls of India. Then from outside the limits of India :

(4) The Pathan and Afghan of the frontier hills.

(5) The Gurkha.

Then we have a further division which is by religion, and also another by country.

For instance, we have the Sikhs, who are largely that portion of the Jat race which embraced the calvinistic reformed Hindu teaching of the Sikh gurus, and who live in that part of Upper India known as the Punjab, the land of the five rivers.

Then we have the Muhammadans of the Punjab, who are of many mixed races, but who largely consist of Rajput tribes converted to Islam at various times in the past. They describe themselves as Rajput rather than Muhammadan.

The Muhammadans of India are either the descendants of conquering or serving foreigners of that faith, or of converts. In whichever category they may claim descent, they will generally be of mixed origin by now, and those who claim Pathan and Mogul descent will have lost the characteris- tics of their race, and even their features, for it is rare to see a sign in these days of the Tartar origin of the Moguls.

Then, again, in the Southern Plateau we have the Deccan, of which the people are largely Mahrattas or Marathi-speaking, and, mixed with them, Muhammadans of varied origin.

For the purposes of describing the military tribes and castes it will be as well to do so by countries and provinces with certain exceptions. The gradual raising of the military standard by the change of times and terrain, and the enervating effect on Asiatics of a few generations of peace, have already been referred to. It has resulted in a gradual enlistment of an increasing number of men of the northern races, whom a cold winter, and a lesser period of the enjoyment of peace, have for the present preserved from military deterioration.

It will be reasonable, therefore, to commence with the races of the north, viz. of the Punjab and the North- West Frontier.

THE MILITARY CLASSES OF THE PUNJAB

The Sikhs. It is not correct to speak of the Sikhs as a race; they are, properly speaking, a numerous religious sect, which, starting as a perse- cuted set of reformers, became a powerful sect embracing many of all the Hindu tribes and races of the Punjab. The first guru or spiritual teacher of the new faith was Baba Nanak, born in 1469, near Lahore. Brought up within the influence of the teaching of a one and only God as conceived in Islam, he taught a reformed or puritan Hinduism, in which simplicity, kindliness, purity, and brotherhood were among the leading principles. Stimulated by repression and persecu- tion, the sect grew and flourished. Nine gurus succeeded father Nanak; the tenth guru, the famous Govind, succeeding his father at the age of fifteen, on the former's suffering death and torture at the hands of the Mogul. In the hands of the tenth guru the religious and peaceful community was changed into a powerful military sect, that constantly obtained fresh recruits and became the champion of the Hindu inhabitants against the Musalman. The faith spread to most of the Hindu tribes of the Punjab, more especially to the vast cultivating race, the Jats, which to this day is spread over the whole of Upper India.

Because the Jats form, perhaps, two-thirds of the Sikhs, the term Sikh (which means disciple) is largely associated with the Jats. These same Jats, however, number many hundreds of thousands who embraced the hostile creed of Islam, while in Rajputana and about Delhi and south of it are numerous Hindus of the same descent who call themselves Jats (q.v.). To the generic title of Sikh or disciple, the warlike Govind added the affix Singh or lion, originally the affix of men of Rajput race.

A Sikh is baptized into his sect and not born into it, so that no man is a Sikh till he has taken the pahul, that is to say, till he has been baptized. Sikhism is an austere faith, demanding some simplicity and rigour of life from its adherents. So much is this so, that for many years there has been a tendency for young men to avoid the pdhul and grow up as ordinary Hindus, for whom life has few irksome restrictions.

But as the value of the Sikh as the simple, faithful soldier, has lain in his adherence to the simple tenets and hardy life of his forebears, no non-baptized Sikh is admitted into a regiment of the Indian Army. So careful are regiments in this matter, and so much are regiments the home of the old ṃartial and simple Sikh principles, that it has been said, not without some shadow of truth, that it is the British officer who has kept Sikhism up to its old standard. The creed of Govind is thus described :

Emerging from his retirement he preached the Khalsa^ the faith of the pure, the elect, and the liberated. He openly attacked all distinctions of caste, and insisted on the equality of all who would join him. Resuscitating the old baptismal rite of the Sikhs, he proclaimed it as the pdhul or gate, by which all might enter the fraternity, while he gave to its members the pershad or communion as a sacrament of union in which the four orders of Hindu society should eat from the same dish;... the higher orders murmured... but the lower orders rejoiced at the new dispensation and flocked in numbers to his standard.... He gave them the outward signs of their faith, in the unshorn hair, the short drawers, and the blue dress. He marked the military nature of their calling, by the title of Singh or lion, by the wearing of steel, and by the initiation by sprinkling water with a two-edged dagger, and he gave them a feeling of personal superiority in their abstinence from the unclean tobacco. But while Nanak substituted holiness of life for vain ceremonies, Govind Singh demanded brave deeds and zealous devotion to the cause as the proof of faith.... Religious fervour was entirely eclipsed by military zeal, and thus for the second time in history a religion became a political power, and for the first time in India a nation arose, embracing all races, all classes, and all grades of society, and banded them together in face of a foreign foe.

Such in brief is Sikhism and its history. The Jdt Sikh forming the bulk of the fraternity are those who have served us most, and who probably make the best soldiers. The Jdt is a peasant farmer before anything else, however. In spite of the military tenets of his faith, his sayings are all of the plough, and a plough is the first toy of the Sikh's son. The Khatris, who have embraced Sikhism, form largely the business class, and have been enlisted in small numbers for their brains... the Jdt being proverbially thick in the uptake,... and have served with distinction. The Lobana, the hereditary carrying class, have always done well as soldiers, though not very largely enlisted. The greater demands of the army on the hardier races of the north have, however, caused the recruiter to closely examine the yield in Sikhs of other classes, with the result that certain regiments enlist no Jot Sikhs, but have been successful in some of the smaller and humbler Sikh communities. For instance, Sanis or gardeners, Kumboh Sikhs, a cultivating race of putative foreign origin, of whom some are Sikhs, the artificer classes, have all been swept into the military net, which only their Sikhism has made possible.

The Jdt race, from whom so many Sikhs were made, is described farther on under Jat and Gujar, but must be referred to here. There is much discussion as to their origin, but it seems probable that they are in reality of a Scythian race, with whom some identify the Jatii of history and the Magyars and gypsies of Eastern Europe. To what extent, and when, they mingled with the Aryan race, and to what extent the distinction between them and the Aryans is social, it is impossible to tell. The Scythian tribes undoubtedly adopted Buddhism soon after their arrival, and later Hinduism. All Jats are cultivators, and the name has become almost the name of an occupa- tion. The inhabitants of the Indus Valley when that river leaves the mountains are largely Muham- madan Jats.

One more Sikh community needs description, since they form so faithful a portion of the Sikh soldiery, and these are the Mazbi Sikhs who serve in the Sikh Pioneer regiments. The term Mazbi means faithful, and was applied to the sweepers of outcaste tribe who brought back the crucified body of Teg Bahadur, the second successor to Guru Govind. Their descendants of outcaste tribe, and probably those outcastes whom they converted to Sikhism, now have the title. They served under Ranjit Singh, and were formed into a pioneer regiment for service before Delhi, since when their courage and general good qualities have made them famous for the work of the military pioneer.

The military services of the Sikhs in our service are well known. The Sikh regiments, whether those raised just before the Mutiny, such as the 14th or 15th Sikhs, the regiments of Ferozepore and Ludhiana, or the 35th and 45th (originally a military police corps), are equally famous, as are those regiments that enlist class squadrons and companies of Sikhs, and the regiments of Pioneers.

Their military reputation, so far as our service is concerned, largely dates from the Mutiny, when the Sikhs flocked to our standards. Since those days, the Punjabi generally, but especially the Sikh, has become a world-wide adventurer. In addition to enlisting in every sort of military or police body that will take him, in Africa, China, or the East generally, he is to be found also as watchman in many private firms. High pay is what attracts him, and wealth to spend on his land when he returns home. These attractions, and the devasta- tion of plague in the last few years, have made the Sikh recruiting -market tight, and there is little doubt that we have, if anything, over-recruited from this nationality. The large number of men they furnish, their importance as a population, and the latent possibilities under- lying the tenets of their creed, all make their description at some length desirable. In appear- ance they are well known : tall, well-knit men, with their long hair pulled up under their head- dress, their beards and whiskers neatly curled up close to the face, and their military bearing all stamp the man, even to those with only a bowing acquaintance with Hindustan. As a fighting man, his slow wit and dogged courage give him many of the characteristics of the British soldier at his best.

INTERNATIONAL LAW AND INTERNATIONAL TERRORISM

The events of 11 September and the subsequent military response by the United States and its allies raise some difficult issues in international law. Does an attack by a non-state terrorist group give rise to the right of self-defence as understood under international law? Under what circumstances was the Taliban regime as the Afghani government itself a legitimate target for military action under the self-defence doctrine? To what extent was the United States entitled to dictate the terms by which the Taliban regime should act before the military action would cease against it and Al Qaeda bases on Afghani soil?

Only the first issue can be answered-yes-with any degree of confidence. The others are clouded with uncertainty. To some extent this uncertainty reflects the shift of international law away from an emphasis on regulating relations between sovereign states (countries) towards having to incorporate the actions of non-state groups within the legal framework. As part of this shift, the responsibility of governments for the actions of non-state groups such as the international terrorist network Al Qaeda is receiving increasing attention. The periodic use of military force by the United States against such organizations and so-called 'state sponsors of terrorism' during the 1990s appears to be forcing a change in accepted state practice and hence (arguably) influencing the boundaries of international customary law. However, given that the United States is likely to be motivated primarily by national interests, it would be useful for the United Nations General Assembly to authorise the International Law Commission to codify exactly what are the principles applying to the doctrine of self-defence under international law.

This chapter begins with a short chronology tracing the major relevant events from 11 September through to the ongoing airstrikes by the United States and its allies during October. This is followed by a review of the status of terrorism under international law. It then looks at the question of legal responsibility for the 11 September attacks, including under what circumstances the Taliban might be deemed to share some form of responsibility. The paper goes on to examine the legal use of force, and whether the events of 11 September give rise to the right of self-defence. Finally it considers what the practical limits of self-defence are in the present case, including role of the United Nations Security Council.

Chronology

11 September-Four commercial United States jetliners on domestic routes are hijacked. The hijackers issue no demands to

authorities. Two of the jets are flown into the twin towers of the World Trade Centre in New York, one into the Pentagon in Washington DC and another crashes in rural Pennsylvania. Around 3 000 people are killed. No organisation claims responsibility for the hijackings. Representatives of the Taliban government of Afghanistan immediately condemn the attacks. Later, Osama bin Laden also denies involvement.

12 September-The United Nations General Assembly and Security Council pass resolutions condemning the events of 11 September as acts of terrorism. The resolutions call for the 'perpetrators, organizers and sponsors' to be '[brought] to justice' and states that those responsible for 'aiding, supporting or harbouring' such persons 'will be held accountable'.

14 September-the United States Congress authorises the use of military force against those involved in the attacks, including those who 'harboured' such persons or organisations 'so as to prevent any future acts of international terrorism'. Also on 14 September, the Australian Government announces the activation of the ANZUS treaty.

17 September-Both Houses of the Australian Commonwealth Parliament pass a resolution which, amongst other things, states that Parliament 'fully endorses the commitment of the Australian Government to support within Australia's capabilities United States-led action against those responsible for these tragic attacks'.

20 September-In an address to a Joint session of Congress, United States' President George Bush states that 'the evidence we have gathered all points to a collection of loosely affiliated terrorist organizations known as Al Qaeda...they are the same murderers indicted for bombing American embassies in Tanzania and Kenya, and responsible for bombing the USS Cole'. Osama bin Laden is named as the leader of Al Qaeda. President Bush demands that the Taliban must 'deliver to the United States authorities all the leaders of Al Qaeda who hide in your land...immediately and permanently close every terrorist training camp in Afghanistan, and hand over every terrorist, and every person in their support structure, to appropriate authorities'. Failure to immediately hand over the 'terrorists' would result in the Taliban 'sharing their fate'.

According to President Bush, the 'war on terror begins with Al Qaeda, but it does not end there. It will not end until every terrorist group of global reach has been found, stopped and defeated.'

21 September-The Taliban refuse to comply with the United States demands unless evidence is produced. The United States rejects the Taliban's position, stating that bin Laden has already been indicted in the United States for the bombings of United States embassies in Kenya and Tanzania in 1998.

6 October-The Taliban offers to detain bin Laden and try him under Islamic law in Afghanistan if the United States makes a formal request and presents them with sufficient evidence. This proposal is rejected by the United States who insist on the fulfilment of their 20 September demands.

7 October-Airstrikes by United States and British planes commence against Al Qaeda training camps and military installations of the Taliban regime in Afghanistan. According to President Bush, 'these carefully targeted actions are designed to disrupt the use of Afghanistan as a terrorist base of operations and to attack the military capability of the Taliban regime'.

7 October-The United States representative to the United Nations delivers a letter to the President of the United Nations Security Council citing the right of self-defence as justification for the airstrikes. The latter states that 'from the territory of Afghanistan, the Al Qaeda organization continues to train and support agents of terror who attack innocent people throughout the world and target United States nationals and interests in the United States and abroad'. It also states that 'we may find that our self-defence requires further actions with respect to other organizations and other States'.

12 October-The United States ceases strikes for one day, pending a response to a renewed demand to hand over Osama bin Laden and the Al Qaeda members. The demand is refused.

13 October-Ongoing airstrikes resume.

November/December-Taliban and Al Qaeda forces are progressively driven out from former strongholds by a combination of Afghani anti-Taliban forces and United States airstrikes. By the end of December, anti-Taliban forces effectively control Afghanistan. Neither the Taliban leader, Mohammed Omar, nor bin Laden are captured or confirmed as killed and their whereabouts are unknown.

14 November-the United Nations Security Council pass a resolution expressing 'strong support for the efforts of the Afghan people to establish a new and transitional administration leading to the formation of a new government'.

22 December-A transitional Afghani administration is sworn in Kabul.

ROLE OF INSTITUTIONS IN MILITARY-POLITICS RELATIONS

The military itself with its senior leadership and their vested interests can be seen as the prime reason for its continued role in politics in Pakistan. Even without direct martial law, the military maintained its influence through its intelligence agencies (ISI's creation of IJI) and otherwise (e.g. as a mediator in the aforementioned political tussle between Ghulam Ishaq Khan and Nawaz Sharif). The role of other institutions that have helped the military with its rule emerges:

The first and foremost reason was a weak parliament. Pakistan was without a constitution of its own until 1956. This weakened the parliamentary system and democratic norms could not develop (PMs were appointed by the head of the state rather than people). Zia did not let any institution strengthen that could serve as a threat to his rule. He weakened the political parties and the 1985 elections were held on non-party basis. The freedom of expression of the Press, one of the pre-requisites of democracy, had always been curtailed during martial laws and censorship laws were enforced. This control over the press reached its limit when in 1982 three journalists were flogged by the martial law regime due to political reasons.

The judiciary was weak during martial law regimes and otherwise when dealing with generals. Several of its decisions have had political fallout. For example, the 1953 decision of Justice Munir upheld the dissolution of the Constituent Assembly and thus weakened the nascent democratic process in Pakistan. After the 1977 coup, the Supreme Court validated the martial law on the basis of "doctrine of necessity". Its role during the Presidential referendum and later during the hearing of the Junejo Government restoration case (decision influenced by the COAS) marred its reputation significantly.

The civil bureaucracy has essentially felt comfortable with whomever is in power, provided it was given a security of service. Ayub Khan's Basic Democracy system was an instrument which made politicians redundant and gave the bureaucracy an outreach at the village level and helped ensure continuity of his regime.

In the Yahya Khan marital law, the bureaucracy was given a diminished role in administration and it was fragmented with the dismissal of 303 civil servants. However, the Zia-ul-Haq martial law saw a revival of the bureaucracy's role and several bureaucrats were given key positions in governance such as Mr Agha Shahi as the Foreign Minister.

The United States, although not an institute, has been perceived as the most significant foreign player in Pakistan's politics. American aid, especially during the Ayub Khan era and as a result of the Afghan War during Zia-ul-Haq's regime, consolidated the dictators' rule. With their extensive military aid to Pakistan in the 50s and commencement of officer training in US military schools, they gave the Pakistan Army an image of a vibrant and elite force occupying important place in national affairs.

Akmal Hussain and Mushahid Hussain claim that according to now-declassified US State Department reports, General Ayub Khan was recognised as the 'King-maker' in Pakistan's politics by the Americans.

The Cold War entered a new phase with the Soviet invasion of Afghanistan in 1979 and Pakistan became a front-line state. For the United States, dealing with a military dictator was much easier in such times. US assistance to Pakistan was resumed in 1983 with a $3.2 billion package. Even though America was opposed to Zia's continuation of Pakistan's nuclear programme, it continued to help him because of the Afghan war and hence helped enormously in the strengthening of his rule.

THE UPPER HAND ON PAKISTANI POLITICS: AN ANALYSIS OF SEASONAL POLITICS

There is in Pakistan a permanent threat of politicization and corruption of the military. Moreover, military officers have a morbid fear of the politicians interfering in military promotions and appointments as this could split the army. Whenever a civilian government starts trying to interfere in this institution, the army has to act in "self defense". This statement is justified by the military officers to justify their intervention in the political affairs. The first army ruler, General Muhammad Ayub Khan, had no fears from the civilian government. Zulfqar Ali Bhutto, an elected Prime Minister did not politicize the military institution. In 1970s, there was deep political chaos in Pakistan which should have been resolved through political means but the army chief, General Muḥammad Zial-ul-Haq, imposed martial law in the country. Every military coup in Pakistan has therefore been carried out by the chief of the army staff, backed by a consensus of the corp. commanders. Army chief does not need to control the country's command if his interests are protected by the civilian governments.

The Pakistan military has long been considered the one institution in the country that functions sufficiently well to deliver international objectives. It has consequently been the partner of choice for many states, not least the United States. Pakistan's history, however, shows that successive military regimes have each led Pakistan to crises, to the detriment of partners' interests; and far from guaranteeing the cohesion and stability of Pakistan, military rule has more often jeopardized it.

Pakistan has suffered four coups in 63 disordered years as a nation. Even some Pakistanis, who believed in democracy but were opposed to Prime Minister Nawz Sharif, welcomed military intervention to change regime in 1999. But if a country is unruly, having generals rule is no solution. The truth is that politicians pave the way for the generals. We have encountered that in our past— every time a politician has gone overboard on their styles of corruption for the country. But as these military generals seized power, martial law would be imposed or a dictatorship would arise in the country. Pakistan failed to establish a strong structure due to this military coup system. Going through the four generals regimes, we can see how Pakistan structure was jolted.

Pakistan's military influence on Pakistani Politics has never been a benchmark as it was considered at the time of crisis. Few Pakistani Generals thought that they would liberate their people from authoritarian, despotic and undemocratic politicians who failed to facilitate and deliver to their people. It is true that Pakistani people always welcomed military man whenever he overthrew an elected prime minister. Some political parties supported them knowingly that a general has no knowledge to run the state institutions. Party leaders also seek their survival to support a man in uniform. Theoretically, all military Generals gave an impression that the state would be prosperous, secure, stable, progressive, democratic and modern. Moreover, all corrupt people would be held with iron hands. Empirically, their policies resembled a mirage. The State divided ethnically, when they centralized all powers in their own hands (few military Generals). Pakistan became more dependent instead of a self-sufficient state.

Indeed, Pakistan's Army is well organized, professionally skilled, equipped and enjoying with modernity. This is the only organization in Pakistan which is fully trusted by the people. On the other hand, selected generals exploited their people's aspirations, dreams and sentiments whenever they got chance to enjoy political power. They could not replace 'shame democracy,' but rather implemented their own agendas which protected their personal interests instead of the national interests. No doubt, the military institution is considered an integral part to protect Pakistan's border/areas from internal and external forces, so it enjoys unique structural positions in Pakistan. In his book on the Pakistani military, Shuja Nawaz mentions how, when his brother General Asif Nawaz was chief of the army staff during Sarif's first government in the 1990s, some of Sharif's own ministers would come to see his brother to throw him out and replace him with someone else.

All four Generals, Muhammad Ayub Khan, Muhammad Yahya Khan, Muhamad Zia-ul-Haq and Pervez Mushrraf, had dismissed or suspended the country's constitution and treated their people as tyrants whenever their power was challenged by them. They did not spare their political rivals and controlled Pakistani society like their own troops (soldiers), those always took their command blindly. They, unfortunately, perceived that Pakistani people did not deserve a western democratic system. If the people wishes are ignored one after the other they always forced dictators to leave and this is what exactly happened with Pakistani Generals in politics who were going to change Pakistan according their own wishes. Why do people rebel? This depends on their level of frustration, anxiety and fear; and when they have lost human dignity, respect and hope and when the rulers are like robbers and hide their criminality with legal sugar-coating.

Why have the military regimes not been achieved political stability, internal/external security and economic objectives? How Pakistan becomes more vulnerable internally? I will explore the answer of these questions. The influence of military establishment on Pakistan's internal security has destabilized the state stability. This statement would be elaborated analytically rather critically. The main purpose of this chapter is to explore the causes or the strains implemented by the military rulers and to illustrate the ideological and security challenges in Pakistan by determined of military regimes regarding federalism which caused ethno – national movement, and promoted religious extremism, it also enhances sectarian conflict and polarization in society.

THE MILITARY IN PAKISTAN

The military has monopoly over most important decisions of the state. A part from being the guards in the external security of the nation, it is a well-accepted political institution. The Pakistani Army has the direct control over Pakistan's nuclear program and foreign policy. The National Command Authority (NCA) was established by the former Chief of the Army Staff and President of Pakistan, General Pervez Musharraf, to assure the west that Pakistan's nuclear weapon is safe.

The Pakistani Army has unique characteristics. It has been called by the civil regimes in the time of crisis. It feels itself the true guardian of the country, in fact, it has proved it whenever the state faces internal security dilemma. The Pakistani military got such a strengthen position has its deep roots in history. Pakistan faced several crises after its inception 1947. It was the army which rescued the nation in times of true crisis. During the disaster of earthquake 2005 and sad flooding situation the army had has always protected the people and has left immensely positive impacts on their minds and heart. In fact, Pakistani army has won the people's mind and heart in their favour no matter what the circumstance is.

Pakistan is a multi-ethnic nation. Internal riots had weakened the civil regime in 1950s. East Pakistan and the West Pakistan, both Pakistani wings were being threatened by the ethno-nationalists. Army curbed the linguistic and ethnic movement when it rose in Sindh and Baluchistan in 1952-54. In 1953 the army assisted the civilian governments when the people stood up against Ahmadya in Lahore. One would be surprised to know that under the 'operation service first' the army also played its role in nation building process; army officers were granted magisterial and executive powers in 1956 to control the widespread hoarding, black-marketing and resulting food shortage in East Pakistan. Earlier in 1951-52, the army conducted an "operation Jute "to stop smuggling of jute to India from East Pakistan. Pakistan was losing a considerable source of revenue. This operation was a healthy cooperation with the civil agencies. Thus army's role started to expand in civilian fields which could not be prevented.

Pakistan could not have the high quality of leadership after Muhammad Ali Jinnah. In the early 1950s, social chaos in Pakistan did make the political organizations weak and corrupt which promoted nepotism. The newly born 'Islamic state' was passing through the gravest situation. Landlords, strong politicians and bureaucrats were holding powers and influence over the public offices. The main stream forces 'Political parties' lost the people's trust. Doubtful circumstances created by the politicians enhanced military's power. Very often elections were avoided by the state elite and when conducted they led political turmoil. The weakness of the political forces is a sign of fragmentation and factionalism among civil society and the political class.

A Worth mentioning fact is that Pakistan's neighbouring countries e.g. India and Afghanistan both created tension and trouble in Pakistan's internal provinces such as NWFP (North Western Frontier Province), currently Khaiber Pakhtunkhawa and Baluchistan. The separatists and ethno movements had been supported either by Afghanistan or India to destabilize Pakistan. Unfortunately, the civil governments have always failed to control the situation. External forces and conflicting neighbouring states also provided strong grip to the army over Pakistan's week institutions. Army's direct interaction and interference in public affairs had affected politicians' credibility. Army's cooperative image toward the people created trust deficit between the people and political leaders, which is still going on.

Usually, because politicians are considered responsible for inviting the army to share their burden during conflicting situation in the country, the military has legitimized its interference by the threat of state destabilization and doubted leadership, the political leadership was perceived as 'security risk' to stage the military coup. As mentioned earlier military rule could not be effective or last long without political co-optation of the same elites who held public offices in the civilian governments. But their cooperation with the military government could never be possible without political fragmentation that the military regime and intelligence agencies under it caused. It was a conscious and well designed effort of military rulers to divide political forces by rewarding those who joined their rule and oppressing those who refused to render the political services they desired from them.

Their regular intervention into the inner functioning of the political parties, elected assemblies, media and other institutions resulted into weakening the political institutions that are necessary for the parliamentary democracy. The tradition of the Generals of Pakistan accusing their political leaders has continued from the first army ruler to the last one."The army meanwhile learned over time to establish patro-client relationships with the bureaucracy and with Islamist parties whom it used in its efforts to fight populist leaders in both East and West Pakistan and fuel the Kashmiri insurgency against Indian rule. Coup d'états in the history of Pakistan have been validated by the superior courts by the misinterpretation of Roman Law" that which otherwise is not lawful, necessity makes lawful".

Therefore, the Pakistan army pushed itself into direct control of governance through sidelining the weak political class. Martial Law was first imposed in 1958.Since then, the military has strengthened its position to become a dominant player in power politics. Over the 63 years of the state's history, the army has experienced direct power four times, and learns to negotiate authority when not directly in control of the government.

The state plays a central role, acting in the interest of other groups, which are; the landed-feudal class, the indigenous bourgeoisie and the metropolitan bourgeoisie. These three groups constitute the ruling power block that competes in the framework of peripheral capitalism.

THE PERVEZ MUSHARRAF GOVERNMENT

As chief executive, Musharraf arrogated virtual total power to himself. The general cited the substantial turmoil in the country and noted that institutions had been systematically destroyed, that the economy was in a state of near collapse, and that only the most drastic measures could even begin to improve the national condition. Musharraf said Pakistan was at a critical crossroads and that the Sharif government had even planned to split and weaken the armed forces. Noting that he could not save both the country and the constitution at the same time, Musharraf chose to sacrifice the latter for the former. Nonetheless, the constitution had not been abrogated—merely held in "abeyance" until better times again allowed for its reinstatement. Careful to point out that martial law had not been imposed, he nevertheless insisted the country could not afford to perpetuate the old politics.

A Chief Executive Secretariat was hurriedly assembled in the waning days of 1999, and by mid-2000 that temporary edifice had undergone restructuring in order to give more administrative powers to the new regime. Ranking military officers assumed the most important positions in the government, and all civilian members of the secretariat had to pass scrutiny by army officers. The massive induction of serving military officers in the secretariat also was aimed at providing Musharraf with the same command and discipline structure found in the Pakistan army. The major dilemma facing Pakistan's new rulers, however, was their lack of experience in civil affairs. Moreover, on-the-job training in the day-to-day life of the country quickly caused strains within the services.

Nawaz Sharif was arrested, charged and tried for high crimes, and, after being found guilty, sentenced to a long prison term. However, under international pressure he subsequently was released and sent into exile (Saudi Arabia), with the understanding that he would remain out of the country for 10 years.

The actions of Pakistan's generals were coldly received by many in the outside world. Washington was quick to criticize the coup leaders, and Clinton signaled his disfavour by altering his March 2000 South Asian itinerary so as to spend only a few hours in Pakistan while stopping in India and Bangladesh for longer visits. However, the strain in U.S.-Pakistan relations was caused by a wide array of issues: Pakistan's sustained political instability, its repeated failure at constructing civil society, the impediments to a resolution of the Kashmir question, and—most significantly—what seemed to be the country's nuclear arms race with India.

As was the case in previous military governments, Musharraf's announced intent was to return Pakistan to civilian rule as soon as feasible. The chief executive's plan to achieve this goal was similar in certain aspects to that put forward by Ayub Khan a generation earlier. Civilian rule had fragmented, and a return to full civilian control would first require the establishment of local democracy—hearkening back to Ayub Khan's "basic democracies"—a system devoid of competitive political parties. However, like the generals before him, Musharraf chose in June 2001 to consolidate his power by forcing the retirement of President Rafique Tarar, dispensing with the title of chief executive, and making himself president. The general also effectively became head of government, since the position of prime minister had been vacant since Sharif's ouster.

In July, as president, Musharraf traveled to Agra, India, where he met with Indian Prime Minister Atal Bihari Vajpayee to discuss regional security and, importantly, the status of Kashmir. No real progress was made, but the meeting set the stage for subsequent summit meetings between Musharraf and his Indian counterparts. The president appeared to be slipping into a role that promised a period of reflection on how to reconstruct the country's domestic and foreign policy, but that all was changed within two months by the new reality created by the September 11 attacks on the United States.

Following Pakistan's humiliating defeat in (and loss of) East Pakistan and Zia ul-Huq's subsequent emphasis on Islamization, the Pakistani army increasingly had been inclined to define its purpose in spiritual terms. Musharraf, long a key planner in Pakistan's military hierarchy, was linked to these trends. Initially, this constituted recruiting Islamist militants for clandestine operations in the Kashmir region. With the Soviet invasion of Afghanistan in 1979, Pakistan—particularly the Federally Administered Tribal Areas (FATA) along the Afghan border—became a safe haven for such militants from all parts of the world. The Pakistani military's Inter-Service Intelligence Directorate (ISI) became the main conduit of the country's support of the Afghan mujahideen fighters based there in their conflict with the Soviet forces in Afghanistan. Such assistance continued following the withdrawal of Moscow's forces in the late 1980s, and the ISI was instrumental in raising the Taliban as a counterforce to the rival groups seeking control of the Afghan state at that time—the strategy being to give Pakistan a dominant role in Afghanistan as that country emerged from two decades of constant warfare.

Pakistan's political landscape changed dramatically with the events of September 11. It was quickly determined that the attacks on the United States had been staged by the Muslim militant organization al-Qaeda, which was operating out of Afghanistan near the Pakistani border with the support of the Taliban regime. Pakistan had diplomatic relations with Afghanistan, but Musharraf hesitated to put pressure on the Taliban to arrest al-Qaeda leader Osama bin Laden. However, as al-Qaeda and the Taliban became judged a single entity, the United States demanded Pakistani assistance as it prepared to move militarily against both organizations. Musharraf chose to side with the U.S.-led coalition against the Taliban.

Musharraf's decision to join the American effort was met with outrage by Islamist conservatives in Pakistan. Thousands of pro-Taliban Pakistani volunteers crossed the border to help in the fight against U.S. troops and their coalition allies when those forces invaded and occupied Afghanistan in the fall of 2001. In the period following the September 11 attacks and the U.S. invasion of Afghanistan, the population of Islamist militants boomed in the FATA, as Taliban and al-Qaeda fighters found refuge over the border in Pakistan. Many more Muslim recruits flocked to the FATA from abroad, eager to join the conflict.

Musharraf was pressured by Washington to take aggressive action against these Islamist operatives in the tribal areas, and the Pakistani military launched a major campaign to combat militants, particularly in mountainous Waziristan. However, the tribal Pashtun region historically had been off-limits to the central government, and Pakistan's military action not only challenged Pashtun tribal autonomy there, but it also affected members of the Pashtun community not involved with the militants. When government forces were met with stiff resistance, the soldiers—often paramilitary and recruited from similar tribal orders—refused to fight or fought with little enthusiasm. Musharraf dismissed a number of army officers deemed sympathetic to the Taliban, and numerous foreign jihadists (including al-Qaeda militants) were arrested by Pakistani authorities and turned over to coalition officials, but the United States continued to accuse Islamabad (and particularly Musharraf) of not doing enough to contain the terrorist threat.

In April 2002 Musharraf, seeking to formalize his position as the head of state, held and overwhelmingly won a referendum granting him an additional five years as president. The referendum also reinstated the constitution, though modified with provisions spelled out in a document called the Legal Framework Order (LFO). In addition to extending Musharraf's term, the LFO expanded the president's powers and increased the number of members of both houses of the legislature. Parliamentary elections followed in October under the limitations imposed by the LFO, and Musharraf's adopted political party, the Pakistan Muslim

League (Q) (PML-Q), took more of the seats in the National Assembly than any other contending party.

The party subsequently forged a coalition government headed by PML-Q leader Mir Zafarullah Khan Jamali, a veteran politician and former Nawaz Sharif supporter. The opposition PPP polled next highest, but it was a coalition of religious parties known as the Muttahida Majlis-e-Amal (MMA) that made the most notable showing—marking the first time a Pakistani religious organization had gained a significant voice in parliament. The MMA was vehemently opposed to Musharraf's policy of confronting Islamist groups, and, after gaining a dominant political role in the North-West Frontier Province, the MMA openly questioned the army's actions in Waziristan.

Musharraf's government had been combating religious extremism at home, banning some of the more militant groups that had long been active in Pakistan and rounding up hundreds of religious activists. However, Musharraf generally had not addressed Islamist violence in Kashmir. Low-level fighting and skirmishing took place along the line of control there until late November 2003, when, unexpectedly, the Pakistani government declared a unilateral cease-fire and sought negotiations with New Delhi. The following month, two attempts were made on the president's life. Acts of political and religious violence continued to escalate, particularly those between Sunni and Shîite factions. Late in December the parliament ratified most provisions of the LFO as the 17th amendment to the constitution, confirming Musharraf's power to dismiss a prime minister, dissolve the National Assembly, and appoint chiefs of the armed forces and provincial governors.

In January 2004 Musharraf sought and received an unprecedented vote of confidence from a parliamentary electoral college. In August Shaukat Aziz, a former banker and minister of finance, took the premiership. Musharraf, however, clearly continued to hold the reins of power, and despite repeated promises to return the country to full civilian authority, he announced at the end of the year that the country was too fragile for him to comply with his own deadlines.

This applied also to the president's refusal to step down as head of the armed forces, despite repeated demands by political opponents that he do so. On the other side of the political spectrum, Musharraf had to contend with constant attacks from the MMA, who accused him of seeking to secularize Pakistan.

The country continued to be subject to increasing incidents of sectarian violence, including suicide bombings at mosques and other public places. Adding to this human-generated calamity, Pakistan suffered a devastating earthquake in October 2005 in the Kashmir region that killed tens of thousands of people and left hundreds of thousands homeless.

In early 2007 Musharraf began seeking re-election to the presidency. However, because he remained head of the military, opposition parties and then the Pakistan Supreme Court objected on constitutional grounds. In March Musharraf dismissed Chief Justice Iftikhar Mohammad Chaudhry, which sparked a general strike of Pakistani lawyers and outbreaks of violent protest in various parts of the country; the Supreme Court overturned the dismissal in July, and Chaudhry was reinstated. In October an electoral college consisting of the parliament and four provincial legislatures voted to give Musharraf another five-year term, although opposition members refused to participate in the proceedings. After the Supreme Court delayed the pronouncement of this outcome (in order to review its constitutionality), Musharraf declared a state of emergency in early November. The constitution was once again suspended, members of the Supreme Court (including Chaudhry) were dismissed, and the activities of independent news media organizations were curtailed. Later in the month, the Supreme Court, reconstituted with Musharraf appointees, upheld his re-election; Musharraf subsequently resigned his military commission and was sworn into the presidency as a civilian.

In the fall of 2007 Nawaz Sharif and Benazir Bhutto—who had also been living in exile—were permitted to return to Pakistan, and each began campaigning for upcoming parliamentary elections scheduled for early January 2008. At the end of December, however, Bhutto was assassinated at a political rally in Rawalpindi, an act that stunned Pakistanis and set off riots and rampages in different parts of the country. Musharraf, having only just lifted the state of emergency, had to again place the armed forces on special alert, and he was forced to postpone the election until mid-February.

Lawrence Ziring

The outcome of the voting was seen as a rejection of Musharraf and his rule; his PML-Q party finished a distant third behind the PPP (now led by Asif Ali Zardari, Bhutto's widower), which captured about one-third of the parliamentary seats up for election, and Sharif's party, the PML-N, with about one-fourth of the seats. In March the PPP and PML-N formed a coalition government. Yousaf Raza Gilani, a prominent member of the PPP and a former National Assembly speaker, was elected prime minister.

Disagreements emerged within the governing coalition in the months following its formation, particularly regarding the reinstatement of the Supreme Court judges Musharraf had dismissed late the previous year, and these disputes threatened to destabilize the alliance. Nevertheless, in August 2008 the coalition moved to begin impeachment charges against Musharraf, citing grave constitutional violations; on August 18, faced with the impending proceedings, Musharraf resigned.

4

Politics of Global Governance

Global governance or world governance is a movement towards political integration of transnational actors aimed at negotiating responses to problems that affect more than one state or region. It tends to involve institutionalization. These institutions of global governance—the United Nations, the International Criminal Court, the World Bank, etc.—tend to have limited or demarcatedpower to enforce compliance. The modern question of world governance exists in the context ofglobalization and globalizing regimes of power: politically, economically and culturally. In response to the acceleration of interdependence on a worldwide scale, both between human societies and between humankind and the biosphere, the term "global governance" may also be used to name the process of designating laws, rules, or regulations intended for a global scale.

Global governance is not a singular system. There is no "world government" but the many different regimes of global *governance* do have commonalities:

"While the contemporary system of global political relations is not integrated, the relation between the various regimes of global governance is not insignificant, and the system does have a common dominant organizational form. The dominant mode of organization today is bureaucratic rational – regularized, codified and rational. It is common to all modern regimes of political power and frames the transition from classical sovereignty to what David Held describes as the second regime of sovereignty – liberal international sovereignty."

DEFINITION

In a simple and broad-based definition of world governance, the term is used to designate all regulations intended for organization and centralization of human societies on a global scale. Forum for a New World Governance ; *Reasons for this Forum for a new World Governance*

Traditionally, government has been associated with "governing," or with political authority, institutions, and, ultimately, control. Governance however denotes formal political institutions that aim to coordinate and control independent social relations, and that have the ability to enforce, by force, their decisions. However, authors like James Rosenau have also used "governance" to denote the regulation of interdependent relations in the absence of an overarching political authority, such as in the international system. Some now speak of the development of "global public policy".

Adil Najam, a scholar on the subject at the Pardee School of Global Studies, Boston University has defined global governance simply as "the management of global processes in the absence of global government." According to Thomas G. Weiss, director of the Ralph Bunche Institute for International Studies at the Graduate Center (CUNY) and editor (2000–05) of the journal *Global Governance: A Review of Multilateralism and International Organizations*, "'Global governance'—which can be good, bad, or indifferent—refers to concrete cooperative problem-solving arrangements, many of which increasingly involve not only the United Nations of states but also 'other UNs,' namely international secretariats and other non-state actors."

In other words, global governance refers to the way in which global affairs are managed.

The definition is flexible as to scope; it applies whether the subject is general (e.g. global security and order) or specific (e.g. the WHO Code on the Marketing of Breast Milk Substitutes). It is flexible enough as to reach; it applies whether the participation is bilateral (e.g. an agreement to regulate usage of a river flowing in two countries), function-specific (e.g. a commodity agreement), regional (e.g. the Treaty of Tlatelolco), or global (e.g. the NPT).

These "cooperative problem-solving arrangements" may be formal, taking the shape of laws or formally constituted institutions for a variety of actors (such as state authorities, intergovernmental organizations (IGOs), non-governmental organizations (NGOs), private sector entities, other civil society actors, and individuals) to manage collective affairs. They may also be informal (as in the case of practices or guidelines) or ad hoc entities (as in the case of coalitions).

However, a single organization may nominally be given the lead role on an issue, for example the World Trade Organization(WTO) in world trade affairs. Therefore, global governance is thought to be an international process of consensus-forming which generates guidelines and agreements that affect national governments and international corporations.

Examples of such consensus would include WHO policies on health issues.

In short, global governance may be defined as "the complex of formal and informal institutions, mechanisms, relationships, and processes between and among states, markets, citizens and organizations, both inter- and non-governmental, through which collective interests on the global plane are articulated, Duties, obligations and privileges are established, and differences are mediated through educated professionals."

Titus Alexander, author of *Unravelling Global Apartheid, an Overview of World Politics,* has described the current institutions of global governance as a system of global apartheid, with numerous parallels with minority rule in the formal and informal structures of South Africa before 1991.

Usage

The dissolution of the Soviet Union in 1991 marked the end of a very long period of international history based on a policy of balance of powers. Since this historic event, the planet has entered a phase of geostrategic breakdown. The national-security model, for example, while still in place for most governments, is gradually giving way to an emerging collective conscience that extends beyond the restricted framework it represents.

The post-Cold War world of the 1990s saw a new paradigm emerge based on a number of issues:

- The growing idea of globalization as a significant theme and the subsequent weakening of nation-states, points to a prospect of transferring to a global level of regulatory instruments. Upon the model that regulation was no longer working effectively at the national or regional levels.
- An intensification of environmental concerns, which received multilateral endorsement at the Earth Summit. The Summit issues, relating to the climate and biodiversity, symbolized a new approach that was soon to be expressed conceptually by the term Global Commons.
- The emergence of conflicts over standards: trade and the environment, trade and Property rights (economics), trade and public health. These conflicts continued the traditional debate over the social effects of macroeconomic stabilization policies, and raised the question of arbitration among equally legitimate objectives in a compartmentalized governance system where the major areas of interdependence are each entrusted to a specialized international institution. Although often limited in scope, these conflicts are nevertheless symbolically powerful, as they raise the question of the principles and institutions of arbitration.
- An increased questioning of international standards and institutions by developing countries, which, having entered the global economy, find it hard to accept that industrialized countries hold onto power and give preference to their own interests. The challenge also comes from civil society, which considers that the international governance system has become the real seat of power and which rejects both its principles and procedures. Although these two lines of criticism often have conflicting beliefs and goals, they have been known to join in order to oppose the dominance of developed countries and major institutions, as demonstrated symbolically by the failure of theWorld Trade Organization Ministerial Conference of 1999.

Context

There are those who believe that world architecture depends on establishing a system of world governance. However, the equation is currently becoming far more complicated: Whereas the process used to be about regulating and limiting the individual power of states to avoid disturbing or overturning the status quo, the issue for today's world governance is to have a collective influence on the world's destiny by establishing a system for regulating the many interactions that lie beyond the province of state action. The political homogenization of the planet that has followed the advent of what is known as liberal democracy in its many forms should make it easier to establish a world governance system that goes beyond market laissez-faire and the democratic peace originally formulated by Immanuel Kant, which constitutes a sort of geopolitical laissez-faire.

Another view regarding the establishment of global governance is based on the difficulties to achieve equitable development at the world scale. "To secure for all human beings in all parts of the world the conditions allowing a decent and meaningful life requires enormous human energies and far-reaching changes in policies. The task is all the more demanding as the world faces numerous other problems, each related to or even part of the development challenge, each similarly pressing, and each calling for the same urgent attention. But, asArnold Toynbee has said, 'Our age is the first generation since the dawn of history in which mankind dares to believe it practical to make the benefits of civilization available to the whole human race'."

Need

Because of the heterogeneity of preferences, which are enduring despite globalization, are often perceived as an implacable homogenization process. Americans and Europeans provide a good example of this point: on some issues they have differing common grounds in which the division between the public and private spheres still exist. Tolerance for inequalities and the growing demand for redistribution, attitudes toward risk, and over property rights vs human rights, set the stage. In certain cases, globalization even serves to accentuate differences rather than as a force for homogenization. Responsibility must play its part with respect to regional and International governments, when balancing the needs of its citizenry.

With the growing emergence of a global civic awareness, comes opposition to globalization and its effects. A rapidly growing number of movements and organizations have taken the debate to the international level. Although it may have limitations, this trend is one response to the increasing importance of world issues, that effect the planet.

Crisis of purpose

Pierre Jacquet, Jean Pisani-Ferry, and Laurence Tubiana argue that "[t]o ensure that decisions taken for international integration are sustainable, it is important that populations see the benefits, that states agree on their goals and that the institutions governing the process are seen as legitimate. These three conditions are only partially being met."

The authors refer to a "crisis of purpose" and international institutions suffering from "imbalance" and inadequacy. They believe that for these institutions, "a gap has been created between the nature of the problems that need tackling and an institutional architecture which does not reflect the hierarchy of today's problems. For example, the environment has become a subject of major concern and central negotiation, but it does not have the institutional support that is compatible with its importance."

World government

Global governance is not world government, and even less democratic globalization. In fact, global governance would not be necessary, were there a world government. Domestic governments have monopolies on the use of force—the power of enforcement. Global governance refers to the political interaction that is required to solve problems that affect more than one state or region when there is no power to enforce compliance. Problems arise, and networks of actors are constructed to deal with them in the absence of an international analogue to a domestic government. This system has been termed disaggregated sovereignty.

Consensus example

Improved global problem solving need not involve the establishment of additional powerful formal global institutions. It does involve building consensus on norms and practices. One such area, currently under construction, is the development and improvement of accountability mechanisms. For example, the UN Global Compact brings together companies, UN agencies, labor organizations, and civil society to support universal environmental and social principles. Participation is entirely voluntary, and there is no enforcement of the principles by an outside regulatory body. Companies adhere to these practices both because they make economic sense, and because stakeholders, especially shareholders, can monitor their compliance easily. Mechanisms such as the Global Compact can improve the ability of affected individuals and populations to hold companies accountable. However, corporations participating in the UN Global Compact have been criticized for their merely minimal standards, the absence of sanction-and-control measures, their lack of commitment to social and ecological standards, minimal acceptance among corporations around the world, and the high cost involved in reporting annually to small and medium-sized business

Issues

Expansion of normative mechanisms and globalization of institutions

One of the effects of globalization is the increasing numbers of rules placed upon businesses, in the global market-place. Jan Aart Scholte asserts, however, that these changes are inadequate to meet the needs: "Along with the general intensified globalization of social relations in contemporary history has come an unprecedented expansion of regulatory apparatuses that cover planetary jurisdictions and constituencies. On the whole, however, this global governance remains weak relative to pressing current needs for global public policy. Shortfalls in moral standing, legal foundations, material delivery, democratic credentials and charismatic leadership have together generated large legitimacy deficits in existing global regimes."

On another level, there is need to set up, in all spheres, an increasing number of networks and institutions operating on a global scale. Proposals and initiatives have been developed at various sources: political parties, unions, regional authorities, and members of parliament in sovereign states.

Formulation and objectives

One of the conditions for building a world democratic governance should be the development of platforms for citizen dialog on the legal formulation of world governance and the harmonization of objectives.

This legal formulation could take the form of a Global Constitution. According to Pierre Calame and Gustavo Marin, "[a] Global Constitution resulting from a process for the institution of a global community will act as the common reference for establishing the order of rights and duties applicable to United Nations agencies and to the other multilateral institutions, such as the International Monetary Fund, the World Bank, and the World Trade Organization."

As for formulating objectives, the necessary but insufficient ambition of the United NationsMillennium Development Goals, which aim to safeguard humankind and the planet, and the huge difficulties in implementing them, illustrates the inadequacy of institutional initiatives that do not have popular support for having failed to invite citizens to take part in the elaboration process.

Furthermore, the Global Constitution "must clearly express a limited number of overall objectives that are to be the basis of global governance and are to guide the common action of the U.N. agencies and the multilateral institutions, where the specific role of each of these is subordinated to the pursuit of these common objectives."

Calame proposes the following objectives:

1. instituting the conditions for sustainable development
2. reducing inequalities
3. establishing lasting peace while respecting diversity.

Reforming international institutions

Is the UN capable of taking on the heavy responsibility of managing the planet's serious problems? More specifically, can the UN reform itself in such a way as to be able to meet this challenge? At a time when the financial crisis of 2008 is raising the same questions posed by the climate disasters of previous years regarding the unpredictable consequences of disastrous human management, can international financial institutions be reformed in such a way as to go back to their original task, which was to provide financial help to countries in need?

Lack of political will and citizen involvement at the international level has also brought about the submission of international institutions to the "neoliberal" agenda, particularly financial institutions such as the World Bank, the International Monetary Fund, and the World Trade Organization (WTO).

Pierre Calame gives an account of this development, while Joseph E. Stiglitz points out that the need for international institutions like the IMF, the World Bank, and the WTO has never been so great, but people's trust in them has never been so low.

One of the key aspects of the United Nations reform is the problem of the representativeness of the General Assembly. The Assembly operates on the principle of "one state, one vote," so that states of hugely varying sizes have the same impact on the vote, which distorts representativeness and results in a major loss of credibility. Accordingly, "the General Assembly has lost any real capacity to influence. This means that the mechanisms for action and consultation organized by rich countries have the leading role."

Gustave Massiah advocates defining and implementing a radical reform of the UN. The author proposes building new foundations that can provide the basis for global democracy and the creation of a Global Social Contract, rooted in the respect and protection of civil, political, economic, social, and cultural rights, as well as in the recognition of the strategic role of international law. The Brussels-based Global Governance Institute is dedicated to a more equitable, peaceful and sustainable global order.

The three 'gaps' in global governance

There is the jurisdictional gap, between the increasing need for global governance in many areas - such as health - and the lack of an authority with the power, or jurisdiction, to take action. Moreover, the gap of incentive between the need for international cooperation and the motivation to undertake it. The incentive gap is said to be closing as globalization provides increasing impetus for countries to cooperate. However, there are concerns that, as Africa lags further behind economically, its influence on global governance processes will diminish. At last, the participation gap, which refers to the fact that international cooperation remains primarily the affair of governments, leaving civil society groups on the fringes of policy-making. On the other hand, globalization of communication is facilitating the development of global civil society movements.

Themes

In its initial phase, world governance was able to draw on themes inherited from geopolitics and the theory of international relations, such as peace, defense, geostrategy, diplomatic relations, and trade relations. But as globalization progresses and the number of interdependences increases, the global level is also highly relevant to a far wider range of subjects. Following are a number of examples.

Environmental governance and managing the planet

"The crisis brought about by the accelerated pace and the probably irreversible character of the impact of human activities on nature requires collective answers from governments and citizens. Nature ignores political and social barriers, and the global dimension of the crisis cancels the effects of any action initiated unilaterally by state governments or sectoral institutions, however powerful they may be. Climate change, ocean and air pollution, nuclear risks and those related to genetic manipulation, the reduction and extinction of resources and biodiversity, and above all a development model that remains largely unquestioned globally are all among the various manifestations of this accelerated and probably irreversible impact.

This impact is the factor, in the framework of globalization, that most challenges a system of states competing with each other to the exclusion of all others: among the different fields of global governance, environmental management is the most wanting in urgent answers to the crisis in the form of collective actions by the whole of the human community. At the same time, these actions should help to model and strengthen the progressive building of this community."

Proposals in this area have discussed the issue of how collective environmental action is possible. Many multilateral, environment-related agreements have been forged in the past 30 years, but their implementation remains difficult. There is also some discussion on the possibility of setting up an international organization that would centralize all the issues related to international environmental protection, such as the proposed World Environment Organization (WEO). The United Nations Environment Program (UNEP) could play this role, but it is a small-scale organization with a limited mandate. The question has given rise to two opposite views: the European Union, especially France and Germany, along with a number of NGOs, is in favor of creating a WEO; the United Kingdom, the USA, and most developing countries prefer opting for voluntary initiatives.

The International Institute for Sustainable Development proposes a "reform agenda" for global environmental governance. The main argument is that there seems to exist an unspoken but powerful consensus on the essential objectives of a system of global environmental governance. These goals would require top-quality leadership, a strong environmental policy based on knowledge, effective cohesion and coordination, good management of the institutions constituting the environmental governance system, and spreading environmental concerns and actions to other areas of international policy and action.

A World Environment Organisation

The focus of environmental issues shifted to climate change from 1992 onwards. Due to the transboundary nature of climate change, various calls have been made for a World Environment Organisation (WEO) (sometimes referred to as a Global

Environment Organisation) to tackle this global problem on a global scale. At present, a single worldwide governing body with the powers to develop and enforce environmental policy does not exist. The idea for the creation of a WEO was discussed thirty years ago but is receiving fresh attention in the light of arguably disappointing outcomes from recent, 'environmental mega-conferences'(e.g.Rio Summit and Earth Summit 2002).

Current global environmental governance

International environmental organisations do exist. The United Nations Environmental Programme (UNEP), created in 1972, coordinates the environmental activity of countries in the UN. UNEP and similar international environmental organisations are seen as not up to the task. They are criticised as being institutionally weak, fragmented, lacking in standing and providing non-optimal environmental protection. It has been stated that the current decentralised, poorly funded and strictly intergovernmental regime for global environmental issues is sub-standard. However, the creation of a WEO may threaten to undermine some of the more effective aspects of contemporary global environmental governance; notably its fragmented nature, from which flexibility stems. This also allows responses to be more effective and links to be forged across different domains. Even though the environment and climate change are framed as global issues, Levin states that 'it is precisely at this level that government institutions are least effective and trust most delicate' while Oberthur and Gehring argue that it would offer little more than institutional restructuring for its own sake.

A World Environment Organisation and the World Trade Organisation

Many proposals for the creation of a WEO have emerged from the trade and environment debate. It has been argued that instead of creating a WEO to safeguard the environment, environmental issues should be directly incorporated into the World Trade Organisation(WTO). The WTO has "had success in integrating trade agreements and opening up markets because it is able to apply legal pressure to nation states and resolve disputes". Greece and Germany are currently in discussion about the possibility of solar energy being used to repay some of Greece's debt after their economy crashed in 2010. This exchange of resources, if it is accepted, is an example of increased international cooperation and an instance where the WTO could embrace energy trade agreements. If the future holds similar trade agreements, then an environmental branch of the WTO would surely be necessary. However critics of a WTO/WEO arrangement say that this would neither concentrate on more directly addressing underlying market failures, nor greatly improve rule-making.

The creation of a new agency, whether it be linked to the WTO or not, has now been endorsed by Renato Ruggiero, the former head of the World Trade Organization (WTO), as well as by the new WTO director-designate, Supachai Panitchpakdi. The debate over a global institutional framework for environmental issues will undoubtedly rumble on but at present there is little support for any one proposal.

Governance of the economy and of globalisation

The 2008 financial crisis exploded, once again, the myth that the all-powerful free-market forces will correct all serious financial malfunctioning on their own, as well as belief in the presumed independence of the economy. Lacking in transparency and far from democratic, international financial institutions have proven incapable of handling the market's critical breakdown.

Free-market economy is incapable of meeting the population's needs on its own. Without regulation and without consideration of social and environmental externalities, free-market capitalism turns into an uncontrollable machine that produces more and more wealth concentrated in fewer and fewer hands, leading the global community into a head-on collision with disaster and chaos. Its capacity to produce is not in doubt: the problem is absence of redistribution, which is the result of absence of political and citizen will to change the rules of the game.

Nonetheless, the debate on the failings of the system has begun to turn in the academic world into solution seeking, which is a step in the right direction. According to Tubiana and Severino, "refocusing the doctrine of international cooperation on the concept of public goods offers the possibility... of breaking the deadlock in international negotiations on development, with the perception of shared interests breathing new life into an international solidarity that is running out of steam."

Stiglitz, on his part, argues that a number of global public goods should be produced and supplied to the populations, but they are not, and a number of global externalities should be taken into consideration, but they are not. On the other hand, he contends, the international stage is often used to find solutions to completely unrelated problems under the protection of opacity and secrecy, which would be impossible in a national democratic framework.

On the subject of international trade, Susan George states that "... in a rational world, it would be possible to construct a trading system serving the needs of people in both North and South.... Under such a system, crushing third world debt and the devastating structural adjustment policies applied by the World Bank and the IMF would have been unthinkable, although the system would not have abolished capitalism."

Political and institutional governance

Building a responsible world governance that would make it possible to adapt the political organization of society to globalization implies establishing a democratic political legitimacy at every level: local, national, regional and global.

Obtaining this legitimacy requires rethinking and reforming, all at the same time:

- the fuzzy maze of various international organizations, instituted mostly in the wake of World War II; what is needed is a system of international organizations with greater resources and a greater intervention capacity, more transparent, fairer, and more democratic;
- the Westphalian system, the very nature of states along with the role they play with regard to the other institutions, and their relations to each other; states will have to share part of their sovereignty with institutions and bodies at other territorial levels, and all with have to begin a major process to deepen democracy and make their organization more responsible;

- the meaning of citizen sovereignty in the different government systems and the role of citizens as political protagonists; there is a need to rethink the meaning of political representation and participation and to sow the seeds of a radical change of consciousness that will make it possible to move in the direction of a situation in which citizens, in practice, will play the leading role at every scale.

GOVERNANCE OF PEACE, SECURITY, AND CONFLICT RESOLUTION

Armed conflicts have changed in form and intensity since the Berlin wall came down in 1989. The events of 9/11, the wars in Afghanistan and in Iraq, and repeated terrorist attacks all show that conflicts can become lethal for the entire world, well beyond the belligerents directly involved. The leaders of a handful of major powers, starting with the biggest of all, the United States, have used war as a means of resolving conflicts and may well continue to do so. If many in the United States believe that fundamentalist Muslim networks are likely to continue to launch attacks, in Europe nationalist movements have proved to be the most persistent terrorist threat. The 'Global War on Terrorism' arguably presents a form of emerging global governance in the sphere of security with the United States leading cooperation among the Western states, non-Western nations and international institutions. Beyer argues that participation in this form of 'hegemonic governance' is caused both by a shared identity and ideology with the US, as well as cost-benefit considerations. Pesawar school attack 2014 is a big challenge to us. Militants from the Pakistani Taliban have attacked an army-run school in Peshawar, killing 141 people, 132 of them children, the military say.<www.bbc.com>

At the same time, civil wars continue to break out across the world, particularly in areas where civil and human rights are not respected, such as Central and Eastern Africa and the Middle East. These and other regions remain deeply entrenched in permanent crises, hampered by authoritarian regimes, many of them being supported by the United States, reducing entire swathes of the population to wretched living conditions. The wars and conflicts we are faced with have a variety of causes: economic inequality, social conflict, religious sectarianism, Western imperialism, colonial legacies, disputes over territory and over control of basic resources such as water or land. They are all illustrations a deep-rooted crisis of world governance.

The resulting bellicose climate imbues international relations with competitive nationalism and contributes, in rich and poor countries alike, to increasing military budgets, siphoning off huge sums of public money to the benefit of the arms industry and military-oriented scientific innovation, hence fueling global insecurity. Of these enormous sums, a fraction would be enough to provide a permanent solution for the basic needs of the planet's population hence practically eliminating the causes of war and terrorism.

Andrée Michel argues that the arms race is not only proceeding with greater vigor, it is the surest means for Western countries to maintain their hegemony over countries of the South. Following the break-up of the Eastern bloc countries, she maintains, a strategy for the manipulation of the masses was set up with a permanent invention of an enemy (currently incarnated by Iraq, Iran, Libya, Syria, and North Korea) and by kindling fear and hate of others to justify perpetuating the Military-industrial Complex and arms sales. The author also recalls that the "Big Five" at the UN who have the veto right are responsible for 85% of arms sales around the world.

Proposals for the governance of peace, security, and conflict resolution begin by addressing prevention of the causes of conflicts, whether economic, social, religious, political, or territorial. This requires assigning more resources to improving people's living conditions—health, accommodation, food, and work—and to education, including education in the values of peace, social justice, and unity and diversity as two sides of the same coin representing the global village.

Resources for peace could be obtained by regulating, or even reducing military budgets, which have done nothing but rise in the past recent years. This process could go hand in hand with plans for global disarmament and the conversion of arms industries, applied proportionally to all countries, including the major powers. Unfortunately, the warlike climate of the last decade has served to relegate all plans for global disarmament, even in civil-society debates, and to pigeonhole them as a long-term goal or even a Utopian vision. This is definitely a setback for the cause of peace and for humankind; but it is far from being a permanent obstacle.

International institutions also have a role to play in resolving armed conflicts. Small international rapid deployment units could intervene in these with an exclusive mandate granted by a reformed and democratic United Nations system or by relevant regional authorities such as the European Union. These units could be formed specifically for each conflict, using armies from several countries as was the case when the UNIFIL was reinforced during the 2006 Lebanon War. On the other hand, no national army would be authorized to intervene unilaterally outside its territory without a UN or regional mandate.

Another issue that is worth addressing concerns the legitimate conditions for the use of force and conduct during war. Jean-René Bachelet offers an answer with the conceptualization of a military ethics corresponding to the need for a "principle of humanity." The author defines this principle as follows: "All human beings, whatever their race, nationality, gender, age, opinion, or religion, belong to one same humanity, and every individual has an inalienable right to respect for his life, integrity, and dignity."

Governance of science, education, information, and communications

The World Trade Organization's (WTO) agenda of liberalizing public goods and services are related to culture, science, education, health, living organisms, information, and communication. This plan has been only partially offset by the alter-globalization movement, starting with the events that took place at the 1999 Seattle meeting, and on a totally different and probably far more influential scale in the medium and long term, by the astounding explosion of collaborative practices on the Internet. However, lacking political and widespread citizen support as well as sufficient resources, civil society has not so far been able to develop and disseminate alternative plans for society as a whole on a global scale, even though plenty of proposals and initiatives have been developed, some more successful than others, to build a fairer, more responsible, and more solidarity-based world in all of these areas.

Above all, each country tries to impose their values and collective prefereences within international institutions such like WTO or UNESCO, particularly in the Medias sector. This is an excellent opportunity to promote their soft power, for instance with the promotion of the cinema

As far as science is concerned, "[r]esearch increasingly bows to the needs of financial markets, turning competence and knowledge into commodities, making employment flexible and informal, and establishing contracts based on goals and profits for the benefit of private interests in compliance with the competition principle. The directions that research has taken in the past two decades and the changes it has undergone have drastically removed it from its initial mission (producing competence and knowledge, maintaining independence) with no questioning of its current and future missions. Despite the progress, or perhaps even as its consequence, humankind continues to face critical problems: poverty and hunger are yet to be vanquished, nuclear arms are proliferating, environmental disasters are on the rise, social injustice is growing, and so on.

Neoliberal commercialization of the commons favors the interests of pharmaceutical companies instead of the patients', of food-processing companies instead of the farmers' and consumers'. Public research policies have done nothing but support this process of economic profitability, where research results are increasingly judged by the financial markets. The system of systematically patenting knowledge and living organisms is thus being imposed throughout the planet through the 1994 WTO agreements on intellectual property. Research in many areas is now being directed by private companies."

On the global level, "[i]nstitutions dominating a specific sector also, at every level, present the risk of reliance on technical bodies that use their own references and deliberate in an isolated environment. This process can be observed with the 'community of patents' that promotes the patenting of living organisms, as well as with authorities controlling nuclear energy. This inward-looking approach is all the more dangerous that communities of experts are, in all complex technical and legal spheres, increasingly dominated by the major economic organizations that finance research and development."

On the other hand, several innovative experiments have emerged in the sphere of science, such as: conscience clauses and citizens' panels as a tool for democratizing the production system: science shops and community-based research. Politically committed scientists are also increasingly organizing at the global level.

As far as education is concerned, the effect of commoditization can be seen in the serious tightening of education budgets, which has an impact on the quality of general education as a public service. The Global Future Online report reminds us that "... at the half-way point towards 2015 *(author's note: the deadline for the Millennium Goals)*, the gaps are daunting: 80 million children (44 million of them girls) are out of school, with marginalized groups (26 million disabled and 30 million conflict-affected children) continuing to be excluded. And while universal access is critical, it must be coupled with improved learning outcomes—in particular, children achieving the basic literacy, numeracy and life skills essential for poverty reduction."

In addition to making the current educational system available universally, there is also a call to improve the system and adapt it to the speed of changes in a complex and unpredictable world. On this point, Edgar Morin asserts that we must "[r]ethink our way of organizing knowledge. This means breaking down the traditional barriers between disciplines and designing new ways to reconnect that which has been torn apart." The UNESCO report drawn up by Morin contains "seven principles for education of the future": detecting the error and illusion that have always parasitized the human spirit and human behavior; making knowledge relevant, i.e. a way of thinking that makes distinctions and connections; teaching the human condition; teaching terrestrial identity; facing human and scientific uncertainties and teaching strategies to deal with them; teaching understanding of the self and of others, and an ethics for humankind.

The exponential growth of new technologies, the Internet in particular, has gone hand in hand with the development over the last decade of a global community producing and exchanging goods. This development is permanently altering the shape of the entertainment, publishing, and music and media industries, among others.

It is also influencing the social behavior of increasing numbers of people, along with the way in which institutions, businesses, and civil society are organized. Peer-to-peer communities and collective knowledge-building projects such as Wikipedia have involved millions of users around the world. There are even more innovative initiatives, such as alternatives to private copyright such as Creative Commons, cyber democracy practices, and a real possibility of developing them on the sectoral, regional, and global levels.

REGIONAL VIEWS

Regional players, whether regional conglomerates such as Mercosur and the European Union, or major countries seen as key regional players such as China, the United States, and India, are taking a growing interest in world governance.

Interdependence among countries and regions hardly being refutable today, regional integration is increasingly seen not only as a process in itself, but also in its relation to the rest of the world, sometimes turning questions like "What can the world bring to my country or region?" into "What can my country or region bring to the rest of the world?" Following are a few examples of how regional players are dealing with these questions.

Africa

Often seen as a problem to be solved rather than a people or region with an opinion to express on international policy, Africans and Africa draw on a philosophical tradition of community and social solidarity that can serve as inspiration to the rest of the world and contribute to building world governance. One example is given by Sabelo J. Ndlovu-Gathseni when he reminds us of the relevance of the Ubuntu concept, which stresses the interdependence of human beings.

African civil society has thus begun to draw up proposals for governance of the continent, which factor in all of the dimensions: local, African, and global.

Examples include proposals by the network "Dialogues sur la gouvernance en Afrique" for "the construction of a local legitimate governance," state reform "capable of meeting the continent's development challenges," and "effective regional governance to put an end to Africa's marginalization."

United States

Foreign-policy proposals announced by the recently re-elected President Barack Obama include restoring the Global Poverty Act, which aims to contribute to meeting the UN Millennium Development Goals to reduce by half the world population living on less than a dollar a day by 2015.

Foreign aid is expected to double to 50 billion dollars. The money will be used to help build educated and healthy communities, reduce poverty and improve the population's health.

In terms of international institutions, The White House Web site advocates reform of the World Bank and the IMF, without going into any detail. Below are further points in the Obama-Biden plan for foreign policy directly related to world governance:

- strengthening of the nuclear non-proliferation treaty;
- global de-nuclearization in several stages including stepping up cooperation with Russia to significantly reduce stocks of nuclear arms in both countries;
- revision of the culture of secrecy: institution of a National Declassification Center to make declassification secure but routine, efficient, and cost-effective;
- increase in global funds for AIDS, TB and malaria. Eradication of malaria-related deaths by 2015 by making medicines and mosquito nets far more widely available;

- increase in aid for children and maternal health as well as access to reproductive health-care programs;
- creation of a 2-billion-dollar global fund for education. Increased funds for providing access to drinking water and sanitation;
- other similarly large-scale measures covering agriculture, small- and medium-sized enterprises and support for a model of international trade that fosters job creation and improves the quality of life in poor countries;
- in terms of energy and global warming, Obama advocates a) an 80% reduction of greenhouse-gas emissions by 2050 b) investing 150 billion dollars in alternative energies over the next 10 years and c) creating a Global Energy Forum capable of initiating a new generation of climate protocols.

Latin America

The 21st century has seen the arrival of a new and diverse generation of left-wing governments in Latin America. This has opened the door to initiatives to launch political and governance renewal.

A number of these initiatives are significant for the way they redefine the role of the state by drawing on citizen participation, and can thus serve as a model for a future world governance built first and foremost on the voice of the people. The constituent assemblies in Ecuador and Bolivia are fundamental examples of this phenomenon.

In Ecuador, social and indigenous movements were behind the discussions that began in 1990 on setting up a constituent assembly. In the wake of Rafael Correa's arrival at the head of the country in November 2006, widespread popular action with the slogan "*que se vayan todos*" (let them all go away) succeeded in getting all the political parties of congress to accept a convocation for a referendum on setting up the assembly.

In April 2007, Rafael Correa's government organized a consultation with the people to approve setting up a constituent assembly. Once it was approved, 130 members of the assembly were elected in September, including 100 provincial members, 24 national members and 6 for migrants in Europe, Latin America and the USA. The assembly was officially established in November. Assembly members belonged to traditional political parties as well as the new social movements. In July 2008, the assembly completed the text for the new constitution and in September 2008 there was a referendum to approve it. Approval for the new text won out, with 63.9% of votes for compared to 28.1% of votes against and a 24.3% abstention rate.

The new constitution establishes the rule of law on economic, social, cultural and environmental rights (ESCER). It transforms the legal model of the social state subject to the rule of law into a "constitution of guaranteed well-being" (*Constitución del bienestar garantizado*) inspired by the ancestral community ideology of "good living" propounded by the Quechuas of the past, as well as by 21st century socialist ideology. The constitution promotes the concept of food sovereignty by establishing a protectionist system that favors domestic production and trade. It also develops a model of public aid for education, health, infrastructures and other services.

In addition, it adds to the three traditional powers, a fourth power called the Council of Citizen Participation and Social Control, made up of former constitutional control bodies and social movements, and mandated to assess whether public policies are constitutional or not.

The new Bolivian constitution was approved on 25 January 2009 by referendum, with 61.4% votes in favor, 38.6% against and a 90.2% turnout.

The proposed constitution was prepared by a constituent assembly that did not only reflect the interests of political parties and the elite, but also represented the indigenous peoples and social movements. As in Ecuador, the proclamation of a constituent assembly was demanded by the people, starting in 1990 at a gathering of indigenous peoples from the entire country, continuing with the indigenous marches in the early 2000s and then with the Program Unity Pact (*Pacto de Unidad Programático*) established by family farmers and indigenous people in September 2004 in Santa Cruz.

The constitution recognizes the autonomy of indigenous peoples, the existence of a specific indigenous legal system, exclusive ownership of forest resources by each community and a quota of indigenous members of parliament. It grants autonomy to counties, which have the right to manage their natural resources and elect their representatives directly.

The *latifundio* system has been outlawed, with maximum ownership of 5,000 hectares allowed per person. Access to water and sanitation are covered by the constitution as human rights that the state has to guarantee, as well as other basic services such as electricity, gas, postal services, and telecommunications that can be provided by either the state or contracting companies.

The new constitution also establishes a social and community economic model made up of public, private, and social organizations, and cooperatives.

It guarantees private initiative and freedom of enterprise, and assigns public organizations the task of managing natural resources and related processes as well as developing public services covered by the constitution. National and cooperative investment is favored over private and international investment.

The "unitary plurinational" state of Bolivia has 36 official indigenous languages along with Spanish. Natural resources belong to the people and are administered by the state. The form of democracy in place is no longer considered as exclusively representative and/or based on parties.

Thus, "the people deliberate and exercise government via their representatives and the constituent assembly, the citizen legislative initiative and the referendum..."and "popular representation is exercised via the political parties, citizen groups, and indigenous peoples."

This way, "political parties, and/or citizen groups and/or indigenous peoples can present candidates directly for the offices of president, vice-president, senator, house representative, constituent-assembly member, councilor, mayor, and municipal agent. The same conditions apply legally to all...."

Also in Latin America: "Amazonia... is an enormous biodiversity reservoir and a major climate-regulation agent for the planet but is being ravaged and deteriorated at an accelerated pace; it is a territory almost entirely devoid of governance, but also a breeding place of grassroots organization initiatives.". "Amazonia can be the fertile field of a true school of 'good' governance if it is looked after as a common and valuable good, first by Brazilians (65% of Amazonia is within Brazilian borders) and the people of the South American countries surrounding it, but also by all the Earth's inhabitants."

Accordingly, "[f]rom a world-governance perspective, [Amazonia] is in a way an enormous laboratory. Among other things, Amazonia enables a detailed examination of the negative effects of productivism and of the different forms of environmental packaging it can hide behind, including 'sustainable development.' Galloping urbanization, Human Rights violations, the many different types of conflicts (14 different types of conflicts have been identified within the hundreds of cases observed in Amazonia), protection of indigenous populations and their active participation in local governance: these are among the many Amazonian challenges also affecting the planet as a whole, not to mention the environment.

The hosts of local initiatives, including among the indigenous populations, are however what may be most interesting in Amazonia in that they testify to the real, concrete possibility of a different form of organization that combines a healthy local economy, good social cohesion, and a true model of sustainable development—this time not disguised as something else. All of this makes Amazonia 'a territory of solutions.'"

According to Arnaud Blin, the Amazonian problem helps to define certain fundamental questions on the future of humankind. First, there is the question of social justice: " ow do we build a new model of civilization that promotes social justice? How do we set up a new social architecture that allows us to live together?" The author goes on to refer to concepts such as the concept of "people's territory " or even "life territory" rooted in the indigenous tradition and serving to challenge private property and social injustice. He then suggests that the emerging concept of the "responsibility to protect," following up on the "right of humanitarian intervention" and until now used to try to protect populations endangered by civil wars, could also be applied to populations threatened by economic predation and to environmental protection.

Asia

The growing interest in world governance in Asia represents an alternative approach to official messages, dominated by states' nationalist visions. An initiative to develop proposals for world governance took place in Shanghai in 2006, attended by young people from every continent.

The initiative produced ideas and projects that can be classified as two types: the first and more traditional type, covering the creation of a number of new institutions such as an International Emissions Organization, and a second more innovative type based on organizing network-based systems.

For example, a system of cooperative control on a worldwide level among states and self-organization of civil society into networks using new technologies, a process that should serve to set up a *Global Calling-for-Help Center* or a new model based on citizens who communicate freely, share information, hold discussions, and seek consensus-based solutions.They would use the Internet and the media, working within several types of organizations: universities, NGOs, local volunteers and civil-society groups.

Given the demographic importance of the continent, the development of discussion on governance and practices in Asia at the regional level, as well as global-level proposals, will be decisive in the years ahead in the strengthening of global dialog among all sorts of stakeholders, a dialog that should produce a fairer world order.

Europe

According to Michel Rocard, Europe does not have a shared vision, but a collective history that allows Europeans to opt for projects for gradual political construction such as the European Union. Drawing on this observation, Rocard conceives of a

European perspective that supports the development of three strategies for constructing world governance: reforming the UN, drawing up international treaties to serve as the main source of global regulations, and "the progressive penetration of the international scene by justice."

Rocard considers that there are a number of "great questions of the present days" including recognition by all nations of the International Criminal Court, the option of an international police force authorized to arrest international criminals, and the institution of judicial procedures to deal with tax havens, massively polluting activities, and states supporting terrorist activities.

He also outlines "new problems" that should foster debate in the years to come on questions such as a project for a Declaration of Interdependence, how to re-equilibrate world trade and WTO activities, and how to create world regulations for managing collective goods (air, drinking water, oil, etc.) and services (education, health, etc.).

Martin Ortega similarly suggests that the European Union should make a more substantial contribution to global governance, particularly through concerted action in international bodies. European states, for instance, should reach an agreement on the reform of the United Nations Security Council.

In 2011, the European Strategy and Policy Analysis System (ESPAS), an inter-institutional pilot project of the European Union which aims to assist EU policy formulation through the identification and critical analysis of long-term global trends, highlighted the importance of expanding global governance over the next 20 years.

STAKEHOLDERS' VIEWS

It is too soon to give a general account of the view of world-governance stakeholders, although interest in world governance is on the rise on the regional level, and we will certainly see different types of stakeholders and social sectors working to varying degrees at the international level and taking a stand on the issue in the years to come.

Institutional and state stakeholders

Members of parliament

The World Parliamentary Forum, open to members of parliament from all nations and held every year at the same time as the World Social Forum, drew up a declaration at the sixth forum in Caracas in 2006. The declaration contains a series of proposals that express participants' opinion on the changes referred to.

Military

The International Alliance of Military for Peace and Security is a platform of expression and discussion of ideas and positions on various topics affecting security and stability, the goal of which is to "discuss issues of security and defense, as well as ways of promoting a new 'Consciousness of Security and Defense' to citizens, which allows them to better understand the risks and opportunities inherent in international relations within a globalizing world and to participate actively in the definition of conditions to ensure the stability of international relations and peace." The Alliance is made up of members of the military and other people interested in issues related to human security.

Some of the member organizations of the Alliance of Military have drawn up a *Charter for the Promotion of an "European Security and Defence Awareness*. This document is written for public opinion and formulates objectives, tasks, and the conditions for adhering to and setting up European-level reinforced military cooperation. One of the Alliance's key goals is to promote the European Security and Defense Policy (ESDP) to a broader public, without wishing to call into question transatlantic partnership and the role of the UN. The actions of national governments and European institutions in the areas of security and defense must be founded on the adherence of European citizens.

Regional organizations

The European Commission referred to global governance in its White Paper on European Governance. It contends that the search for better global governance draws on the same set of shared challenges humanity is currently facing. These challenges can be summed up by a series of goals: sustainable development, security, peace and equity (in the sense of "fairness").

Non-state stakeholders

The freedom of thought enjoyed by non-state stakeholders enables them to formulate truly alternative ideas on world-governance issues, but they have taken little or no advantage of this opportunity.

Pierre Calame believes that "[n]on-state actors have always played an essential role in global regulation, but their role will grow considerably in this, the beginning of the twenty-first Century... Non-state actors play a key role in world governance in different domains... To better understand and develop the non-state actors' role, it should be studied in conjunction with the general principles of governance." "Non-state actors, due to their vocation, size, flexibility, methods of organization and action, interact with states in an equal manner; however this does not mean that their action is better adapted."

One alternative idea encapsulated by many not-for-profit organisations relates to ideas in the 'Human Potential Movement' and might be summarised as a mission statement along these lines: 'To create an accepted framework for all humankind, that is self-regulating and which enables every person to achieve their fullest potential in harmony with the world and its place in existence.'

The use of the word 'humankind' is instead of 'mankind'. There are many examples of the use of the word 'humankind' and possibly therefore of this choice e.g. in the opening narration of the TV series Wonders of the Universe by Professor Brian Cox (physicist).

'Self-regulation' is meant to invoke the concept of regulation which includes rule-making such as laws, and related ideas e.g. legal doctrineas well as other frameworks. However its scope is wider than this and intended to encompass cybernetics which allows for the study of regulation in as many varied contexts as possible from the regulation of gene expression to the Press Complaints Commission for example.

World Religious Leaders

Since 2005, religious leaders from a diverse array of faith traditions have engaged in dialogue with G8 leaders around issues of global governance and world risk.

Drawing on the cultural capital of diverse religious traditions, they seek to strengthen democratic norms by influencing political leaders to include the interests of the most vulnerable when they make their decisions. Some have argued that religion is a key to transforming or fixing global governance.

Proposals

Several stakeholders have produced lists of proposals for a new world governance that is fairer, more responsible, solidarity-based, interconnected and respectful of the planet's diversity. Some examples are given below.

Joseph E. Stiglitz proposes a list of reforms related to the internal organization of international institutions and their external role in the framework of global-governance architecture.

He also deals with global taxation, the management of global resources and the environment, the production and protection of global knowledge, and the need for a global legal infrastructure.

A number of other proposals are contained in the World Governance Proposal Paper: giving concrete expression to the principle of responsibility; granting civil society greater involvement in drawing up and implementing international regulations; granting national parliaments greater involvement in drawing up and implementing international regulations; re-equilibrating trade mechanisms and adopting regulations to benefit the southern hemisphere; speeding up the institution of regional bodies; extending and specifying the concept of the commons; redefining proposal and decision-making powers in order to reform the United Nations; developing independent observation, early-warning, and assessment systems; diversifying and stabilizing the basis for financing international collective action; and engaging in a wide-reaching process of consultation, a new Bretton Woods for the United Nations.

This list provides more examples of proposals:

- the security of societies and its correlation with the need for global reforms— —a controlled legally-based economy focused on stability, growth, full employment, and North-South convergence;
- equal rights for all, implying the institution of a global redistribution process;
- eradication of poverty in all countries;
- sustainable development on a global scale as an absolute imperative in political action at all levels;
- fight against the roots of terrorism and crime;
- consistent, effective, and fully democratic international institutions;
- Europe sharing its experience in meeting the challenges of globalization and adopting genuine partnership strategies to build a new form of multilateralism.

Dr. Rajesh Tandon, president of the FIM (Montreal International Forum) and of PRIA (Participatory Research in Asia), prepared a framework document entitled "Democratization of Global Governance for Global Democracy: Civil Society Visions and Strategies (G05) conference." He used the document to present five principles that could provide a basis for civil society actions: "Global institutions and agenda should be subjected to democratic political accountability."

- Democratic policy at the global level requires legitimacy of popular control through representative and direct mechanisms.
- Citizen participation in decision making at global levels requires equality of opportunity to all citizens of the world.
- Multiple spheres of governance, from local to provincial to national to regional and global, should mutually support democratization of decision making at all levels.
- Global democracy must guarantee that global public goods are equitably accessible to all citizens of the world.

Vijaya Ramachandran, Enrique Rueda-Sabater and Robin Kraft also define principles for representation of nations and populations in the system of global governance. They propose a "Two Percent Club" that would provide for direct representation of nations with at least two percent of global population or global GDP; other nations would be represented within international fora through regional blocs.

Academic tool or discipline

In the light of the unclear meaning of the term "global governance" as a concept in international politics, some authors have proposed to define it not in substantive, but in methodological terms. Global Governance, thus defined, becomes an analytical concept that provides a specific perspective on world politics different from that of conventional international relations theory. Some universities, including those offering courses in international relations, have begun to establish degree programmes in global governance.

REFLECTIONS ON SOUTH ASIAN MILITARY POLITICS

Building a military establishment that is loyal to the Constitution and supports the democratically elected government poses special challenges in post-colonial environments. In this chapter, I am going to examine how this objective has been approached in the two pivotal states of South Asia: India and Pakistan. The question I wish to find an—and not necessarily *the*—answer to is: why has India been successful in creating democratic civil-military relations and why has Pakistan failed so completely on this score? A hefty book would, no doubt, be necessary to produce a fully comprehensive explanation that addresses all the relevant issues that have a bearing on this subject.

My ambition in this chapter is far more modest. I am interested primarily in the *origins* of Indian and Pakistani military politics as I believe they go far in demarcating the overall patterns for the entire post-Independence period. My purpose, then, is not to examine the entire post-Independence period but to cover a time-span sufficient to recognise the basic trends that shaped civil-military politics in these countries. India succeeded in placing its armed forces under firm and virtually unchallenged state control right from the beginning. My coverage, therefore, will stop in 1975, when the handling of the "Emergency" confirmed, yet again, the generals' lack of political ambition. Civil-military relations in Pakistan have been far more "eventful" than in India. In this case, I will look at the period starting with Independence and ending with 1988, the end of Gen Zia-ul-Haq's dictatorship that heralded the arrival of a civilian government, once again. This study makes three arguments. First and most important, by the end of the first post-colonial decade, the patterns for the drastically different military politics of India and Pakistan were already set. Second, of the numerous reasons for the evolution of different civil-military relations in the two countries, several lie in the circumstances of the 1947 Partition and in the immediate post-Partition. Third, the British colonial period left behind profound legacies most of which have positively influenced military affairs in the subcontinent. After a short examination of the British legacy, I look at the impact of Partition on Indo-Pakistani military affairs. I continue with some comparative commentary on the two armies, followed by an exploration of the main themes of Indian and Pakistani civil-military relations.

The British Legacy

Few imperial powers succeeded in leaving behind such a durable impact on their subject peoples as the British did in India and, to a lesser extent, Pakistan. The British were more successful colonisers than their European rivals, or—and there is an important lesson here—the more recent vintage of American and other Western "democracy promoters" for several reasons.1 They may not have been less exploitative or racist than others, but they were more effective because they worked hard at understanding the people they were governing, recruited individuals who were prepared to spend their careers in the provinces of a single alien nation, and then invested in teaching them the local language and culture. Moreover, the British established effective bureaucracies and integrated local elites into the governing structures on every level. In some cases, Indians occupied high positions in the bureaucracy so that at the time of Independence, a fairly high percentage of the elite Indian Civil Service was staffed by Indians. In short, the British thought about and planned for the long-term. That bureaucracies and large organisations are resistant to change is a truism but it is interesting that after more than six decades of independence, no other Indian or Pakistani institution retains as much of its British origins as the armed forces.

The British India Army (BIA) originated in the army first created by the British East India Company to protect its personnel and property. When the conquest of India began in earnest in the late 18th century, the British faced native troops who had a reputation for individual bravery and some of whom were equipped with cannons and muskets. The British advantage lay primarily in organisation, training, and drill which paid dividends in battlefield discipline. British commanders soon realised not only that a few of their troops could prevail over the large but disorganised Indian forces but also, later on, that the Indians themselves were amenable to discipline.

The British India Army served the empire with distinction. Even if most *sepoys* (native Indian soldiers) were highly disciplined and unswervingly obedient to the British, mutinies did occur, and two of them are noteworthy. About 70,000 sepoys joined the Mutiny of 1857, 30,000 remained loyal to the British, and an equal number were disarmed or deserted. This was a significant turning point in Indian history: had all the *sepoys* mutinied at the same time, British rule in India quite conceivably could have been ended.3 After 1857, the colonisers changed their personnel policies and paid more attention to the "divide-and-rule" principle.4 The second significant mutiny broke out in February 1946—after the high morale of World War II in the BIA eroded—and was joined by 7,000 sailors, a quarter of the navy's strength. The rebels hoisted the flags of the two native political forces, the Congress Party and Muslim League, on the vessels, which encouraged the rioting on shore. The mutiny—that clearly suggested the slipping away of imperial authority—stunned both the government in Delhi and the Congress Party.

During World War II, the Indian National Army (INA) posed an even more important challenge to the BIA. Established in 1942 principally by Subhas Chandra Bose in collaboration with the

Japanese occupying force in Southeast Asia, the INA—its recruiting message was "what's the use of fighting with/for your colonial masters when you can fight for your freedom?"—wanted to overthrow the British Raj with Japanese assistance. The INA's first members were BIA prisoners-of-war captured by the Japanese. They were joined by expatriate Indians from Burma and Malaysia and, in time, also by BIA personnel. According to British military intelligence, in 1944, 20,000 Indian (BIA) troops had gone over to the Japanese, two out of every seven captured. In 1945, they identified a hard core of 7,600 INA fighters who were devoted to their charismatic leader, Bose, had actively assisted the Japanese, and in some cases committed "horrendous war crimes." The INA's potential to cause frontline soldiers to surrender was taken seriously by the government though, in the end, it did not make a major impact on the war.

The INA's size was dwarfed by the BIA – 1,789,000 Indians were fighting with the British in World War II in Africa, Asia, Europe, and the Middle East. India was also a major source of industrial material in support of the war effort. The BIA also played an important role in handling the sporadic rioting, civil unrest, non-cooperation and resistance from Gandhi and the Congress during the war; its Indian officers and Non-Commissioned Officers (NCOs) did not participate in the struggle for their country's independence which put them in a curious position once it was achieved.

Several attributes of the British India Army made a lasting impact on its successor forces:

Separating the Army from Politics: Although in the early years, some of the pro-consuls who governed British India were military officers, the BIA quickly settled into a position that remained outside and above politics. The principle of the army's political subordination was clear and the division between the civil and military spheres was unambiguous: the army was responsible for recruitment, training, discipline, and strategic advice. Beyond that, civilians made the decisions, including when and in the service of what objective the army should be deployed.

Recruitment: One of the pillars of the BIA's success was the careful recruitment of soldiers and prospective NCOs and officers.

After 1857, recruiters generally avoided enlisting Bengalis and drew from the region in the west, e.g. Punjab, which had largely remained loyal to the British at the time of the Mutiny. In any event, the British firmly believed in "martial races," that people originating from the northwest corner (Punjab) of India, the Sikhs, the Gurkhas of Nepal, and members of the Kshatriya (warrior) castes were better suited for military service than others (such as Bengalis or Sindhis). Most of the soldiers were middle class peasants, promotion was based solely on ability and merit, and the BIA developed a distinctive and powerful *esprit de corps.* The obedience of the vast majority of rank-and-file soldiers was the result of attracting politically reliable and pliable individuals.

Training and Professionalism: The British provided rigorous and modern training to native Indians and a career that was attractive to many. The cream of the crop received officer training at Sandhurst in England but training was on-going in the garrisons and bases of the three armies headquartered in Madras, Bombay and Calcutta. After the opening of the Indian Military Academy at Dehradun in 1932, all Indian officers were trained there. Until 1939, the officer corps was relatively small and tight-knit, but the need for a much larger force in World War II required its quick expansion and the abandonment of some recruiting principles.

Religion and Caste: Perhaps the greatest achievement of the British in the military realm was the creation of a personnel system based on competition and excellence rather than religious identity. That religion was not a central issue in the BIA was the consequence of careful British policy in this regard. To avoid tensions, most units were organised by religion and soldiers took a religious (Hindu, Sikh, or Muslim) oath administered by regimental priests. Because the British were particularly concerned with Muslim recruits after the Mutiny of 1857, there were no all-Muslim regiments. Nonetheless, Muslims were well represented among the ranks of the prestigious King's Commissioned Officers and Viceroy's Commissioned Officers; in fact, they held slightly more than their proportionate share (roughly one-third) of positions.

Aid to the Civil Power: The British developed a system – called "aid to the civil power" – for contingencies when local disturbances could not be contained by law enforcement personnel. In such cases, authority was passed from the civil administrator to the local military commander for the duration of the conflict. Though the danger that the loyalty of *sepoys* and Indian officers would be tried by these manoeuvres against the civilian population that few of them desired was real, there were hardly any cases of insubordination or desertion. In any event, there were conscious efforts to use troops from other regions (thus, south Indians might be used to put down riots in Bombay).

The Partition and Its Impact

The partition of British India into an independent India and Pakistan in 1947 remains *the* formative moment in the political path of the subcontinent that explains many of the profound differences between the two states and their armed forces. More specifically, it helps one understand not so much why India became a democracy – with civil-military relations befitting a democracy – but, far more so, why Pakistan did not. The Muslim movement in British India was distrustful of democracy due to its conviction that in an independent India, the large Hindu majority would marginalise the Muslims. The main Muslim political organisation, the All-India Muslim League, announced its support for a separate state, to be named Pakistan, in 1940. It has been argued that the League's long-time leader, Mohammed Ali Jinnah, did not really want an independent Muslim state but overplayed his hand by making such excessive demands – e.g., a separate Muslim electorate, guaranteed seats in Parliament – that the Hindus could not accept it. In this sense, by the mid-1940s, Pakistan had become a virtual inevitability. Although Jinnah wanted a homeland for Muslims, but not an Islamic state, in its final stages the campaign for Pakistan became a religious movement.

The most ardent support for an independent Pakistan originated principally from the minority Muslim provinces – in fact, most of Pakistan's leaders came from there. In the provinces where Muslims were in a majority, they expected to retain political control and, therefore, did not see the need for a Muslim state. On Independence Day, Jinnah (originally from Bombay) became governor-general and his close associate, Liaquat Ali Khan (who spent most of his life in north India), became prime minister. Resentment built up quickly against these "foreigners," called Muhajirs, in the new state because they monopolised leadership positions and designated their mother tongue, Urdu, as the country's official language even though Urdu language and tradition was alien to much of Pakistan – and certainly to all of Bengali-speaking East Pakistan, where the majority lived. Many Muslims still felt that their interests lay with India or were simply unable to emigrate and stayed there: they now comprise the world's largest religious minority.

The British ruling on the boundaries of the two states was based in part on the result of the 1945-46 elections for the Constituent Assembly and various other legislative bodies. The Radcliffe Award – named after its author, Cyril Radcliffe, who had never set foot in India and worked from outdated maps and census information – was presented in August 1947. Pakistan was carved out of five provinces of British India – including two partitioned provinces, Punjab and Bengal – and some princely states. The arrangement required the relocation of as many as ten million people – some six million Muslims from India to Pakistan and four million Hindus and Sikhs to India – and its announcement was followed by extensive riots in several regions, particularly in the Punjab. The ethno-religious bloodletting that took place there and elsewhere after Independence – a series of massacres and counter-massacres, looting and arson – claimed the lives of at least half a million people. The fact that the British did not make the necessary preparations to help accommodate the population exchange exacerbated the situation. The matter of the princely states' accession on the eve of Independence heightened the animosity between Muslims and Hindus and brought the armed forces into the conflict. Although parts of the army became embroiled in the violence and could not be relied upon to reestablish order, most of the military units in the area – British, Indian, and Pakistani – tried to contain the killing and prevent even more destruction.

The eastern part of Bengal – what became East Pakistan and, after the 1971 civil war, the independent state of Bangladesh – was slightly more populous than the western part, and about 85 per cent Muslim, with a 15 per cent Hindu minority. All in all, the population of Pakistan was about one-fourth of that of India. There were many disagreements that can be traced back to the hastily prepared Partition and the pro-India sympathies of Lord Mountbatten – the last viceroy of the British Empire and independent India's first governor-general (1947-48). The feud regarding the state of Jammu and Kashmir could not be resolved and eventually led to a war in October 1948, ending with a United Nations-brokered ceasefire in the following January. This issue has not been settled and has been the source of numerous serious conflicts – some armed – between the two states.

Muslim suspicions about Hindu intentions were only reinforced by India's handling of the division of British India's assets. Delhi refused to release large amounts of funds that were Pakistan's due and cut off the flow of water of the Indus river despite a water sharing agreement because it did not want to aid Pakistan while they were embroiled in an armed conflict in Kashmir. In protest against Indian policies, Mahatma Gandhi started a well-publicised fast in January 1948 which he declined to break until the government adopted an "honourable" course regarding the release of Pakistan's property. India's inequitable treatment extended to the BIA's military equipment that was to be divided between the two successor states. The Delhi government failed to honour its pledge to deliver Pakistan its share: for instance, only three per cent of the Pakistani portion of 165,000 tons of ordnance stores was delivered by April 1948 and none of its allocation of 249 tanks was ever transferred.

The Pakistani share of institutions and infrastructure amounted to important naval bases in Karachi and Chittagong, the Staff College at Quetta, the Royal Indian Service Corps School at Kakul, and some other facilities such as regimental training centres. In terms of armed force personnel, Pakistan's inheritance was a paper army of roughly 150,000 officers and men in 508 units – 40 per cent of them still on Indian soil on Independence Day (14 August 1947). In fact, the staff of the new Pakistani General Headquarters arrived only in October 1947 in Rawalpindi – but without many key documents because Indian officials refused to release them.

The officers of the BIA were told to choose between the Indian or the Pakistani armed forces. For Muslim officers who lived in India – and for the far fewer Hindu and Sikh officers living in Pakistan – Partition meant having to leave their homes, uprooting their families, and losing their property. After Partition, nearly all Muslim officers went to Pakistan and virtually all Hindu officers moved to, or remained in, India proper.

The departure of Muslim officers to Pakistan after Partition was not unexpected given their background and the opportunities that opened up in a new and understaffed army. A few Muslim officers stayed in the new Indian Army and some actually managed to rise high in the hierarchy.

During the politically tense years leading up to Partition, a remarkable amity prevailed among most Hindu, Muslim and Sikh officers. Field Marshal Mohammed Ayub Khan, the Pakistani leader of the 1950s and 1960s, recalled in his memoirs that in 1947, the senior Indian officer of the BIA, Gen K M Cariappa asked him to support efforts to keep the army undivided which, of course, Ayub could not do as "the army was the instrument of sovereignty and the shield of the people."

In spite of their different post-Independence development, at the time of Partition, the two armies were not that different from one another. They came from the same body, shared a single ethos and institutional culture, and played no role in the political movement that led to Independence. Owing to the shortage of high-ranking officers, both the Pakistani and Indian armed forces employed British officers for more than a decade after Independence. Pakistan's 150,000-man army should have had 4,000 officers but there were only 2,500; to fill this deficiency, the government retained 500 British officers and accelerated the promotion of native officers to fill higher ranks. The first Indian Chief of the Naval Staff, Vice Admiral Ram Dass Katari, assumed office only in April 1958 – nearly eleven years after Independence – with the retirement of his predecessor, Vice Admiral Stephen Hope Carlill. The real difference lay in the political culture in which the two armies were to function. The very nature of the creation of Pakistan goes far in explaining their different evolution.

Two Different Armies

In both the Indian and Pakistani Armies, recruitment along the lines of the British "martial races" principles continued for decades after Independence. In India, officers and NCOs from the Punjab were over-represented, while regions like Madras, Kerala, let alone West Bengal, had produced far less than their fair share of recruits. The Indian government had decided to abolish caste-identity as the organising principle of military units decades ago. The units of the two relatively young Services, the air force and the navy, have been for long completely integrated.

The abolition of all units based on ethnic, religious, or caste identity has not been completed in India though it has been the subject of an on-going public debate. Opponents have argued that people from similar backgrounds fight better together and sacrifice more readily for one another than those in mixed units. In any case, only a few single-group regiments remain in the army; these units go back a long way – some trace their histories to the 18th century. Conversations with military officers indicate that pure regiments are the repositories of tradition and history and are often characterised by extraordinarily high morale and pride in service.

Three types of infantry battalions emerged: pure (single-caste or ethnic group), mixed (regiments segregated by company) and totally mixed battalions that were open for anyone eligible for military service. Although concerted efforts were made to make the army more representative, in 1974, Punjabis still comprised over 15 per cent of the army, several times more than their share of the population.35 In 1978-1982, 57 per cent of the cadets attending the Indian Military Academy came from the northwest, suggesting that the over-representation of this region in the Indian armed forces has declined hardly at all since Independence.

Their numerical strengths in the officer corps notwithstanding, Sikhs, particularly, have been concerned about the lack of Sikhs in the high command. The 1984 government assault on the Golden Temple in Punjab to remove Sikh militants precipitated a Sikh mutiny in the army, including about 2,000 personnel. It showed that the armed forces – often viewed as a symbol of national unity, hardened in battles against the Chinese and the Pakistanis – can be an example of ethno-religious rift. These chasms have been bridged, however, and, according to one of the country's top military experts, "With its multi-religious, multi-lingual, and multi-cultural composition, the army is a shining example of the national goal of achieving 'unity in diversity'."

As in armed forces everywhere, the appeal of the military profession is negatively correlated with the fortunes of the national economy. Under the British and in the first couple of decades of Independence, the military – along with the elite administrative services – was the occupational bailiwick of the upper middle class. Since then, there has been a gradual shift toward the lower middle class, given the profession's fading lustre owing to faraway deployments, considerably lower salaries, and fewer advancement opportunities than for comparable civil service personnel. By one calculation, the total benefits of company and battalion commanders fell between 60-70 per cent in real terms during 1947-1982.39 This trend has served to eradicate the elitist aura surrounding the officer corps and diminish its social status. The occupational prestige of soldiering is far higher in Pakistan for several reasons: national defence is a higher priority, the Pakistani economy offers fewer promising employment opportunities, and the military's dominant socio-political rule practically ensures that its personnel would be better provided for. Pakistani society has a genuine connection to the armed forces; as in Turkey and Indonesia there is a profound social connection, rooted in history and traditions, that is missing in India.

The Indian Army is the largest volunteer military establishment in the world. Until 1977, soldiers enlisted for seven years with an additional eight years in the reserves; since then, they have enlisted for seventeen years. The threshold of entry for enlisted men has been relatively low — little more than a successful physical exam and literacy. Although a generation or two ago, many officers' sons followed their fathers into the armed forces, this is no longer the case: new cadets tend to be the sons of NCOs and come from small towns. Unlike in the rest of Indian society, corruption is not a major problem in the armed forces partly because its disciplining structure remains excellent.

Since Independence, both the Indian and Pakistani militaries have become highly professional forces with rigorous training and educational requirements. One of the basic tenets of Indian military training is that armed forces and politics do not mix; for decades, junior officers were taught to be political illiterates. Although the Indian Army may no longer get the best and the brightest young people, entry into the profession remains competitive. The new National Defence Academy (NDA) opened its doors in 1955 – the ceremony witnessed by the Shah of Iran, Soviet leader Nikita Khrushchev and his Defence Minister, Marshal Georgy Zhukov. Its success persuaded the Ethiopian government to request the NDA's help in setting up a similar institution, the Haile Selassie Military Academy. One of the key differences between the two armies is that in Pakistan, the Muslim identity of military personnel is supposed to prevail over historical and cultural differences.

Because officially, all Muslims are equally eligible to bear arms and serve in the armed forces, the ethnic imbalances in the Pakistani Army are all the more noticeable. Bengalis, long considered unsuited for military life, suffered harsh discrimination under this system and constituted only a small percentage of military personnel.

Even though they were Pakistan's majority population, in the 1960s, they made up only 7 per cent of the Pakistan Army – their proportion in the bureaucracy was 24 per cent. Not surprisingly, Bengali grievances fuelled their drive for independence. For many years, Pakistani officers were actually taught that the country's "core area" was Punjab and the other regions were merely "invasion routes," something that could not but increase the defiance of Baluchi, Bengali, Sindhi, and other non-Punjabi citizens. With the loss of East Pakistan in 1971, the discrimination against those of Baluchistan and Sindh backgrounds appeared even sharper.

On the other hand, the British regard for the martial virtues of Punjabis and, to a lesser extent, Pashtuns, continued; some experts even talked about the "Punjabisation" of the Pakistani armed forces. Political activists from Baluchistan and Sindh have called the Pakistani armed forces the instrument of the Punjabi-Pashtun ruling elite, not of the federation of Pakistan. In the 1980s, 75 per cent of soldiers came from three districts of Punjab and two districts of the Northwest Frontier Province that contained only 9 per cent of Pakistan's male population. Nevertheless, Punjabis and Pashtuns (who share ethnic identity with roughly 50 per cent of Afghans) are divided on a number of issues, especially on their views of the Taliban in Afghanistan and in the Northwest Frontier. Most Pashtun pilots, for instance, refuse to shoot at, or bomb, the Taliban.

Another major difference between the two armies is that while the Indian Army's personnel remain relatively isolated from mainstream society, Pakistani officers and NCOs are much more integrated into it. Pakistani soldiers spend as many as 200 days a year away from their units – annual or casual leave, vacation, holidays, weekend – and during this time, they return to civilian life. Perhaps this close social proximity makes the military more acceptable and its appearance in other – including political – roles, more palatable. Upon retirement, Pakistani officers, particularly those who achieved higher ranks, are often rewarded with lucrative jobs in the country's large defence-related civilian sector as bureaucrats, advisers, and experts. This has not been a widespread practice in India – particularly given its far larger military establishment and proportionately smaller defence sector – though in recent years, retired officers, appalled by the politicians' shabby treatment of armed forces personnel – have entered the political arena.

5

Democratic Control Over the Military

All Bulgarian Governments after 1989 invariably place the accession of Republic of Bulgaria to European political and economic organizations among their main goals. Although to a different degree, they seek national security guarantees in the cooperation with European and Euroatlantic security structures, including NATO. Both the declared goals and concrete political and diplomatic steps aim increased security and economic prosperity, but on a deeper level, they reflect the dominant endeavor of the Bulgarian people to join democratic Europe.

The countries in Western Europe and North America demonstrate a rich spectrum of historical traditions, forms of state government, and vast cultural diversity. Nevertheless, all they share in certain ways some signs - a multiparty political system, division of power and authority, market economy, respect for human rights, etc. In this respect, the integration of Bulgaria in Europe relates not so much to the introduction of a specific state model or the achievement of certain level of economic development, but to the acceptance of a relevant value system.

Among the basic principles of democracy is the principle of civil control over the military. In their strive for democratization, all post-communist countries confronted the problem of transforming one model of civilian control – the communist party control – with another – democratic control over the armed forces. As a whole, the necessity of this transformation was accepted positively. However, its implementation encountered a number of obstacles, created by lack of traditions, impossibility to implement directly models of civil-military relations, functioning successfully in the US and Western Europe, and lack of people, prepared to guide and lead the armed forces in conditions of political pluralism.

The establishment of effective civil control is crucial for the democratic development of Bulgaria, both in the sense of preventing excessive military involvement in politics and as a guarantee that no more than the necessary resources for the military security of the state will be allocated, and that these resources will be spent effectively. At the same time, the achievement of effective democratic control over the military turned into a requirement for integration of countries from Central and Eastern Europe (CEE) in international political, economic, and security organizations. For example, although NATO has not announced officially *criteria* for accession to the Alliance, the Study on NATO Enlargement postulates that "Prospective members will *have to have*:

- Demonstrated a commitment to and respect for OSCE norms and principles, including the resolution of ethnic disputes, external territorial disputes … ;
- Shown a commitment to promoting stability and well-being by economic liberty, social justice and environmental responsibility; „
- *Established appropriate democratic and civilian control of their defense forces;* …

However, a number of authors reason that the Study practically enacted *criteria* which new members must fulfill, encouraging harmonization of their security and defense policy with those of the Alliance and achievement of effective democratic civil-military relations. Illustrative in this respect is Jeffrey Simon's conclusion that if NATO adopts conditions for *effective* civilian oversight of the military, then "most of the Visegrad states would not currently qualify." Furthermore, despite the purposeful efforts of these and other CEE countries, two years later Chris Donnelly declared that "no post-communist country has yet achieved a totally satisfactory degree of democratic control and good civil-military relations. In all cases, as societies transform, their armies lag behind." Regarding

Bulgaria in particular, the US Congressman Christopher Smith announced a similar conclusion in May 1997.

These conclusions surprised part of the Bulgarian political and military leadership. Bulgaria has a new democratic Constitution and new laws on defense, the armed forces, and other security organizations. Roles and responsibilities of Parliament, President, Government, and General Staff are specified according to the principle of civilian control. The Minister of Defense is civilian. But this is only the formal side of the issue. To illustrate the role of formal institutions in civil-military relations, we need to examine their theoretical foundations.

THEORETICAL APPROACHES TO THE CIVIL CONTROL OVER THE MILITARY

Civil-military relations present a topic of significant interest at least since the beginning of the written history of the mankind. But the question the Romans asked in the 1sr century "Who is to guard the guardians?" is still to receive its definite answer.

More often than not, in premodern times one person embodied the roles of the state leader and the supreme military commander. Among the examples are almost all Bulgarian Khans and Czars of the First and the Second Bulgarian states. But even in such cases the issue of the civilian control was not irrelevant. Dramatic is the example from the Bible of the relations between King David and his chief of staff Yoav and the way, in which the otherwise loyal military leader imposed his views on the state politics.

Ancient thinkers examine the other side of the coin, too. More than 2,500 years ago, the Chinese general Sun Tzu focused the attention on the "ways in which a ruler can bring misfortune upon his army." When a ruler, ignorant of military affairs, participates in their administration, "this causes the officers to be perplexed. ... If one ignorant of military matters is sent up to participate in the administration of the army, then in every movement there will be disagreement and mutual frustration and the entire army will be hamstrung." The military strategist concludes that "he whose generals are able and not interfered with by the sovereign will be victorious. ... To make appointments is the province of the sovereign; to decide on battle, that of the general." There is no universally accepted time period for the emergence of the modern civil-military relations. Scientists suggest that their beginning coincides with the rise of the modern nation state, the emergence of professional officer corps, or the advent of large-scale standing armies. However, the theory of the civil-military relations as a separate area of scientific research was established only after World War Two with the works of Huntington, Janowitz and Finer.

Theoretical Breakthroughs

In a book published for the first time in 1957, *Samuel Huntington* examines civil-military relations as a system of interrelated elements. Its major components are :

- formal structural position of military institution in government;
- informal role and influence of military groups in politics and society;
- nature of military ethics and dominant ideologies of nonmilitary groups, and neither of these alters without causing changes in the other elements of the system.

The theory, proposed by Huntington, is based on the concept of professionalism. The main focus of civil-military relations is on the officer corps and the state. The author convincingly proves that the modern officers are professionals and form a particular type of functional group with highly specialized characteristics of expertise, responsibility, and corporateness. The distinctive sphere of competency, characteristic for all officers independent on service or branch, is the management of violence. The responsibility is in guaranteeing the military security of the state. The corporate character of the officership is formed by complex procedures and requirements for access to the profession, an explicit system for promotion and appointments, the system of military education, a clear cut hierarchy and staff organization, esprit and competence of the officer corps. The behavior of the officer within the military structure is guided by a complex of regulations, norms, customs, and traditions. The professional behavior towards society is based on the understanding that his expertise may be applied only for purposes, approved by society through its political agent, the state.

Huntington examines three forms (military, internal and situational) and two levels (operative and institutional) of the national security policy and defines civil-military relations as the principal institutional component of the military security policy. Although the public debate is usually focused on operative issues such as size, recruitment, organization, equipment, deployment, mobilization, etc., the long-term character of the decision-making process is based on the established (conscientiously or not) model of civil-military relations.

Any system of civil-military relations involves a complex equilibrium between authority, influence and ideologies of military and nonmilitary groups. The goal is to achieve an equilibrium which maximizes military security with the least sacrifice of other social values. Huntington identifies two main models of civil-military relations *-subjective* and *objective* civilian control. In the first model control is achieved through maximizing the power of particular civilian groups in relation to the military. The latter involves minimization of military power by professionalizing the military, thus guaranteeing their neutrality and political sterility. It is this abstract model *-the objective civilian control* - that maximizes military security of the state while minimizing danger to democratic values.

The second pillar in the fundament of the new theory was the work of *Morris Janowitz,* published in 1960. Studying in detail the professional character of the US officer corps, the author concludes that the armed forces have preserved their professional distinctiveness, integrity, and professional ethics, adequate to support civilian supremacy.

Thus, Huntington and Janowitz focused the attention on professional autonomy and introduced a sense of balance in the study of civil-military relations. For too long the problem of civilian control has been interpreted only in the sense of potential military intervention in civilian affairs. The introduction of the principle of professional autonomy brought in focus the other side of the coin - the overinvolvement of civilian political authorities in military affairs. Janowitz emphasizes that "civilian supremacy is effective because the professional soldier believes that his political superiors ... are prepared to weigh his professional advice with great care." Furthermore, Janowitz develops the concept of common responsibility and introduces the term *unanticipated militarism,* which develops from "a lack of effective traditions and practices for controlling the military establishment, isolation between civil and military leadership, as well as failure of civilian political leaders to act relevantly and consistently. Under such circumstances, a vacuum is created which not only encourages an extension of the tasks and power of military leadership, but actually forces such trends."

Applying methods from sociology, Janowitz studies how the trends in the evolution of civil society influence military organizations, and how military leaders react to that evolution. He established research directions, set of categories and concepts, and even the terminology of civil-military relations. His fundamental thesis is that from the beginning of the 20th century the boundaries separating the military from civilian society had progressively weakened. Thus, military organizations are forced to participate more actively in the life of society and yet maintain its *relative* autonomy, competence, and cohesion.

While Huntington and Janowitz examined primarily Western experience in civil-military relations as a function of nature and character of the armed forces, *Samuel Finer* studied civil-military relations as a reflection of the nature and character of society. He provides a conceptual and classification system with methodological tools for categorizing and evaluating military intervention. His central thesis is that the level of military intervention in a given country is a direct function of the political culture of that society and the level of development of civil organizations. The lower the level of political culture, the higher the level of military intervention in politics and public affairs.

Developments in civil-military relations theory

The three works established the theoretical fundament of civilian control. In the following years, the growing scientific field of civil-military relations attracted modern hypotheses and methods from sociology, political science, organizational theory, theory of communication, etc.

According to *Charles Moskos,* there are always forces unifying and dividing civil and military components of society. In some areas trends of increased integration between military and civilians are active, and in others the tendency is towards traditional isolation of the military. Therefore, Moskos prefers to examine *pluralistic* military, functioning in the spectrum be-tween civilian and strictly military activities. The new military is segmented. Some organiza-tional units are isolated from civilian society and others are more closely connected with it. Thus, Moskos introduced a more realistic concept of the corporateness of the military profes-sion. His realism brought forward the division of motivations for military service. The reasons for selecting the military profession may be not only institutional, but also occupational, and their prevalent nature to a high degree defines the status of civil-military relations.

Amos Perlmutter offered a unified theory of civil-military relations valid for all countries in the world. He rejects the view that a clear-cut division between civilian and military functions exists. The assumption "that professionalism removes military from politics" is based on classical traditions of administrative theory, that is built on the premise that policy making is distinguished from policy implementation. The modern administrative theory is fusionist, recognizing that bureaucracy and politics are symbiotically connected. Perlmutter agrees with Huntington that politics is beyond the scope of military competence in the sense that the military plays no active role in elections, but states that the military's role in formation and implementation of the policy on national security forces it to accept and support a political attitude.

The concept of subjective and objective models of civilian control was further elaborated by *Peter Feaver*. He reasons that neither civilian nor military leadership has ever followed the prescriptions of the classic theory of division of responsibilities and proposes instead the *assertive-delegative* framework. Feaver proves that although the delegative control is closely related to the Huntington's objective civilian control, civilians do not always un-reservedly support its ideal division of labor. Instead, they prefer to exercise direct super-vision over the military, including supervi-sion over military operations. Without com-pletely undermining the professionalization of the officer corps, the assertive control preserves the institutional basis for division of labor, but in the framework of a conflictual pattern of civil-military relations. Empirical evidence exists, that the assertive control is prevalent in Western democracies, and the U.S. in particular. Similar is the conclusion is made by *Stephen Cimbala* who reasons that during the Gulf War the American civil-military relations were characterized by a unusual combination of *assertive* and *permissive* control.

Samuel Sarkesian expands Huntington's theoretical framework studying three areas of civil-military relations as systemic interaction between civilian elites, military, and political-social system. Certain factors, i.e., the process of democratization, not only influence the separate elements of the systemic relationship, but may alter the balance among them. Furthermore, the military may play an enhanced role in national security decision-making and still maintain their political neutrality.

Focusing the attention on the role of culture in the social-political system, *Rebecca Schiff* proposes to reconsider the theory of civil-military relations. In an alternative approach, designated as *theory of concordance,* she accounts for the central role of culture in the interaction of three components - military institutions, political elites and citizenry. The new theory encompasses the institutional division of civilian and military responsibilities as just one model of civil-military relations, typical mainly for the United States. Depending on cultural, historical, and political peculiarities, the pattern of civil-military relations in a certain country may be based on either division or integration of civilian and military responsibilities, and cultural factors exert paramount influence over the potential for military intervention in politics. Among those factors are value system, attitudes, perceptions, and symbols, shaping not only the national view on the role of the military, but also the military view on their own role. Concordance does not require a particular form of government, decision-making process or set of institutions. Concordance may take place in the context of increased dialogue, recognition of the views of the other side, and shared values among political elites, military, and society. Whether based on law or lasting historical and cultural values, concordance is achieved in countries with a process of active debate on issues concerning the social composition of the officer corps, the process of political decision-making, recruitment method, and military style.

In another study of the role of cultural factors, *Kemp* and *Hudlin* reason that the nature of civil control and the limits in its implementation depend on the degree, to which soldiers accept the support for the civil supremacy as their moral obligation. The rationale is partially based on the inherent *vagueness* in the relation "political ends-military means", implicitly accepted as a basis for institutional civilian control. The authors pay special attention to the fact that civilian leadership not only defines the goals, but also decides where to draw the boundary between ends and means, policy and implementation.

The last theoretical development to be examined combines the previous two approaches in the principle of shared responsibility. According to *Douglas Bland,* problems in mature democracies appear not when the military seize civilian control, but when politicians, because of either incompetence or negligence, abandon their responsibilities. Politicians in democratic societies act as defenders of neutrality and integrity of the armed forces not only because democracy requires it, but also because otherwise the high command would be defenseless. Bland questions main points in the Huntington's theory concluding that "mature democratic states guard against political abuse of the armed forces by dividing certain aspects of control over defense policy and the military between politicians and soldiers." The acceptance of the shared responsibility encourages consensus-building on issues of underlying principles, national strategy, and defense resource spending. Even without being declared publicly, the consensus provides a stable basis for control of defense policy and clear directions for the work of lower command and administrative levels.

Conceptual framework of the current study

For the last seven years the CEE countries, including Bulgaria, are undergoing a unique transition from authoritarian one-party rule to democracy and from a command to a free-market economy. Main component of the process of democratization is the establishment of democratic civilian control over the armed forces. Democratizing civilian control has a paramount importance for the success of democratic transformation and, at the same time, presents a significant theoretical challenge.

Naturally, it is expected that scholars from the countries in transition will be active participants in the quest for deeper understanding of this unique process. Bulgarian scientists also contribute to the analysis of transformations in civil-military relations. The Bulgarian Institute for International Studies cooperated with the NATO Defense College in preparing and conducting the NDC 1994 Seminar on "Democratic and Civil Control over the Armed Forces." In early 1996, the Institute for Security and International Studies, Sofia, published the first monograph on civil-military relations in Bulgarian. It was quickly followed by two more books, published by non-governmental organizations.

These publications and the accompanying seminars acquainted Bulgarian politicians, officers, cadets, students and journalists with the concept of democratic civilian control over the military. However, they examine civil-military relations mainly in the framework of the institutional theory. This framework does not allow to detect and analyze the whole spectrum of current problems. Therefore, in order to evaluate the present situation in the area of civil-military relations and to identify directions and means for improvement, we examine a conceptual framework that partially combines the institutional and sociological approaches previously outlined.

An abstract scheme is proposed that separates the realization of civil-military relations in three areas within two layers. The first layer covers the formal basis of civilian control encompassing accepted laws and other legislative documents, procedures, and organizational structures, as well as their institutionalization. The second layer is the "cultural" layer. It accounts for the value system of the actors in civil-military relations, their level of education and training, perceptions, attitudes, and behavioral patterns. The three main areas of interaction are "political elites-military" (military leadership in particular), "political elites-society", and "military-society."

With the understanding that this representation is a simplification of reality, allowing for some overlap and disguising complex interactions, it provides a conceptual framework for identification and systemic examination of the principle components of current civil-military relations in Bulgaria.

CIVIL-MILITARY RELATIONS DURING TRANSITION FROM COMMUNISM TO DEMOCRACY

The Bulgarian state was founded in 681. After the Russian-Turkish war, 1977-1978, the Bulgarian statehood was restored. The Third Bulgarian state fought several wars for unification of the territories with predominantly Bulgarian population, and actively participated in both World Wars. Except for brief periods of time, the state maintained strong *army*. The officer corps had a distinct social composition and practically all officers were graduates of a single military school. The military profession and the army had high prestige. With no exceptions, the reasons for losing wars were attributed to political actors, whether the Monarch or the Government.

The Bulgarian military has a record of intervening in politics. The original source lists one more event: With the advance of the Soviet army during World War Two, on September 9, 1944, Bulgarian army officers took part in the overthrow of the week-old West oriented Government of Muraviev. It is questionable whether the participation of Bulgarian military played a significant role in those events. Indisputable, however, is that 1944 brought an abrupt change in the model of civil-military relations.

In the following 45-year period, the development of civil-military relations in Bulgaria obeyed a completely different pattern. In conditions of strong Soviet influence, the Bulgarian Communist

Party exercised effective political control over the Armed Forces. However, in decisions on doctrine, strategy, planning, composition, deployment, education and training, etc., essential was the role of the direct ties between Bulgarian military and the Soviet General Staff. The military had a monopoly over defense information and the word 'transparency' was practically unknown. Civilian expertise on defense issues was virtually unavailable, and the citizenry did not play any significant role in defense and national security decision-making. Nevertheless, at least in the last decades of the period, there were factors supporting the professionalization of the military, among them:

- A set of strictly observed educational requirements for officer commission and advancement;
- A system of promotion, based mostly on merit and experience ; £ Well structured, and to a high degree closed, system of military education and training; £ The system of the General Staff.

There were also factors working against the professionalization of the military. Most important among them were the following:

- Through the "apparatus" of political officers, the communist party exercised both high-level and in-place control over the military;
- The structures of military counterintelligence were subordinated not to the military authority, but to the Ministry of Internal Affairs;
- A trend of growing occupational motivations in choosing the military profession in the 70s and the 80s;
- Following the Soviet model, the army and the system of military education were highly compartmentalized, providing good promotion and advancement opportunities to officers from certain branches and substantially limiting other officers, thus lowering the cohesion of the officer corps.

Nevertheless, as a whole, the army had a high prestige. It was never used against the Bulgarian people. Moreover, military officers played an important part in the best known plot against the regime of the communist party under Todor Zhivkov. All these factors influenced the process of establishing democratic civil control over the armed forces after 1989.

Establishing civil control (institutional layer)

The first step towards institutionalization of the democratic changes in Bulgaria after November 10, 1989, involved the abolition of Article 1 of the 1971 Constitution on the leading role of the Bulgarian Communist Party in all state and public affairs. This step was followed by the so called "depolitization" of the military, when all officers and NCOs were asked to leave either the communist party or the military.

The new Constitution of the Republic of Bulgaria, adopted in 1991, set a firm basis for the establishment of civil control over national security and defense policy, as well as over the armed forces. It is also fundamental for the interaction between society and the political elites, thus guaranteeing indirect influence of the citizenry over the military. Although with some delay, other laws followed, most important for the civil control being the Law on Defense and the Armed Forces (LDAF). This Law preserved the obligatory military service for all healthy men, which is the most important formal component of the interaction between military and society.

The detailed analysis of the legislative documents shows that they provide a solid basis for the institutionalization of democratic civil control. The Constitution and LDAF delineate roles and responsibilities of the People's Assembly (the Parliament), the generally elected President, the Council of Ministers, the civilian Minister of Defense, the Chief of the General Staff, and the judicial branch. Moreover, the comparative analysis shows that in the development of the normative base of civilian control Bulgaria is ahead of most countries in CEE, including the Visegrad countries. The process of building organizational structures and developing procedures for civilian control is also nearing completion.

However, some provisions of the operative legislature do not support the establishment of effective democratic control over the armed forces:

- The approach to defining roles and responsibilities of Parliament and President (Supreme Commander of the Armed Forces) is inconsistent and somewhat contradictory. Situations when the President and the majority in Parliament are from different political parties create conditions for subjective civilian control, and such attempts were already made;
- In the instituted interaction between President and Government, the President may effectively block the moves of the Government;
- A number of parallel structures were created;
- Article 8 of the LDAF states that "Civilian control over the Armed Forces is exercised by the bodies, envisioned in the Constitution and this Law." Thus, LDAF recognizes *only* the institutional form of civilian control and, potentially, may create obstacles to civil control by media, non-governmental organizations, and citizens;
- LDAF reintroduced the *Inspectorate* as an instrument of the civilian Minister of Defense for exercising civilian control. It has seven Inspections, including separate inspections for "Civil Control of the Land Forces," "Civil Control of the Air Force," and "Civil Control of the Navy." However, the three Inspections are lead by senior military officers, and most of the "civilians" at the Inspectorate (one third of its personnel) are recently retired officers. Thus, the overreliance on military expertise and the corporate spirit of the officership may jeopardize the idea of using the Inspectorate as an agency for civilian control over the military putting instead additional weight on the side of the General Staff in its conflictual relationship with the civilian Minister of Defense;
- As a whole, the LDAF was developed and adopted under very strong influence of the military leadership while the Bulgarian Socialist Party had absolute majority in Parliament. As a result, provisions were included which increased retirement age and gave the military substantial benefits at the time they leave active duty. Although such

benefits may be well deserved, in the current financial situation these provisions pose significant limitations on the options, available to the new civilian leadership in its efforts to reform the military establishment;

- A law regulating rights, responsibilities, educational requirements, and career opportunities of the state employee (civil servant) is still in the making. Hence, civilian experts at all levels, who are subject to frequent reshuffling and political caprice, have no incentives to specialize in the field of defense and security.

Although there are imperfections in operative legislature, established procedures, and relevant organizations, the changes in the last six years created conditions for institutionalization of effective democratic control over the armed forces.

However, these are necessary but not sufficient conditions. Therefore, the effective functioning of democratic control requires deeper changes in the second— cultural— layer of civil-military interaction.

Building civil control (cultural layer)

Bulgarian society almost anonymously welcomed the democratic changes launched on November 10, 1989. The military, being used to work under civilian (political) control, accepted the principle of civilian control of defense and national security. Problems appeared mainly because of:

- ack of relevant political culture and modest (during the first couple of years even missing) civilian and military expertise in democratic procedures in formulation and administration of national security policy, military and defense policy, and oversight of modern armed forces;
- Lack of a defense community, able to provide the political leadership with alternative solutions to national security and defense problems. Political decision-making depends to a very high degree on military advise;
- Insufficient number of civilian experts in defense and national security issues both on political and administrative level. Thus, even the civilian Minister of Defense almost

completely depends on the advise and technical assistance of the military;

- The military's understanding of the concept of boundaries between rights and responsibilities of political authority and military (predominantly dichotomous). Even though they accept the principle of civilian control, most senior military leaders consider the responsibility for the formulation of military doctrine, force structure, planning and conduct of operations, promotions, military education and training, as entirely theirs and examine civilian participation as unacceptable. This fact should not be surprising, because historically that has been the case in Bulgaria since regaining independence in 1878;
- Lack of traditions in citizen participation in discussions on issues of state importance, and in particular in the national security decision-making process and in overseeing state expenditures. Low level of societal awareness and misunderstanding of the real problems of defense and the military. As a rule, low level of competency of mass media in covering the problems of the armed forces.

Therefore, no matter what the normative base, it allows for different expectations, interpretations, and actions of the players in the civil-military interaction. The current pattern of civil-military relations depends mostly of the cultural level, and has the following manifestations:

Interaction "political elites - military"

During the first years of democratization events typical for the Huntington's abstract model of subjective civilian control were witnessed, most important being the politically inspired confrontation in the early 90s between the Chief of the General Staff General Petrov and the Chief of Staff of Land Forces Lieutenant-General Liutskanov. This confrontation culminated in the 1992 Plovdiv meeting of commanders from the Land Forces, organized by General Liutskanov. The then Chief of the General Staff, General Petrov appeared announced, and whatever the plan was, it did not succeed. Soon after that General Liutskanov retired from the army and became advisor to the Union of Democratic Forces. Years later, the former President's Adviser on National Security Lieutenant-General Stoyan Andreev declared that General Petrov's visit prevented a coup d'état, planned to keep the then Prime Minister Philip Dimitrov in power.

In the fall of 1994, the contradictions between the Minister of Defense and the Chief of the General Staff (having the support of different political parties) aggravated, and this time General Petrov was the one to leave the army.

The two-year cycle in spreading rumors for coup d'état was confirmed in late 1996 after the assassination of the former Prime Minister Andrei Lukanov. In conditions of very high inflation, skyrocketing prices and extreme devaluation of the Bulgarian currency, rumors for a coup in the making found support in the news of a meeting between the Prime Minister Videnov and the members of the Military Council of the General Staff.

The latest plan for a coup was "unveiled" by mass media in April 1997. This time, the "plan" relied heavily on Retired General Liutskanov's participation. However, the information was published only a week before the parliamentary elections, and it should be evaluated respectively.

Another source of tension is the peculiar understanding of the principle of civilian control by part of the political elites. In February 1997, a politician was appointed as a Head of the National Intelligence Agency, and he was promoted directly to the rank of Colonel. Another example is the promotion of a journalist— Head of the Press Office of the Ministry of Internal Affairs— to the rank of Major, and then to Colonel. Such decisions not only demonstrate misunderstanding of the principle of civilian control, but pose a direct threat to the professionalization of the officer corps.

A third sign of subjective control is the use of mass media to solve organizational, mostly personnel, issues. The leakage of information to mass media is turning into a pattern, and judging by the character of information it is most probably provided by officers. This pattern contradicts major principles of military ethics, acts against the unity of the officer corps and the corporateness of the military profession.

Finally, the strong dependence of the political elite on the military for expert advice still continues. Recently retired officers form the main source of advice to all major political parties. Furthermore, they fill in key positions for exercising civilian control. A typical example is the appointment of recently retired flag officers as "civilian" ministers. Not contradicting operative legislature, but descriptive of the level of political culture is also the fact, that three of the five candidatures for the post of Minister of Defense in the new Government, discussed by media in the spring of 1997, were those of very recently retired generals.

Interaction "political elites - society"

So far, the indirect role of the relations between society and political elites over civil-military relations is quite limited. Public scrutiny of the military leads to parliamentary oversight only in extreme cases, such as the 1994 tragic road accident in which fourteen soldiers were killed. Mechanisms for access of citizens to the executive branch on issues of national security and defense are almost nonexistent. However, the undeveloped political culture of society is but one of the reasons. Ineffective state-owned economy, lost markets, high unemployment rates, rising crime, and spreading corruption are in the focus of public attention. The percentage of the GDP for defense purposes and the ineffective use of resources by the military account for a very small part of the state expenditures, and were never mentioned among the reasons for the current severe economic crisis.

In such conditions, expertise in defense and security would barely improve the chances of a politician for reelection. As a result, politicians rarely put the effort to improve their knowledge and understanding of defense and security issues. Instead, they often are content with formal declarations for good relations with the military and "respect for their difficult mission," participation in military parades, and show of presence at military facilities and exercises.

Interaction "military - society"

Since November 10, 1989, conflict and splitting of Bulgarian political parties, trade unions, sport organizations, etc., became the norm rather than an exception. The pervert culmination came with the first ever split of the eleven-hundred-year-old Bulgarian Orthodox Church. In such conditions, society as a whole, and Bulgarian military as its integral part, do not examine previously mentioned conflicts between senior military leaders as extraordinary events.

Secondly, Bulgarian society in general does not understand the concept of civil *control* over the armed forces. The reasons are partially linguistic. The word "control" exists in the Bulgarian language but the meaning is more one-sided than in English. It means rather to "check", "supervise", or "oversee" and the meaning to "regulate", "direct", or "guide" is simply missing. The immediate consequence of using the world "control" is misleading public opinion. It creates confusion even among political elites and the military.

Military traditions in regard to secrecy and isolation combined with the barely developed civil society prevent even humble citizen attempts to question decisions on doctrine, structure, and deployment, as well as military effectiveness in utilizing societal resources.

Finally, both media and the public eagerly discuss the potential for and spread rumors related to a military regime. Experts in social psychology reason that although people respect the army, they "would not support any dictatorship, independent of whose interests it serves. ... As a really extreme measure, though unpopular, the people would accept an 'enlightened' marshal law if convinced that it will improve and not aggravate the situation."

From the brief examination of the problems we may conclude that, as a whole, the legal base of the democratic civilian control in Bulgaria is established. Nevertheless, it is possible to further develop the legislature, in particular regarding the role of society in exercising civil control, as well as to improve some of the operative laws and regulations. However, the main problems are in the second–cultural–layer of civil-military interaction. Even though the normative base and the organizational structures are well developed, they do not suffice. Deep transformation in perceptions, attitudes, and behavioral patterns of political elites, the military and society is required to ensure effective and democratic civil-military relations. The Bulgarian system of military education may contribute in important ways to the acceleration of this transformation. But first, let's examine the current challenges to military education in Bulgaria.

CIVILIAN CONTROL OF THE MILITARY

The United States has engaged in relatively few sustained military efforts since 1789. As a result, American public interest has focused primarily on domestic matters, while attention to foreign affairs and national defense has been sporadic.

In general, public-opinion polls show that most Americans are relatively indifferent toward foreign policy matters, and only at times of international crisis is their interest heightened.

Yet a primary motivation in founding the United States was, as the Constitution puts it, to "provide for the common defense." One-third of the 18 enumerated powers in Article I Section 8 of the U.S. Constitution deal with military and foreign policy matters. It is no accident that many of the initial issues of *The Federalist Papers* dealt with the defense requirements of the United States.

In constructing a new national government, the Founders understood the importance of establishing a government that could properly defend the country.

An effective, unified military and foreign policy required strong executive leadership of the military. At the same time, they realized that if military force was not adequately controlled, it could be used to seize control of the government and threaten democracy.

The Founders had a genuine fear of the abuse of military power, a concern that a strong executive could, over time, degrade into dictatorship or demagoguery. History had taught them that this abuse was not infrequent. Thus, they believed it was necessary to demonstrate that under the new Constitution the military would be subject to civilian authority in order to protect democracy. In *Federalist* No.28, Alexander Hamilton wrote,

Independent of all other reasonings upon the subject, it is a full answer to those who require a more peremptory provision against military

establishments in times of peace to say that the whole power of the proposed government is to be in the hands of the representatives of the people. This is the essential, and, after all, the only efficacious security for the rights and privileges of the people which is attainable in civil society.

The Founders recognized the importance of a standing army for protection and defense but believed that considerable care should be taken in order to preserve liberty and prevent abuses of power. As James Madison explained in *Federalist* No.41,

Security against foreign danger is one of the primitive objects of civil society....[But a] standing force?.is a dangerous, at the same time that it may be a necessary, provision. On the smallest scale it has its inconveniences. On an extensive scale its consequences may be fatal. On any scale it is an object of laudable circumspection and precaution. A wise nation will combine all these considerations; and, whilst it does not rashly preclude itself from any resource which may become essential to its safety, will exert all its prudence in diminishing both the necessity and the danger of resorting to one which may be inauspicious to its liberties.

The clearest marks of this prudence are stamped on the proposed Constitution. The Union itself, which it cements and secures, destroys every Pretext for a military establishment which could be dangerous.

The Constitution, therefore, vests responsibility for raising and maintaining an army — that is, paying for it — in the Congress, in order to prevent the presidency from becoming too powerful. In addition, Congress, not the executive, is given the power formally to declare war so as to prevent rash and unalterable decisions. At the same time, however, the Constitution designates the president as commander in chief of the U.S. Army and Navy, and state militias, thus giving the office sufficient power to resist foreign attacks and defend the fledgling nation.

Yet, like many principles in the Constitution, the details of civilian control are never clearly spelled out in the Constitution. Civilian control of the military in 1789 was vastly different from civilian control today. In fact, the Founders never envisaged a professional military class and, therefore, could not have foreseen the nature of civilian control today. Consequently, civilian control of the military in America has evolved as a matter of custom and tradition as well as from constitutional legalities.

A tradition of citizen-soldiers

The Constitution itself does not discuss the creation of a permanent military establishment. The Founders were not acquainted with the concept of career military service. They viewed military service in wartime as an attribute of all citizens. While George Washington was the most obvious soldier-statesman, many delegates to the Constitutional Convention had held military rank during the American Revolution. In fact, the idea that there existed a division between civilian and military classes was almost non-existent.

The Founders' view can be inferred from Article I, Section 6 of the Constitution:

No Senator or Representative shall, during the Time for which he was elected, be appointed to any civil Office under the Authority of the United States, which shall have been created, or the Emoluments whereof shall have been increased during such time; and no Person holding any Office under the United States, shall be a Member of either House during his Continuance in Office.

This clause rejects the idea that members of Congress could also serve in executive or judicial posts. It reflects the basic constitutional principle of separation of powers, the belief that each branch of government must be separate and distinct from all other branches. Nowhere in this clause, however, or anywhere else in the Constitution, are senators or representatives prohibited from being appointed to military offices. Since the Founders believed these individuals would be the most capable in American society, they assumed some would naturally serve as commanders of the military during times of crisis. In fact, the clause's inclusion in the Constitution was defended on the grounds that military offices were an exception. The Founders viewed the military as nonprofessional; essentially, the military consisted of a standing army or a citizen militia, and standing armies existed only when a nation was at war. As Elbridge Gerry, a delegate to the 1787 Constitutional Convention, explained, "Standing armies in time of peace are inconsistent with the principles of republican Governments, dangerous to the liberties of a free people, and generally converted into destructive engines for establishing despotism."

The principle of civilian control, then, embodied the idea that every qualified citizen was responsible for the defense of the nation and the defense of liberty, and would go to war, if necessary. Combined with the idea that the military was to embody democratic principles and encourage citizen participation, the only military force suitable to the Founders was a citizen militia, which minimized divisions between officers and the enlisted.

The Founders thus reduced the regular army after the Revolutionary War and relied on state militias to defend the western frontiers. These cutbacks reflected American democracy's fear of military institutions and of the military function, in part rooted in experiences with British military rule during the colonial period. Throughout the 19th century and early 20th century, these fears became embedded in American politics and society. America's deep cultural heritage of anti-military feeling, along with its geographic isolation, has thus produced a legacy of civilian control of the military.

The Anglo-Saxon cultural heritage, dominant at the time of the nation's founding, was another, more general, reason for this aversion to the military and military institutions, especially during peacetime. The British reaction to the Cromwellian period of the 1640s, when the British army was used to suppress political opposition, was a vivid memory in the 18th century. In addition, one of the major tensions leading to the American Revolution was the stationing of British troops on American soil after the French and Indian Wars (1754-63). The colonists rejected such an intrusion based on their concept of their rights as Englishmen, on the grounds that this would be unacceptable in Great Britain. This same wary attitude was reflected throughout the Revolution itself. In order to get the Continental Congress to authorize and provision the army, General George Washington had to assure Congress he would not use that army to usurp its authority. Thus, even in the heat of battle, Americans were suspicious of military authority.

Geography also played an important role in American attitudes toward the military. Throughout the 19th century, broad oceans acted as a buffer to the North American continent and America's neighbors did not present a serious threat. With its isolation, the United States was virtually immune from significant military threats from Europe and Asia. The abundant natural resources of the United States also made it virtually independent from the rest of the world.

At the beginnings of the Republic, then, four basic premises conditioned how most Americans saw civilian control of the military. First, large military forces were viewed as a threat to liberty, a legacy of British history and the army's occupation in the colonial period. Second, large military forces threatened American democracy.

This notion was linked to the ideal of the citizen-soldier and fears of establishing an aristocratic or autocratic military class. Third, large military forces threatened economic prosperity. Maintaining large standing armies represented an enormous burden on the fledgling economy of a new nation. Finally, large military forces threatened peace. The Founders accepted the liberal proposition that arms races led to war. Thus, civilian control of the military arose from a set of historical circumstances and became embedded over time in American political thought through tradition, custom, and belief.

Early presidents as military commanders

The commander-in-chief clause of the Constitution states that, in addition to his other duties, "The President shall be Commander in Chief of the Army and Navy of the United States, and of the Militia of the several States, when called into actual Service of the United States." This clause has been fundamental throughout U.S. history, as it has provided a standing invitation for civilian control of in military affairs. The same principle that permitted the framers of the Constitution to envision the possibility that senators might become generals during war permitted them to accept a civilian president as military commander in chief. What is crucial here is that the U.S. president, himself, is subject to the constraints of democratic government in all his functions, and thus less likely to use the military to increase executive power in general by means of military command.

The extent that the Founders expected the president to exercise military functions can be seen in their failure to curb the personal authority of the president to lead troops on the field of battle. The intention and expectation of the time was that the president could, and should, assume personal command of the military in the field. Presidents throughout the 19th century did not hesitate to do this. As the first president, George Washington clearly established this precedent in suppressing the Whiskey Rebellion, a violent insurrection in 1799 of farmers in Pennsylvania against the government's excise tax. Although the rebellion was small and confined to a limited area, Washington attributed the violence to nothing less than the subversion of the government. Washington declared that if the rebels were not subdued, "We may bid adieu to all government in this Country." To demonstrate federal authority, Washington gathered a military force that rivaled the entire Revolutionary army, and he personally led the army's march across Pennsylvania.

Other presidents followed Washington's lead. Although ineffectual, President James Madison organized and designed the defense of the capital against British forces in 1814. During the Mexican-American War in the 1840s, President James K. Polk exercised his authority as commander in chief by personally directing the American army against the Mexicans. While Polk did not command the army in the field, his strategies were the basis for the army's actions. Throughout the 19th century, presidents continued to command the army by personally formulating military strategies and participating in exclusively military matters. Most notable in exercising this broad grant of authority was President Abraham Lincoln.

Lincoln was faced with the most severe and serious threat to American democracy ever. Confronted by the secession of Southern states and the disintegration of the Union, Lincoln used his executive powers to their fullest extent in order to preserve the nation. He delayed one session of Congress from April to July

1861. Then, relying on his power as commander in chief, Lincoln assembled the militia, enlarged the army and navy without congressional authorization, called out volunteers for service, spent public money without congressional appropriation, suspended *habeas corpus*, and instituted a naval blockade of the Confederacy. In July he told Congress:

No choice was left but to call out the war power of the [executive branch of] the Government; and so to resist force, employed for its destruction, by force, for its preservation....These measures, whether strictly legal or not, were ventured upon, under what appeared to be a popular demand, and a public necessity; trusting, then as now, that Congress would readily ratify them?.Now it is insisted that Congress, and not the Executive, is vested with this power. But the Constitution itself, is silent as to which, or who, is to exercise the power; and as the provision was plainly made for a dangerous emergency, it cannot be believed the framers of the instrument intended, that in every case, the danger should run its course, until Congress could be called together; the very assembling of which might be prevented, as was intended in this case, by the rebellion?.It was with the deepest regret that the Executive found the duty of employing the war-power, in defense of the government, forced upon him.

But Lincoln's exercise of power did not stop there. In spring 1862, Lincoln participated in the direction of the Union armies. He personally determined the plan of operations and directed the movement of troops through executive war orders. Lincoln, however, was the last president to be so directly involved in formulating detailed military policies.

Lincoln's use of the commander-in-chief power helped confirm the president as the prime director of the nation's military forces. Throughout the 19th century, indeed, as in the 18th century, there existed no clear distinction between political and military competence. Most men of politics were capable of military command, and the exercise of military functions by the president created little difficulty perhaps because, in spite of the extensive powers assumed by Lincoln, presidents continued to respect overall constitutional constraints on their authority. During that period, a clear political-military hierarchy evolved: The president was at the top with the secretaries of war and the navy, giving direct orders to uniformed commanders in the field. Political and military responsibilities, therefore, remained mixed. The president frequently had previous military experience and generals became involved in politics. By the time the 19th century closed and the 20th century opened, the idea of a combination military commander/president had become more difficult to sustain. The advent of new technology, military professionalism, and the emergence of the United States on the international scene altered the relationship between politicians and military commanders. Still, the strong principle of acceptance of civilian control established in the 19th century served to solidify this tradition into the 20th century, if in a somewhat different form.

A shifting balance in the 20th century

The 20th century brought the onset of major war. When Woodrow Wilson was elected president in 1912, the United States' objectives were overwhelmingly domestic. When war broke out in Europe in 1914, Wilson chose neutrality for the United States. However, belligerent attacks on American economic interests and the rights of neutrals led Wilson to ask Congress for a declaration of war against Germany.

Following World War I, Wilson failed to get Senate ratification of the League of Nations treaty, plunging the United States into isolation. Subsequent presidents were faced with a Congress reluctant to involve itself in international affairs. In 1929-1930, Congress passed a series of high tariffs, culminating with the Smoot-Hawley Tariff Act. These tariffs were meant to protect the American economy from outside interference, and further isolated the United States. In 1935, 1936, and 1937 Congress passed a series of Neutrality Laws meant to ensure that the United States would avoid another European war.

The height of isolationism was reached during the Franklin Roosevelt administration. Faced with the crisis of the Great Depression, Roosevelt supported American neutrality as early as 1935 and stressed domestic priorities over foreign policy. It was only in the late 1930s that Roosevelt began to see the importance of American involvement in European affairs.

Ironically, it was the same conservative Supreme Court that attempted to limit Roosevelt's "New Deal" economic reform policies in the domestic sphere that finally established the presidency as the leading player in foreign affairs, reinforcing the president's control and direction of the military. In the 1936 case of *United States v. Curtiss-Wright Corporation*, the Supreme Court drew a fundamental distinction between presidential power in domestic and foreign affairs, stating that the president is the "sole organ of the federal government in the field of international relations — a power which does not require as a basis for its exercise an act of Congress."

The Court argued that the inherent authority of the president in foreign affairs found sanction in the Constitution, history, and present necessity.

By the time the Roosevelt administration became preoccupied with international concerns as clouds of war gathered over Europe, the world had changed significantly.

First, the technological revolution made it difficult for any president to be totally versed in the nature and strategies of war. Second, World War II was a global conflict.

These factors would challenge the idea of day-by-day civilian direction of the military during the war and afterwards. Yet, civilians today, for the most part, the president and his staff — as well as the secretary of defense — remain firmly in control of the nation's military establishment. It should be noted also that the constitutional "power of the purse" — the fact that the U.S. Congress appropriates all money for the military — enables senators and congressmen who are willing to devote time to the subject to exercise influence and control.

The advent of the Cold War in 1945 meant a complete end to the American tradition of isolationism and ushered the United States to a leadership position in world affairs. As a vast number of servicemen returned home from World War II, many moved into civilian roles in the government, academic life, and in business, establishing for the first time numerous relations between military services, American companies, and other sectors of society. The armed forces, previously somewhat isolated from American society, were now much more actively involved in it. The change resulted in major shifts in public and elite attitudes about the military. The fear of the military that had prevailed in the 19th century was largely replaced in the Cold War era by an understanding and appreciation for the role of military force in American foreign policy.

The combination of technical advances and American engagement in world affairs required new governmental institutions to control, organize, and monitor the military forces and institutions.

The National Security Acts of 1947 and 1949 established greater centralized control with the creation of the Joint Chiefs of Staff and the Department of Defense. The cabinet-level office of the secretary of defense, reporting to the president, soon became the link between the military and its civilian command.

In 1958 the Defense Reorganization Act strengthened the power of the secretary of defense, and Robert McNamara's strong influence while serving in this job in the 1960s solidified the power and authority of the defense secretary's office. These changes served to maintain the power of the presidency in military affairs, under new circumstances. Throughout the Cold War, the locus of strategic authority continued with the president. The executive branch, through the National Security Council in the White House and the secretary of defense, exercised critical authority over such issues as force levels, weapons procurement and deployments, and the use of force.

The failure of American military forces in the Vietnam War to achieve their immediate war aims had the effect of decreasing further the power and authority of the professional military vs. civilian authority. Once again, many Americans distrusted military solutions and military options. A greater caution in committing to military force even developed in the military itself. Since the 1970s, many military leaders have been reluctant to use force, arguing that the limited use of military force for political purposes without a clearly stated objective will result in failure.

This reluctance stemmed from two sources. First, the failure in Vietnam brought with it a post-Vietnam "syndrome." Presidents, military leaders, Congress, and the public all expressed suspicions about the ability of force to achieve American goals. Second, Congress asserted its authority in an attempt to control presidential use of force which had driven the U.S. role in Vietnam. In 1973, Congress passed the War Powers Act over President Nixon's veto. It was designed to limit the president's power to commit armed forces abroad without congressional approval.

According to the act, its purpose was "to fulfill the intent of the framers of the Constitution?and insure that the collective judgment of both the Congress and the President will apply to the introduction of United States Armed Forces" into conflict abroad. The act attempts to redress the growth of presidential war-making power by requiring presidential consultation and reporting, and outlining congressional action to thwart presidential use of force.

Despite its attempts, the War Powers Act remains largely symbolic due to congressional reluctance to use it and presidential claims that the act is unconstitutional.

In fact, the act may have strengthened presidential use of force by authorizing the introduction of forces prior to congressional approval.

Throughout the 20th century, in general, civilian control of the military, whether on the part of the president or Congress, has been strengthened and further institutionalized in American government and society. The increasing power of weaponry has further accelerated this trend towards firmer civilian command and control of military forces and institutions, by necessity.

The limits of military advice

As the United States enters a new century, the most likely problem is not that the professional military would ignore or in any way oppose civilian control. Rather, the issue is that civilian leaders may not have the technical expertise by background and experience to deal with the complex and dangerous problems of the 21st century. The challenge is for the civilian leadership to work effectively with military professionals to ensure that the president and his staff have access to necessary technical expertise and information that is required for effective decision-making.

The nature and extent of military influence in American foreign and defense policy has waxed and waned over American history. The military's influence depends on a number of factors, including the public's perception of threats and military structures and roles established in law and tradition. The American military itself is far from monolithic in character, but by now the best way to describe the role of military leaders in American democracy is as expert advisors. As General Matthew Ridgway, top military commander during World War II and the Korean War, explained,

The military advisor should give his competent professional advice based on the military aspects of the programs referred to him, based on his fearless, honest, objective estimate of the national interest, and regardless of administration policy at any particular time. He should confine his advice to the essential military aspects.

The professional officer, in short, should be an expert in making judgments about how force can be used most effectively. In other matters, he defers to civilians. Thus, the U.S. Constitution and American tradition have restricted the military to administrative and instrumental roles in the policy process.

As the United States moves into the 21st century, military leaders are not asked when and where to wage war. They are asked a far more restricted question: How can the military be most effectively used at a particular time and for a given strategic purpose? In 1983, Ronald Reagan did not ask the military whether the U.S. armed forces should enter Grenada and stabilize a threatening situation, but how to accomplish the mission. Nor did Presidents Bush or Clinton ask military commanders whether to evict Iraq from Kuwait, or protect Kosovar Albanians from the Serbians. They asked only how to accomplish those objectives quickly and with minimal casualties. So, custom, tradition, and legality have combined to firmly establish civilian control of the military in American politics and society.

The American experience may provide valuable lessons to countries struggling with the challenges of an emerging democracy. Perhaps the most obvious of these challenges is the threat of military commanders seizing power. There are two important principles that can reinforce civilian control. First, a newly emerging democracy would do well to establish solid constitutional foundations as the basis for civilian control of the military. Despite some ambiguities, the U.S. Constitution divides military power between the legislature and the executive, a division aimed to preventing abuses of power.

Also, the Constitution clearly establishes the president, a popularly elected civilian leader, as commander in chief of the armed forces. The crucial element here is that the president's powers are defined and limited as a whole, and that Congress, the U.S. courts, and the electorate, have substantial power. Thus, the president's command of the military does not lead to command of other sectors.

The president's primarily civilian status has been borne out through the country's history. Only four presidents — Washington, Jackson, Grant, and Eisenhower — had significant careers in the military prior to becoming president. Each of them understood the need to keep military and political functions separate and distinct. General Dwight Eisenhower carried this principle so far while he was commanding Allied forces in Europe during World War II that he did not vote.

The second key principle requires that the military serve in an administrative, not a policy-making, role. Eisenhower's refusal to vote while in the army is representative of his belief that military decisions must not be clouded by political decisions.

Generals should not be involved in the political decision-making process. Instead, they should proffer advice regarding the use of the military in achieving policy-makers' goals, and as to the probable success of the military outcome. It should be left to the political leaders to decide if the military option should be pursued.

This second principle is much more difficult to accomplish than constitutional protections. While a written constitution specifying the proper division of power between military and political leaders is an excellent first step, the challenge is convincing the military that its role is a subservient one. The primary obstacle to civilian control of the military is often a culture that has glorified the military. Changing that culture is a difficult, but necessary, task if the military is to be brought under civilian control. This will take time and education. Old leaders who distrust civilian leaders must be replaced by new ones willing to work with and for the civilian leadership.

Obviously, if the civilian leadership is popularly elected, its legitimacy in the eyes of the people helps it control the military. This task is a difficult one but no more difficult than the task of building a sound, democratic government. It must be made clear that a military that sees itself as but one element of a democratic society will be stronger, not weaker, as a result, as its actions are more likely to reflect the sovereign will of the people it serves.

6

National Authorization to Use Military Forces

Once an international institution decides that military forces should be used, the issue of authorization then shifts to the national level. The concept involved in Article 43 of the United Nations Charter was that military forces made available under these agreements would be committed without further national authorization. Since NATO has maintained standing military forces in the territory covered by Article 5, these forces would automatically become engaged if an attack occurred. However, the Article 43 agreements were never put in place and NATO forces have never been attacked in the territory covered by Article 5. The issue of national authorization thus has arisen every time that the UN or NATO has decided that military forces should be used.

The nine countries in this study have handled the issue of national authorization in different ways. As we expected, in all nine countries the debate at the national level has been deeper and more extensive the larger and more risky the military operation and the murkier the legal basis for action. Some of the nine have developed explicit formal guidelines. Norway and Japan have enacted laws that govern their participation in military operations conducted under the auspices of the United Nations. The United States has enunciated policies. While the others have not done this, their actions have followed implicit guidelines. The extent to which the legislature has been involved in the decisions to assign countries military forces to international military operations has varied across the nine countries and with the type of operation. Another issue that has varied among the countries is the conditions under which their political authorities are willing to assign military forces to international operations.

Except in the cases of Japan and Germany, monitoring and observation missions have been handled relatively simply. Executives in countries other than Japan and Germany have routinely assigned military personnel to such missions acting on their own authority.

Frequently, however, they have only felt free to assign those personnel that volunteered for these missions. Until the passage of the peacekeeping law in 1992, Japan's governments felt that they could not assign personnel of Japan's Self-Defense Forces outside of Japan. The same is true for Germany. Germany could not readily deploy its forces outside the NATO area until the constitutional court ruling of 1994.

Traditional peacekeeping has also been relatively unproblematic. Since all four traditional peacekeeping operations occurred before 1990, neither Germany nor Japan participated in them. The number of personnel required in traditional peacekeeping has generally been modest.

In Norway the legislature has given the executive authorization to assign up to a certain number of military personnel to UN traditional peacekeeping operations, though this authorization is limited to personnel who volunteer for such missions. In Canada and India, the executive branch of government routinely assigned personnel to traditional peacekeeping missions without raising the issue with their parliaments. The United States regularly provided transport and support services for traditional peacekeeping missions on the basis of executive decisions, and the president felt no need to request congressional authorization.

The other three types of uses of military forces, where the costs and potential risks are greater, have been more complicated. Because it is the extreme use of military forces, it is useful to start with enforcement operations. In at least some of the nine countries what has happened concerning enforcement has conditioned attitudes toward more modest uses of military forces.

We can start with the situation in the United States. President Truman felt that he had the authority to commit U.S. military forces in Korea.. USA, Senate, "Memorandum of July 3, 1950, prepared by the U.S. Department of State on the Authority of the President to Repel the Attack in Korea." in Military Situation in the Far East: Hearings Before the Senate Committee on Armed Services and the Committee on Foreign Relations, 82nd Congress, 1st session, Pt. 5 (Washington, D.C.: Government Printing Office, 1950) pp. 3373-81. Whether this case constituted a precedent for future authorizations to deploy U.S. military forces has been debated at length.

While Truman did consult with congressional leadership before ordering U.S. forces into combat, he acted without formal congressional authorization. Since the Korean War the authority of the executive to act without formal congressional authorization has become problematic. Congress insisted that it had to provide authorization for the use of U.S. military forces in the Gulf War. The British Parliament, the French *Assemblée* Nationale, and the Canadian Parliament all authorized their country's executive to deploy their national military forces to secure compliance with the Security Council resolution.

The involvement of the legislature in these four countries differed. In the United States, a republican president faced a congress controlled by democrats. The outcome of the vote was in question until the last minute. In the other three countries, the outcome of the vote was never in question. In all four of the countries, however, the involvement of the legislature was seen as a useful instrument in mobilizing popular support for the operation. Comparison of these two episodes suggests a trend toward increasing legislative involvement, but two cases do not provide a strong basis for generalizations.

In the case of the United States, however, the precedent established in the Kuwait case makes it likely that congressional authorization would be essential for the United States to participate in any enforcement action. This probably also applies to deploying U.S. military forces in peacekeeping plus state-building operations and using force to ensure compliance with international mandates.

As the number of instances in which military forces were used under international institutions increased in the 1990s, both the executive and legislative branches took steps seeking to define the cases in which the United States would participate in such military actions. The executive branch's views were embodied in Presidential Decision Directive 25 (PDD-25), which was signed in May 1994.

According to PDD-25 the U.S. could vote for a UN resolution establishing a military operation only if there were a threat to international peace and security. PDD-25 further specified that the U.S. could vote for deploying military forces under Chapter VII of the UN Charter only if the threat to peace and security were significant. In addition, it specified that the U.S. could vote for deploying military forces under Chapter VI of the UN Charter only if a cease-fire were in place. PDD-25 also specified that for the U.S. to vote for a deployment of military forces there should be an identifiable end-point to the UN operation. PDD-25 directed that the United States should participate in a UN operation only if it advanced U.S. interests and if U.S. participation were essential for the success of the operation.

Congress has demanded that it be informed before the United States votes for the use of military forces under the auspices of the United Nations. The acts authorizing expenditures for the Departments of State and Defense for Fiscal Year 1998, which were adopted in 1997, require that the executive branch notify Congress fifteen days before the U.S. votes for a resolution authorizing the deployment of military forces under UN auspices.

In Operation Allied Force, the 1999 Kosovo air war, Congress refused to give the president broader authority "to use all necessary force and other means, in concert with United States allies, to accomplish United States and North Atlantic Treaty Organization objectives in the Federal Republic of Yugoslavia (Serbia and Montenegro)." The president acted on his own authority. Congress did, however, authorize the participation of U.S. forces in IFOR, SFOR, KFOR.

The U.S. position may be summarized as follows. First, the debate about Kosovo has not affected the authority of the president to deploy a limited number of military forces under his authority as commander in chief and under the authority vested in him under the UN Participation Act. There is an effective limit of about 1,000 forces under this authority. Second, there seems to be broad agreement among constitutional lawyers that deployment of substantial U.S. military forces would require specific congressional authorization, and the practice in the Kuwait crisis and with respect to IFOR, SFOR, and KFOR was in accord with this view. PDD-25 and the State and Defense Department Appropriations acts deal with traditional peacekeeping and peacekeeping plus state-building. There is a clear demand for legislative participation in decisions about such operations. Finally, the War Powers Act applies to the deployment of U.S. military forces in multilateral military operations although when and what is to be applied may remain unclear.

Although the debate in the United States has gone further than that in other countries, it has gone on in other countries as well. Five of the other eight countries in this study have parliamentary systems. Because of this, the debates and the legislative history in these countries have been less complex. Moreover, the parliamentary systems ensure that there will not be the partisan division between the executive and legislative bodies that frequently prevails in the United States.

In all of the countries in our study, there have been parliamentary discussions about the use of military forces under the auspices of international institutions. Often these discussion have ended with a resolution taking note of what the government was doing or planned to do. Such resolutions carry the implicit threat that in some future instance parliament could take a negative decision.

Even in Canada with its long history of participation in international peacekeeping, there was an attempt in 1995 to adopt legislation that would ensure that parliament would be involved before the Canadian military forces were committed to UN operations, but a proposed bill requiring this was defeated. In general, legislatures have become more concerned with UN military operations as the number of these operations has increased and as national military establishments have been reduced after the end of the Cold War and in response to budgetary pressures. There has been an increase in the demand for military forces to serve under international auspices and a decrease in the forces available for such service. This contradiction has heightened legislative concern.

In the decisions that Japan and Germany adopted in 1990s allowing them to participate in UN military operations, legislative approval is required in both cases for the deployment of troops. The German case is interesting because the constitutional court concluded that deployments outside the NATO area are permissible as long as they receive specific "constitutive approval" from the Bundestag for each deployment. This carefully crafted formula enabled all political parties in Germany to accept the overall concept of deployment of Germany forces outside of Germany by assuring them that they would always have a voice in the decision to deploy before any commitment to do so is made.

The practice that has been established in many countries in the Kuwait case and with respect to IFOR, SFOR, and KFOR and the legislation that has been adopted in many countries has in effect negated the automatic commitment to use military forces for collective action envisaged in the doctrine of collective security. In the legislative debates that occurred in the United States, the United Kingdom, France, Canada, and Norway the question of whether or not the UN had authorized the military operation was an important issue. In all cases, there were individuals and groups within the legislative bodies for whom UN authorization was an essential condition for giving legislative consent for the authorization to use the national military forces.

A second issue that has arisen concerns the conditions under which states will commit their military forces to an international operation. The Japanese peacekeeping law establishes the most stringent conditions. According to the law Japanese Self Defense Forces may only be deployed if a cease-fire has been established and if the host country gives its consent. In addition, the rules of engagement that Japanese Self Defense Forces must follow permit them to use deadly force only in response to direct attacks upon themselves. They may not use deadly force to defend the forces of another country. In effect, the Japanese peacekeeping law precludes the deployment of the Japanese Self Defense Forces in enforcement operations and operations that involve using force to ensure compliance with international mandates. India also insists on having host country consent. In addition, it will not allow its forces to be deployed in a conflict that involves a significant Muslim population.

As mentioned above, through Presidential Decision Directive 25 and legislation the United States has also specified a variety of conditions for the involvement of U.S. forces.

The record indicates that under existing conditions democratic states are going to make independent decisions about the uses of their military forces under the auspices of international institutions. None of the nine countries whose practices we have reviewed has made an automatic commitment to engage its military forces except those six countries whose forces would be engaged were there an attack that called into play NATO's Article 5 commitment.

States have handled decisions about the uses of their military forces in operations conducted under the auspices of international institutions in ways that have been shaped by their national constitutions and traditions. Because of the separation of powers, the legislature has been more involved in the United States than in the other eight states, but legislatures have been involved in the others as well. Legislative approval when the governing party controls a parliamentary majority may be pro forma, but it is seen as an important instrument for gaining popular legitimacy. Traditionally executives have had considerable freedom to use military forces, particularly in parliamentary systems.

Do these national decisions to use military forces under the auspices of the UN and NATO meet standards of democratic accountability? Several things are clear. Five of the nine countries, France, India, the Russian Federation, the United Kingdom, and the United States, have used their military forces unilaterally in the period since the end of World War II. In terms of democratic accountability, their decisions to deploy their military forces unilaterally or collectively have been taken by roughly the same procedures.

Another point is that when large-scale and potentially dangerous military operations have been mounted; there have been many opportunities for enlightened public understanding. It was more than half a year between the time that Iraq invaded Kuwait and Operation Desert Storm began.

An almost equal time elapsed between the time that the initial warnings were given to Serbia about its operations in Kosovo and Operation Allied Force began. The media provided vast amounts of information about the issues. There were public and legislative debates.

Karen Mingst points out the influences of political culture as well as political and societal relationships within democracies that work in tandem with the formal and legal constitutional set-ups to ensure accountability in decision making. She notes that democratic accountability is more complicated than constitutional structures and includes "indirect accountability through the political culture..." The question is whether these forms of political activity provide sufficient accountability for decisions to act taken at an international level. Or does the decision-making process at the international level have to accord with democratic principles independent of domestic political processes? If so, how would these international processes work? How do national debates affect the shaping of future international policy and law?

The implication of the fact that when serious risks are involved national governments will insist on deciding whether or not to deploy their military forces in an operation conducted under the auspices of an international institution is that such operations will never be automatic as the doctrine of collective security demanded, they will always be conducted by coalitions of the willing. In many cases, such coalitions are likely to be organized on a regional rather than a universal basis; that is, regional leadership will be necessary. Another implication is that probably only the United States can provide leadership for the most dangerous operations, enforcement actions. Only the United States has the military capacity to conduct such operations with a strong probability of success. At the same time, the U.S. has one of the most complicated structures for committing its armed forces.

INTERNATIONAL AUTHORIZATION TO USE MILITARY FORCES

The intent of the UN Charter was to centralize authority concerning the use of military force in the Security Council. Under Article 42, the Security Council could authorize the use of military forces. Under Article 51 states could individually or collectively take military action in their own self-defense, but this action had to be reported to the Security Council and the authorization was limited until the Security Council had taken action. Under Chapter VIII of the Charter regional organizations could use force but only with the authorization of the Security Council. The voting arrangements in the Security Council were intended to ensure that military action would have broad international support and that effective action would be feasible, that is action would be taken only with the consent of the five permanent members, the states that at the end of World War II were assumed to have the greatest capacity to enforce the peace.

In practice, the United Nations Security Council, the United Nations General Assembly, and the North Atlantic Council have all given authorization to use military forces. The General Assembly's role was not foreseen in the Charter. Whether or not any institution other than the UN Security Council can authorize the use of military forces for purposes other than self-defense has been contested, as have the legal bases for deploying forces.

Decisions involving monitoring and observation missions have not been controversial. The practice became well established in the early years of the United Nations, and the League had undertaken similar tasks. Monitoring and observation missions have had the consent of the host states. The UN Security Council authorized all of the eighteen monitoring and observation missions.

Debates have arisen with respect to decisions about the other uses of military forces. Nevertheless, thirty-seven of the forty uses of military forces under the auspices of the UN and NATO in the other four categories have had the authorization of the UN Security Council. The only three instances when the Security Council did not authorize the initial deployment of military forces were UNEF I in 1956—a traditional peacekeeping operation, the United Nations

Security Force in West New Guinea (West Irian – UNSF) in 1962—a peacekeeping plus state-building Operation, and NATO's Operation Allied Force in 1999—a force to ensure compliance operation. The General Assembly authorized the first two, and the North Atlantic Council the third. Although the Security Council authorized the initial deployment of military forces in the Korean case, subsequent decisions about the military operation were taken by the General Assembly under the Uniting for Peace Resolution. This was true also in the case of the UN Operation in the Congo. In all, the UN Security Council authorized fifty-five of the fifty-eight uses of military forces, or almost ninety-five percent of them.

The United States and the United Kingdom were early proponents of the view that when the Security Council cannot act because of the veto decisions of the UN General Assembly or the North Atlantic Council constitute appropriate authorization for the use of military forces. The United States and the United Kingdom were co-sponsors of the Uniting for Peace Resolution in 1950, which allowed the General Assembly to act in crisis situations when the Security Council could not act because of the inability of the permanent members to reach unanimity. The UK's position, however, changed with the use of the Uniting for Peace Resolution to authorize UNEF I following the British and French attack on the Suez Canal in 1956. Even their Western allies have opposed this view on occasion, and the People's Republic of China and the Soviet Union and later the Russian Federation consistently opposed it. India abstained from voting on the Uniting for Peace Resolution, but voted for the authorization of UNEF I and UNSF. Japan's peacekeeping law explicitly accepts General Assembly authorization.

The essential question is under which if any circumstances should the UN structure and law be bypassed keeping in mind that the system exists precisely to restrain the use of force? And if it should be bypassed, then on whose authority and judgment? And how much force is authorized? Are regional organizations valid sources for authorization? Can states act unilaterally?

UN Secretary-General Kofi Annan expressed the dilemma clearly in a contribution to the *Economist*. He wrote:

To those for whom the greatest threat to the future of international order is the use of force in the absence of a Security Council mandate, one might say: leave Kosovo aside for a moment, and think about Rwanda. Imagine for one moment that, in those dark days and hours leading up to the genocide, there had been a coalition of states ready and willing to act in defence of the Tutsi population, but the council had refused or delayed giving the green light. Should such a coalition then have stood idly by while the horror unfolded?

To those for whom the Kosovo action heralded a new era when states and groups of states can take military action outside the established mechanisms for enforcing international law, one might equally ask: Is there not a danger of such interventions undermining the imperfect, yet resilient security system created after the second world war, and of setting dangerous precedents for future interventions without a clear criterion to decide who might invoke these precedents and in what circumstances.

If the United Nations were a democratic institution these questions would be less vexing. A body that was democratic might be able to act in a way that would be broadly regarded as legitimate. It could subject proposed policies to public scrutiny, debate the issues, and take decisions by some form of majority vote. However, the UN structure is not democratic. The Security Council was set up to provide an effective response to threats to the peace by those states that were assumed in 1945 to have the most powerful military forces. Unanimity among these states was seen as an essential condition for collective action. Because of this, the veto was given to the five permanent members of the Council. While these states remained militarily powerful in 2000, other states such as Germany, India, and Japan were at least as powerful if not more powerful than some of them. The justification for giving the five the special privilege of the veto had eroded. All organs of the United Nations further fail to meet the democratic criterion requiring the inclusion and equality of all adults. Representation and voting in the United Nations are based on the doctrine of the sovereign equality of states not the inclusion and equality of all adults. China with more than 1.2 billion people and Liechtenstein with only 31 thousand each have one vote in the UN General Assembly. According to this criterion, neither the Security Council nor the General Assembly provides democratic representation. Even if one took a broader notion of representation grouping states by their geographical regions, the Security Council would fail the test. Asia the most populous region of the world is seriously underrepresented.

Finally, more than a third of the 188 member states of the United Nations do not have governments that even under the most lenient interpretation could be regarded as democratic. Their representatives may or may not represent the wishes of the citizens of these countries.

Yet on issues of war and peace, the United Nations is at the apex of the international political and legal structure. There is no other organization that has universal membership and a mandate to deal with issues of war and peace. States clearly prefer to have the Security Council's authorization when they use military forces. Because of the importance of the UN in the legal and political decision-making processes within states, Security Council authorization bestows a legitimacy that cannot be gained in any other way. This legitimacy is important for gathering domestic support for using of military forces.

The legal grounds for authorization in the fifty-eight cases that have occurred have varied from measures to facilitate the pacific settlement of disputes under Chapter VI of the UN Charter, through threats to the peace as established under Article 39, Chapter VII of the UN Charter, to the necessity of preventing genocide and violations of humanitarian law. When Article 39 of the UN Charter and Article 5 of the North Atlantic Treaty were drafted, threats to peace were generally conceived as cross border military attacks. The North Korean attack on South Korea and the Iraqi attack on Kuwait involved clear violations of Article 2, Paragraph 4 of the United Nations Charter. The international law involved in the other fifty-six cases in which military forces were deployed under the auspices of the UN and NATO has frequently been less clear and has sometimes been contested. The humanitarian concerns that have compelled the deployment of international operations within states and without clear authorization by the UN Security

Council have raised the most difficult questions as Operation Allied Force in Kosovo demonstrated.

That many contemporary conflicts stem from intra-state rather than inter-state violence tests a key assumption of international law — that states are sovereign within their own territory. However, if the international law prohibiting genocide and providing for human rights protection appears to overcome, or even requires overcoming, the concerns of intervention in the internal affairs of states, new standards and procedures must be developed if international relations are not to revert to the unregulated unilateral great-power interventions of the nineteenth century. As the international community explores this issue, it may be useful to recall that the initial impulse to control the cross-border use of military forces came from within states. The debates at the dawn of the 21st century taking place within states as to the level of commitment to humanitarian operations may provide a basis for building an international consensus on the purpose and scope of these operations. The controversy surrounding NATO's out of area operations demonstrate the complexities of this problem. The central question is whether NATO can legitimately take decisions to use military forces in out of area operations without authorization by the UN Security Council. NATO's decisions relating to the International Force (IFOR), the Stabilization Force (SFOR), and the Kosovo Force (KFOR) were all taken within a framework provided by UN Security Council resolutions. Operation Allied Force, the air war against Serbia, did not have this mandate. As in the UN Security Council's expansion of the concept of threats to peace, in NATO's out of area operations what constitutes a basis for intervention is also an issue.

The debate in October 1998 in NATO and preparation of the Activation Order authorizing the air strikes that started in March 1999 in Kosovo highlighted these issues. The legal basis for NATO's taking action was a central concern. France, Germany, and Italy initially maintained that explicit authorization by the UN Security Council would be required for the NATO Council to authorize any out of area military operation.

Russia, China and many other countries including India have maintained this consistently. Britain, in contrast to its allies, felt that international humanitarian law provided an adequate legal basis. The U.S. assumed adequate authority from Resolution 1199 in which the Security Council acting under Chapter VII demanded that all parties in Kosovo "cease hostilities."

NATO countries eventually were able to build the required consensus to take a decision, and at its 50th anniversary summit in 1999, NATO adopted the Alliance's Strategic Concept, which called on the alliance to make "full use of every opportunity to help build an undivided continent by promoting and fostering the vision of a Europe whole and free." This suggested that NATO might again take such action. Yet, it remains uncertain whether NATO could ever again achieve the consensus required to repeat such an operation in Kosovo or elsewhere. Moreover, the legitimacy of NATO's decision was contested by states, particularly those who were not members of the alliance.

The broad issues of whether any institution other than the UN Security Council can authorize the deployment of military forces and what constitute legitimate grounds for intervention thus are far from resolved.. See the debate in countries whose policies have been examined in this study have taken on the issue of international authorization. As can be seen, there is disagreement about the legitimacy of General Assembly and North Atlantic Council authorizations. Further unresolved are the legal bases for deploying military forces in operations that do not involve repelling cross border attacks. Is progress in resolving these issues unlikely until the UN Security Council has been reformed? Will making the Security Council more representative of the world's population and changing its procedures so that the majority will could be implemented enhance its authority for the majority of states: Are these essential conditions for moving the Security Council and its procedures toward conformity with democratic tenets?

INTERNATIONAL DEPLOYMENT OF CANADIAN FORCES

Parliament's Role

With thousands of Canadian Forces (CF) personnel deployed overseas in peace support and other military operations, there has been debate over Parliament's role in authorizing the international deployment of Canadian Forces. Some argue that Parliament should be involved in related discussions much sooner and have more formalized authority over the final decision, while others counter that such requirements would hinder the government's ability to respond quickly to crisis situations around the globe.

To clarify the question of Parliament's role in the engagement of Canadian Forces overseas, this chapter examines: the legal and constitutional authority for the commitment of Canadian military personnel abroad; the process whereby Canada has deployed its military (both in times of war and of peace); and the focus of the debates surrounding those deployments. Ultimately, this chapter seeks to explore the appropriate degree of parliamentary involvement in making key defence decisions and how Parliament's role in such matters could be strengthened without compromising Canada's ability to respond swiftly and effectively to international crises.

Legal And Procedural Requirements

As a matter of Canadian constitutional law, the situation is clear. The federal Cabinet can, without parliamentary approval or consultation, commit Canadian Forces to action abroad, whether in the form of a specific current operation or future contingencies resulting from international treaty obligations.

Under the Canadian Constitution (*Constitution Act, 1867,* sections 15 and 19), command of the armed forces – like other traditional executive powers – is vested in the Queen and exercised in her name by the federal Cabinet acting under the leadership of the Prime Minister. As far as the Constitution is concerned, Parliament has little direct role in such matters.

Of course, Parliament, especially the House of Commons, plays an indispensable though indirect role by voting or withholding funds and by retaining or withdrawing confidence in the government of the day. Moreover, short of an actual vote, there are other mechanisms that enable parliamentarians to hold the government accountable for its decisions and to register their own views. These include questions to ministers, debates on the *Estimates,* and take note debates.

Although Parliament has a specific statutory role in some national emergencies under the *Emergencies Act* and with respect to the active status of the Canadian Forces under the *National Defence Act*, Cabinet is required to seek parliamentary approval only in the event of conscription or specific states of emergency. Without consulting Parliament, Cabinet can deploy troops by an order in council. Section 32 of the *National Defence Act* only "requires that Parliament (unless it is dissolved at the time) be sitting whenever any element of the Canadian Forces is placed on 'active service' by the Governor in Council, or within ten days thereafter. Although the *Act* does not specifically give Parliament any say in the matter, the requirement may reinforce Cabinet's accountability to Parliament at such times by ensuring that parliamentarians are on hand to question and challenge the government."

The effectiveness of section 32 in this regard can be limited, however, when Cabinet simply issues "blanket" active service orders. For example, the Canadian Forces have been on active service continuously since 1950 in furtherance of Canada's NATO commitments. Nonetheless, Cabinet has adopted the practice of issuing specific active service orders for major UN deployments.

Of course, Cabinet is accountable to Parliament and ultimately to the electorate for its decisions. But given the potentially far-reaching and irrevocable nature of those decisions, it seems reasonable to consider whether the generally *ex post facto* scrutiny of executive policy in this area is sufficient. After all, legislatures of other countries (for example, the United States and Denmark) appear to have a greater role in foreign policy decision-making than does the Parliament of Canada. Moreover, past Canadian practice also seems to have allowed for more regular involvement of Parliament in foreign policy matters.

Analysis

According to Professor Kim Richard Nossal, "one of the most deeply rooted traditions in Canadian foreign policy is the idea that only Parliament should decide to commit Canadian forces to active service overseas." The application of this theory to practice – whether for an offensive deployment or for peace operations –

has been inconsistent. To complicate matters, since the early 1990s it has become more difficult to distinguish offensive from non-offensive missions, because peace support operations have increasingly become high-risk for personnel. Involvement of Parliament in this decision-making has ranged from no consultation at any time to a full debate and vote in the House *before* the making of a formal commitment. In many cases, however, debate came only after the government had made its decision, or so close to a deadline that it had little influence on the final decision.

Although the current government has increased the *frequency* of parliamentary debate on deployment, more deployments have been at issue. Apparently, the government has not established criteria (such as the size of the force or the duration of the commitment) to guide whether or not a given deployment will be debated. In some cases, it was only after opposition parties complained publicly about the lack of parliamentary debate that a government proceeded to hold discussions within the House of Commons. Some would argue that little appears to have changed over the years to strengthen parliamentary oversight in this area. Even individual government-party Members of Parliament outside Cabinet have little input into decisions on the use of the Canadian military, let alone any real power to affect those decisions.

Debate on changes in mandates or other actions during a mission are even rarer than those on initial deployment. Typically, mid-mission decisions are not brought back to the House. According to Art Eggleton, former Minister of National Defence, this reflects a precedent established in World War II and Korea, whereby:

Parliament was involved in the first-principle debates to commit or not to commit [Canadian Forces for international deployment]. The nature and extent of that commitment – where, when, how, and with what Canadian troops would engage the enemy – was not something for parliamentary review. This same model has applied to the initial peacekeeping deployments to recent conflicts in the Middle East and Cyprus. Parliament debated [the] commitment in principle, and the Government, advised by its military staffs, defined and managed that commitment subject, after the fact, to parliamentary review.

To complicate matters further, many decisions must be based on factors beyond Canada's control: "the reactive nature of Canada's foreign policy means that much of the agenda is not the Canadian government's to set." In many instances, unilateral action by other countries (such as the United States), alliances (such as NATO), or multilateral institutions (such as the United Nations) make parliamentary input impossible. It would not be diplomatically feasible to withhold all comments on Canada's position from foreign representatives until after a parliamentary debate, particularly when most such decisions seek to address emerging crises within compressed timeframes. Moreover, "once Canada commits troops, it has written off its right to act independently, and has become just another 'troop contributing nation' participating under a common policy adopted by the UN; and Canada becomes 'locked in'. Subsequent Parliamentary involvement is largely ineffective."

The parliamentary calendar places yet another constraint on Canadian governments' ability to engage Parliament actively before deciding how to proceed. Professor Nossal notes that, when combined with the "huge distances" that separate many Members' constituencies from Ottawa, the fact that Parliament is not constantly in session renders meaningful input on its behalf into the making of day-to-day foreign policy near impossible: "Instead, the folk who are on duty ... 24-hours a day, 7 days a week, and 52 weeks a year – ministers in cabinet, or, more properly, their officials – are perfectly placed to deal with the unpredictable rhythms of world politics. ... Decisions can rarely wait until the members are reassembled and parliament organized for a debate."

Nonetheless, when the international deployment of Canadian Forces *has* been debated in the House of Commons, those debates did *not* typically focus on geopolitical reasons or interests that prompted Canada to become involved (or not). Strong support for a given military operation usually existed across party lines, especially if the mission in question had been authorized by the United Nations Security Council and/or if deployment had already occurred – that is, the engagement of Canadian Forces was *de facto*.

Rather, debate tended to focus on the ability of Canada and the armed forces – given the current environment of limited human, material and financial resources – to take on new commitments. Many challenges to the government revolved around providing adequate equipment and personnel to ensure the Canadian military was not overstretched and could complete its assignments without causing undue risk, either physical or mental, to its personnel. Questions seemed to focus more on whether Canadian Forces should be deployed *if/when* they did not have the proper resources to do the job safely, rather than on whether they should be sent at all.

Other questions from opposition Members inquired about the details of a deployment (its objectives, degree of risk, size, cost and expected duration), whether appropriate resources were available, and if there were any conditions on participation. Members of Parliament also wanted assurances that all other options had been exhausted and that solutions to the original source of conflict would continue to be pursued. They wanted to know about the government's long-term plans, particularly in the event of escalation.

Of course, the major challenge to the government in most cases was to justify why Parliament had not been consulted or asked to vote with respect to these matters. Typically, opposition parties have not argued against the deployment of Canadian Forces. Ultimately, the problem is seen to be with the political process, not the actual act of deploying troops.

In Professor Nossal's view, "when Canadian prime ministers say that parliament will decide such important matters [as the deployment of military forces overseas], they in fact do not really mean it. They do not mean it because they know formal parliamentary approval to be legally and constitutionally unnecessary. ... [T]he use of the Canadian Forces abroad, whether to go to war or to engage in peacekeeping, is, in British parliamentary systems, the prerogative of the executive." Indeed, we are once again faced with the fact that, with the possible exception of a declaration of war, there is no legally required role for the Canadian Parliament to approve Canada's participation in external military operations, despite attempts to change this situation.

Attempts To Change Practice

In its April 2000 report, the Standing Senate Committee on Foreign Affairs considered the lack of parliamentary approval of overseas deployments of Canadian Forces to be "unacceptable" and stated that "Parliament should always be consulted ... when Canadian troops are deployed abroad." It also noted that the 1994 Special Joint Committee on Canada's Defence Policy and the 1997 Commission of Inquiry into the Deployment of Canadian Forces to Somalia had called for enhanced parliamentary oversight of defence matters and made recommendations to that effect, with little impact. In his May 1996 Report, the Auditor General of Canada had done the same. In addition, Members of Parliament have used private Members' motions and opposition days in an attempt to require such a vote, at least in the House of Commons, *before* a decision is made. However, the government has consistently defeated these initiatives.

For example, Reform MP Chuck Strahl introduced a private bill, Bill C-295, in the House on 7 December 1994. The bill proposed amending the *National Defence Act*to provide for a vote in Parliament before Canada could commit to overseas operations, according to certain basic requirements. For example, the operations would have to be UN-authorized and involve a minimum of 100 CF personnel for at least one month. The mission would have to have specified objectives and duties as well as a clear role for Canada, while the government would have to establish a clear end date and its maximum planned expenditure for that mission. However, it did allow certain exceptions for outstanding circumstances. The bill was defeated on second reading on 19 June 1995.

Reform MP Bob Mills' similar attempt on 23 October 1996 was also eventually defeated. On 10 June 1998, Parliament began consideration of another private Member's motion (M-380) by Mr. Mills. In speaking to his motion, Mr. Mills explained that it had a three part approach. First, in an information session of two hours, Members of Parliament would sit in the House of Commons as a committee of the whole to hear from military, foreign affairs and academic experts and be informed of the history of the part of the world to which it was proposed troops would be dispatched.

Second, in a debate of two hours, speakers from each party would present their party's opinion on the proposal from a military and foreign affairs perspective. Finally, all Members would vote on whether to deploy CF personnel to the operation under consideration. If passed by the House, the motion would be transferred to a committee, which could then make appropriate adjustments.

The opposition parties argued for a change in how information on the activities and commitments of Canadian Forces was brought to the House, in order to achieve greater accountability, transparency and legitimacy as well as to avoid the "top-down" Cabinet decision approach to engaging Canadian Forces abroad. In the view of the opposition, special take-note debates took place too late to influence the outcome, and key players from the government were frequently absent from the chambers for the duration of any such debates. The opposition also expressed concern about the military's lack of capability, in view of funding, equipment and personnel deficiencies, to continue to participate so widely around the world; and argued that voting would ensure a more democratic process, involving elected representatives to a greater extent and bolstering formal support for the government's actions in a true expression of Parliament's sentiment.

The government countered with references to its constitutional legal right to make such decisions independent of the legislature. It maintained that requiring a vote would "handcuff" it and deprive it of the necessary flexibility to respond quickly and decisively to emergency situations through the dispatch of troops on short notice. Government members noted that "additional steps in the deployment process risk[ed] delaying [its] ability to respond" and could compromise alliance commitments under NATO and NORAD.

Finally, the government asserted that parliamentary procedure on the issue of military deployments had progressed significantly and would continue to do so without requiring a formal vote. As an example, it cited the practice that had emerged of consulting Parliament (when it was in session) through take-note debates in which all Members had an opportunity to express their views.

Moreover, the government had attempted to involve all parties in its decision-making even when Parliament was not in session: during the situation in Haiti (when Parliament was in recess), the government informed the appropriate porte-parole from each of the opposition parties of the government's intentions, and requested their agreement for action without recalling Parliament. The government also pointed out that it had pursued other means of involving Parliament in its decisions, such as having ministers appear before standing committees.

The motion was debated in the House on three separate occasions (10 June 1998, 29 October 1998 and 4 February 1999) before being defeated on 9 February 1999, despite support from most members of all four opposition parties.

Later, on 19 April 1999, during its allotted day, the Bloc Québécois moved:

That this House demand that the government submit to a debate and a vote in this House the sending of Canadian soldiers to the Balkans who may be involved in military or peacekeeping operations on the ground in Kosovo and the Balkan region.

The Bloc's main complaint concerned the lack of ongoing information about the mission. The Liberals responded that the motion was "imprecise at best" and that, if the House did not support the government, the opposition should introduce a motion of non-confidence. Government members further argued that the motion: dealt with a hypothetical situation; would set an unworkable precedent by requiring micro-management of the mission, thereby undermining day-to-day efficiency; and would hinder the deployed forces' ability to respond swiftly and flexibly to new crises. Ultimately, the motion failed to pass.

Another attempt to have a compulsory vote came, interestingly, from the Senate. In its April 2000 report, the Standing Senate Committee on Foreign Affairs argued that:

While the requirement of an explicit and timely vote in Parliament on external military action may ultimately be deemed to be undesirable or infeasible on policy or procedural grounds, the idea should not be rejected out of hand as being incompatible with Canadian parliamentary democracy. Indeed, such a practice could have salutary effects in terms of enhancing both the involvement of parliamentarians in foreign and military affairs and the democratic legitimacy of such decisions.

Consequently, the Committee recommended: That both Houses of Parliament have the opportunity to debate and approve at the earliest possible moment Canadian participation in any military intervention or external conflict situation, including peacekeeping and peacemaking missions, with the Government clearly spelling out Canada's interest in the situation and the scope of Canadian involvement.

The government did not respond to the report. Following the 11 September 2001 terrorist attacks, the Bloc Québécois revived the issue of requiring a vote before Canadian armed forces are committed. In an Opposition Day debate on 25 September, it moved the following motion:

That this House urge the government, in any reprisals taken in reaction to the terrorist strikes in New York on September 11, not to commit Canadian armed forces in any offensive action until the House of Commons has been consulted and has voted on the matter.

The then Minister of Defence, Art Eggleton, said that while the government agreed that Parliament should be consulted, it would not agree to a vote on committing the armed forces because this was the responsibility of the government. In the event, the motion was defeated.

After the election of a minority Parliament on 28 June 2004, the opposition parties once again put forward the idea of votes on Canadian participation in armed conflicts. On 9 September, the leaders of the opposition parties – Stephen Harper of the Conservative Party of Canada, Gilles Duceppe of the Bloc Québécois, and Jack Layton of the New Democratic Party – announced they would be seeking a series of changes to the Standing Orders of the House of Commons. Among these, they said "MPs should be allowed to vote on all opposition motions, including on the ratification of international treaties and on Canadian participation in armed conflicts...." In February 2005, all Opposition Days were made votable on a trial basis, expanding the capacity of opposition parties to precipitate votes on international treaties and initiatives.

Other Options For Parliamentary Scrutiny

The most obvious, although limited, means of exercising Parliament's authority over the international deployment of Canadian Forces consists of its ability to withdraw confidence from the government in the House of Commons and to refuse to do the government's supply (money) business. As long as Parliament uses neither of these powers, it implicitly approves the government's exercise of its executive powers. To withdraw support or deny a supply bill would be difficult, however, in view of a government majority and the claims of party loyalty. Furthermore, as the Senate committee notes: "denying funds to the Government and withdrawing confidence are rather blunt instruments for expressing dissenting views on such issues. Moreover, the opportunities for scrutiny and dissent that are offered by the Supply process cannot always be used in an effective or timely fashion. In the case of Kosovo, for example, it was only in November 1999, five months after the action had ended, that Parliament had an opportunity to vote funds expressly earmarked for that operation."

Alternatively, Parliament can be involved in decisions to deploy Canadian Forces by other means, for example, through hearings in committees and briefings by public officials. (It has been noted that committee activity has increased since 1969.) Standing committees have already been used as a forum for more ample debate on international deployments. For example, in April 1998, a special joint meeting of the House standing committees on foreign affairs and defence was held to discuss possible Canadian participation in a peacekeeping force in the Central African Republic. As a member of the government explained: "This option was chosen because of the need to make a decision and deploy troops as rapidly as humanly possible. Both ministers attended the special meeting and a unanimous resolution in favour of Canadian assistance was adopted."

In addition, the Department of National Defence (DND) makes available a monthly update of its *D PK POL Peace Support Operations*

SITREP. This non-classified document identifies those peace support operations since 1945 to which the Canadian Forces have provided personnel, their role, and the size and duration of the commitment. It also mentions operations in which Canada has chosen not to participate. Regular reporting by the Department to, and scrutiny of this list in, the House of Commons Standing Committee on National Defence and Veterans Affairs and the Standing Committee on Foreign Affairs and International Trade, as well as the Standing Senate Committee on National Security and Defence and the Standing Senate Committee on Foreign Affairs, would ensure some awareness among parliamentarians of Canada's military commitments overseas. The Department has also begun to offer occasional operational briefings which may be of interest to committee members and, indeed, all parliamentarians. (Transcripts of these briefings are available on the DND Web site.)

Finally, the House committees regularly review their respective departments' *Main Estimates*. This exercise provides an excellent opportunity to scrutinize departmental planning and budgeting, and to comment accordingly. In its April 2000 report, the Senate Standing Committee on Foreign Affairs acknowledged the importance of this and recommended that it be afforded the same opportunity.

In a February 2004 paper, Douglas L. Bland and Roy Rempel proposed some specific reforms for security and defence committees. These included having the parliamentarians assigned to these committees undergo security clearance procedures and having experienced military officers appointed to the committees to assist in research projects. Professors Bland and Rempel noted that such reforms would require political cooperation in the national interest.

Conclusion

In 1999, Professor Bland commented on the view that "Canadian politicians are not interested in defence policy. Neither are they conversant with nor much interested in the Canadian Forces, except in a kind of folksy regard one has for the family pet." The vibrant debate over Parliament's role in the international deployment of the Canadian Forces, however, suggests that

Canadian politicians want very much to have a say in how the military is used to fulfil Canada's foreign policy. Furthermore, it is ultimately the responsibility of Parliament to hold the government accountable for its decisions, including those related to military operations. Evidently, practice has been inconsistent on this matter. Even the current practice of holding take note debates, which do not involve a vote, is applied erratically and without a clear rationale. Professor Nossal concluded that:

The historical record suggests that the Canadian legislature is simply not well positioned to participate in such decisions [on the deployment of Canadian Forces]. And suggests that members of Parliament should reconcile themselves to the essentially *ex post facto* role that Canadian parliaments have historically played in this respect: in other words, to assess, via debate and discussion, executive decisions already taken. The element of discussion is crucial, for the putting of different views, and the subjection of particular perspectives to critical analysis, all combine to make better policy.

Indeed, constitutional requirements are not likely to change. As long as a majority government holds power and opposes a mandatory vote, it is improbable that any attempt at change will succeed (unless it is initiated by the governing party itself). This does not preclude greater parliamentary involvement through other means, such as scrutiny in committees, review of the *Estimates*, and so forth. In addition, recent changes implemented by the government have moved toward greater all-party involvement and input on deployment of forces (although not always *before* a decision is made).

As a minimum, Members of Parliament and Senators can insist that they be provided with as much information on engagement as possible – on the mandate, terms and objectives of a mission, risk factors, number of Canadian troops to be employed, duration, cost, other participants, and Canada's interest in the region – before any debate takes place. "Effective oversight need not derive from Parliament micro-management of Cabinet. Rather, the key to effective oversight is proper information to Parliament." One thing is certain: the debate will continue.

7

Pre-emptive Military Action and the Legitimate use of Force

From the "just war" doctrines of the Middle Ages to the Westphalian concept of a sovereign state's "right" to wage war for whatever ends the sovereign judged right to the contorted efforts of 19th Century legal scholars to avoid the problems of the legitimacy of "war" by defining all kinds of military operations as something other than "war" to the futile efforts of the League of Nations and the Kellogg-Briand Pacts to – with various reservations and ambiguities – "outlaw" war to today's discussion of the distinctions between preventive and pre-emptive use of force and the rise of "humanitarian intervention" as a politically correct form of warfare, practical political and military leaders, as well as legal scholars and scholars of international relations, have wrestled with the question of when use of military force is a legitimate instrument of statecraft.

It remains sadly the case that cannon are still the last argument of kings. Not the sincere efforts of leaders and citizens to substitute international institutions and international diplomacy for military power, not the terrible costs of two massive Europe-based world wars, not those of countless smaller internal and international wars throughout the world since 1945, not even the potential consequences of war fought with nuclear, chemical, and biological weapons, as well as the massively increased potential lethality of conventional technology, have fundamentally changed the fact that the threat and use of force are the ultimate instruments of international relations. Moreover, it is a necessary qualification to the proposition that diplomacy is preferable to force that where vital interests, or at least conflicts over perceived vital interests, are at stake, and where willingness to provide inducements is not unlimited, diplomacy and negotiation are unlikely to succeed unless there is seen to be a real cost to refusal to compromise.

The consequences that can be imposed by other means of pressure are puny compared to those of military force. The states (not to mention non-state actors) whose actions are most dangerous and most essential to be constrained are the least likely to be much affected by "international opinion." In such states, the prospects of affecting regime action by appeals to the good sense or innate caution of the citizenry are minimal simply because the regime will have been careful to insulate itself very thoroughly from such public pressures. Even the most powerful international instrument of pressure short of military force – economic sanctions – has a very feeble potential for deflecting such states' actions. Indeed, it is, in some sense too simple even to say that it is an absolute principle that force is a last resort. Certainly, the risks and costs of military force make it both prudent and moral to refrain from its use while there is a reasonable prospect that other means may be effective. But the principle of using force only after exhausting non-military alternatives necessarily implies a willingness to recognize that, at some point, they have been exhausted, and that waiting too long may mean waiting until military options are no longer effective at acceptable costs.

In the limited time and space available, rather than try to cover the whole huge field, it seems appropriate to focus on two specific questions that have come to the fore in the face of fundamental changes in the international security environment since the end of the Cold War:

- When is use of force justified? (Herein of pre-emption)
- Who can legitimately decide on the use of military force? (Herein of unilateralism)

Unilateralism, multilateralism, and international decision-makers. Of the two issues, the second, "unilateralism," is relatively the easier, because the dichotomy between "unilateralism" and "multilateralism" is to a large degree an illusory one. To be sure, there are today a few in the United States who prefer – or at least affect to prefer – unilateral action as a matter of both principle and expediency. They see American military power as so overwhelming that there is no need for the assistance of others. Equally important, they see American purposes as so noble and the perspectives of other governments as so narrow, even craven, that it is not only possible, but necessary, for the United States to ignore their views. The conclusion these "unilateralists by preference" draw is that involvement of other nations in decision-making about American use of force is unwise in that it risks diluting the clarity of American purposes, while involving other nations in actual operations is pointless because they can add nothing significant to American capabilities and including them merely complicates operations.

Conversely, there is a sharply contrary view that decisions on use of military force must always and only be made on a multilateral basis, and indeed, must be made by international institutions, preferably, and perhaps exclusively, by the United Nations. There are some in the United States – and there appear to be many more in other countries – who insist, or at least affect to insist, that only formal approval by the United Nations can legitimate the use of military force, except perhaps in the case of immediate defense by a certifiably innocent victim against direct military attack across a recognized international border by acknowledged forces of a foreign state.

There is, however, in international law – and more in international practice – widespread acceptance of the concept that, in the end, all decisions on use of military force are unilateral, in the sense of being made by nation states, but those decisions must, for reasons of both prudence and principle, be made in the light of the opinions and interests of others so as to gain their support. The great weight of American opinion takes a view that can fairly be described as "unilateral if necessary, but multilateral if possible – and multilateral should almost always be possible."

To begin with the first element – the reservation of the ultimate right of unilateral action – the current US administration is by no means the first to espouse the notion that the United States has the right, even the duty, to act alone if the nation's vital interests are at stake, and that, in the end, it is the United States and no one else that makes that decision. The quotation at the top of this chapter is indeed from a National Security Strategy document, but it is drawn from that of President Clinton in 1999, not that of President Bush in 2002.

Nor is the idea that decisions on military force are ultimately national decisions confined to superpowers. Indeed, it seems very likely that, in extremis, every country would take that position. Certainly, even those, like the current German government, who are most enthusiastic in theory for multilateral decisions on use of force, insist on reserving the right to make a separate national decision on whether a multilateral approval of military action is sufficiently justified – or sufficiently serves their own nation's goals and principles – to require actually participating in the action. And there are numerous examples of nations that, in general, regard themselves as adherents of a multilateral approach who proven nonetheless ready to use their military forces for their national aims without bothering much about international opinion, as Spain did last summer over the occupation of a disputed Mediterranean island. To point this out is not accuse Germany or Spain or anyone else of hypocrisy or even to call into question the soundness, much less the sincerity, of their general commitment to multilateral decision-making, but only to observe that it has its limits.

But if unilateralism in theory is all but universal, unilateralism in practice is very hard even for a superpower on a matter of any difficulty. First, in most situations, there may not be much of a practical option of truly unilateral action. American military operations are almost always greatly facilitated by having the cooperation and support of others. The US may have overwhelming capability in many, perhaps most, forms of military power, but the direct military contributions of other nations remain highly useful. The military capability gap is real, but it is not infinite, and many allies can make very helpful contributions, in specialized areas like special operations forces, in capabilities where cutting edge technology is not required, and increasingly also where other nations are, albeit on a smaller scale, approaching American capabilities in fields like precision strike or naval forces. Even setting aside direct military contributions, the United States is, in almost all circumstances, heavily dependent on other countries for bases, overflight rights, and access, and usually for even more direct support in the form of intelligence, cooperation in applying economic and political instruments, and, very importantly, in dealing with the aftermath of conflict. Certainly that was the case in Afghanistan. The Bush Administration's National Security Strategy may exaggerate a little when it says, "There is little of lasting consequence that the United States can accomplish without the sustained cooperation of its allies and friends in Europe," but the basic point is correct – and not just about Europe.

And, of course, there are powerful political and psychological dimensions to international support. America, however patriotic even jingoistic and ostensibly disdainful of foreigners our popular culture, is far from unilateral by preference when it comes to military operations. Opinion polls consistently show – in a variety of contexts – that public support for American military operations is far higher where the United States has the support of its allies than where it would be alone. In part, this reaction is no doubt the sensible one that Americans like others to share the costs and risks, but it also appears to reflect a more complex judgment about international affairs: The American public has more confidence that the decisions of our government are right if they are shared and supported by other countries, as evidenced both by their formal positions and statements and by their willingness to send their own military forces to join in.

Moreover, in most situations, it is not that hard for the United States to garner international support. This is in part the consequence of the obvious fact that the United States has a wide variety of levers of influence and persuasion at its disposal. And the United States need not shy from using those levers. Accepting that the use of military force requires – or is at any rate immensely helped by – international support does not require that the United States be neutral about whether that support is forthcoming. Forced to choose between the United States and its adversaries, most countries will, whatever their misgivings, realize that their interests counsel considering the consequences of opposing the United States on an issue so important to it that the use of military force is an issue.

But the proposition that, in the end, the United States can usually count on the support of those countries that matter does not rest simply – on the proposition that frustrating the Americans would have a price. At bottom, those interests of the United States that plausibly could involve the use of American military force are also the interests of much of the rest of the world. An American diplomacy geared to exhausting non-military alternatives as means of meeting fundamental challenges will, if non-military means fail after being seriously applied, in most cases, also convince many other countries that resort to military force is not only justified, but required in their own interest, not just that of the United States.

However, to say that international support for the use of military force is, in most cases, both necessary and obtainable, is not necessarily to say that the only legitimate source of international support is action by the United Nations. The interesting and much-disputed legal issues of how the UN Charter, in particular Article 51 (reserving the inherent right of individual and collective self-defense against armed attack) should be interpreted – and what, to a practicing lawyer is an equally important issue – who has the legitimate authority to interpret it authoritatively are matters more for scholars than practitioners of international relations.

Of course, formal UN support is desirable, both for its own sake, and for its impact on the actions and attitudes of individual countries whose support may be essential. But insofar as the issue is legitimacy, it is hard to make the case that only UN action suffices. In practice, whether "the United Nations" has given its sanction for use of military force means, as a practical matter, whether there is a Security Council resolution that can plausibly be read as authorizing military force.

That, in turn, means whether there is a negative vote by Russia or China. Strictly speaking, of course, the UK or France could also veto, and, in theory, a UN Security Council resolution authorizing the use of military force could fail by reason of not having the affirmative votes of a majority of the Security Council, even if no permanent member voted against it. As a realistic proposition, however, it is indeed hard to imagine a use-of-force situation where a resolution to which none of the "Perm 5" objected enough to use a veto could not get a majority (even if one or more permanent members abstained)-and it is still less plausible that France – not to mention the UK – would exercise a veto in a situation where Russia and/or China would not (always laying aside the – presumably no very unlikely – of a case like Suez in 1956 where the interests of France or the UK were uniquely at issue.)

It follows that to require United Nations approval as an absolute condition of legitimate use of military force is to say that no military action of which Russia or China (or, in principle, France, Britain, or, indeed, the US) strongly disapproves is legitimate, no matter how broadly the action is otherwise supported, or how well justified in other international legal or political terms. To illustrate the point – NATO could legitimately point to various UNSC resolutions as supporting its intervention to reverse Milosevic-led Serbia's expulsion of the ethnic Albanian population of Kosovo in 1999. There was, however, no authorizing action by the Security Council in classic "all necessary means" words, and it is not clear that had one been sought, Russia (or China) would have withheld a veto. That intervention was, nonetheless, broadly regarded as legitimate, whether as a "humanitarian intervention" or as a means of forestalling a spreading conflict in a region of Europe that has bred a host of wars in living memory.

Would a failed attempt to get a formal Security Council authorization really have changed things? For most of the world, the Kosovo intervention was legitimate and would still have been so had a UNSC effort produced a veto. For to say that a UNSCR is essential amounts to saying that – not "the international community" – but Russia, China – and, in principle the other permanent members or alternatively, a majority-blocking group of the non-permanent members – are the absolute custodians of the legitimacy of international force. In these terms, the choice between "unilateral" action and "multilateral" is not between a strictly national decision and a UN Security Council Resolution, but one between efforts to garner as much support from other countries as possible, and an insistence, even a preference, for acting alone. In such efforts, the actions of formal regional institutions like NATO and of informal ad hoc groups like the coalition that fought the first Gulf War (admittedly with UNSCR blessing) and may fight a second one, count for as much as a UN Security Council hamstrung by a veto.

Pre-emption: When does the Right to Self-defense Arise?

The question of "pre-emption" is a much more difficult issue. The concept that "defense" is legitimate, while "offence"– more pejoratively "aggression" – is not, lies deep in all discussions of use of military force. In practice, the distinction has always been hard to draw. Indeed, a good deal of effort has been spent – without notable success or general acceptance in practice – in attempting to abolish the distinction by aspiring to abolish force entirely as a means of settling disputes – by a sort of "no fault" renunciation of force. But the principle of "self-defense" has survived, and is, in fact, formally and explicitly recognized in the UN Charter as an "inherent" right, not one created by the Charter.

Lurking in the concept of "self-defense" is the question of at what point the right arises, of where on the spectrum of prevention, pre-emption, and response, military action is justified. The American government has, especially but not exclusively since the attacks of September 11, 2001, stressed the right of pre-emption in certain circumstances, specifically against terrorists and against rogue states threatening to acquire nuclear and other mass destruction weapons.

So far as the United States striking at terrorists is concerned, the issue is hardly one of pre-emption. Once hostilities have been started by others, it is no longer "pre-emption" for the victim to seek to destroy the source, not just to frustrate specific attacks in the future from the same source. The United States has already been – indeed was years before September 2001 – the victim of attack by the coordinated terrorist groups that are the targets for American attacks today. And, beginning at least with the embassy bombings in 1998, the United States was prepared to use force to destroy Al Qaeda operations and leadership where there was sufficient intelligence of their location, entirely independent of any indication that a specific new attack was being planned. There are, to be sure, many difficult legal, moral, political, and practical issues raised by the "war" on terrorism, and by the American determination to, in the words of President Bush's National Security Strategy, "destroy the threat before it reaches our borders." For example, since terrorists are non-state actors, the sovereignty of other countries is, by definition, involved in American attacks on them. Countries in whose territory terrorists are operating have a responsibility to suppress the operations, and the Administration has declared that it will regard countries that give sanctuary to terrorists as subject to military attack just as much as the terrorists themselves. The sovereignty questions raised by this position – and other issues of legality and legitimacy – are real and sometimes difficult issues, but they are not about pre-emption, but about the conduct of a "war" that does not fit traditional patterns.

The Bush Administration has, however, squarely relied on pre-emption in also enunciating a potentially more far-reaching doctrine of anticipatory action against rogue states that are in the process of acquiring nuclear, chemical, and biological weapons. The NSS says, "We must be prepared to stop rogue states... before they are able to threaten or use weapons of mass destruction against the United States, our allies, or friends." To an important degree, this doctrine is less innovative than either its advocates or its critics profess to believe. Perhaps most important, it is, in its terms, limited to the particular issue of rogue states seeking to acquire WMD; it is not a claim to use force pre-emptively (and unilaterally) whenever the American government judges US interests to be a stake.

Critics, however, argue that the Administration is claiming that self-defense is not limited to "pre-emption" in the sense of forestalling an imminent attack, but "preventive war," in the sense of using military force where the only threat is a vague and uncertain one of possible conflict at some indefinite point in the future. Such "preventive" war, it is argued, is not only in violation of international law, but an unbounded invitation to use of force on mere suspicion of the ambitions or intent of another nation, and indeed an negation of the very concept of international law.

However, far from ignoring international law, the United States government has advanced a sophisticated legal argument for the legitimacy of its position regarding pre-emption against rogue state WMD that is squarely based on international law principles. The argument begins with the proposition that international law unquestionably recognizes a right of self-defense and moreover acknowledges that exercising that right of self-defense does not require absorbing the first blow. As the NSS puts it, under long-recognized international law principles, "nations need not suffer an attack; they can lawfully take action to defend themselves against forces that present an obvious danger of attack."

The classic and widely accepted formulation of that right was stated by Daniel Webster, as American Secretary of State in the 1840's during negotiations about a British cutting out operation in American waters in Lake Ontario against the American ship *Caroline* that was being used to supply rebels in Canada. He wrote the British Minister, Lord Ashburton, that a nation has a right to act first where the "necessity of self-defense is instant, overwhelming, and leaving no choice of means, no moment for deliberation." The Administration argues that Webster's formulation must be "adapted to the capabilities and objectives of our adversaries." The traditional concept of "imminence" assumed a context where the need for mobilization and other preparation meant that there was a realistic prospect of warning of an attack. Stressing that its claim of a right to pre-empt is limited to action "to eliminate a specific threat to the US or our allies and friends," the Administration argues for a standard of "necessity" that recognizes that terrorists and rogue states with WMD would have at their disposal "weapons that can be easily concealed, delivered covertly, and used without warning." Accordingly, it is lawful to "take anticipatory action to defense ourselves, even if uncertainly remains as to the time and place of the enemy's attack."

On balance, the Administration has the better of the legal argument: Webster's formulation – which was adopted in the course of a protest against, rather than a defense of, a pre-emptive operation and therefore takes a restrictive view – speaks of a "necessity of self-defense" that is "instant, overwhelming," etc. Critics argue that only an immediate prospect of specific attack can met that standard. But, in Webster's formulation, it is the "necessity" that must have those characteristics, and such a necessity may exist without an immediate prospect of attack. The right of anticipatory self-defense by definition presupposes a right to act while action is still possible. If waiting for "imminence" means waiting until it is no longer possible to act effectively, the victim is left no alternative to suffering the first blow. So interpreted, the "right" would be illusory. The Administration is accurate when it points out that once a rogue state has achieved a serious WMD capability, effective action to eliminate the capability may well have become impossible. The problem is not so much that WMD be used with little warning – attacks with conventional weapons have all too often achieved tactical surprise – but that surprise use could be decisive and that the capability can be so successfully concealed that pre-emption is operationally impossible even if warning were available. On this basis, a strong case exists that the right of "self-defense" includes a right to move against WMD programs with high potential danger to the United States (and others) while it is still feasible to do so.

The problems with pre-emption, unfortunately, are not lack of legal legitimacy, but operational practicality. A right of pre-emption is one thing; a meaningful capability to pre-empt is quite another. Exercising the right pre-supposes, both logically and practically, that there is some military operation that will achieve the desired result of eliminating the WMD capability that is targeted at an acceptable cost, taking into account the enemy's possible reactions.

The first operational issue with pre-emption is whether the proposed operation will actually eliminate the WMD capability targeted. The problem is not (usually) whether there is a means of executing a pre-emptive attack once targets are identified, but knowing what and where to strike. Precision weapons require precision intelligence, and pre-emption requires that intelligence be comprehensive as well as precise. Too much attention to action movies and too little to the realities of intelligence collection have tended to obscure the difficulty of knowing enough about a nation's WMD programs to have much confidence of eliminating them by pre-emption. Still more difficult operationally is dealing with what the enemy may do in response, even if his WMD capability has been successfully negated.

The contemporary cases of Iraq and North Korea illustrate the operational problem in some of its dimensions: In the Korean case, there is no question about the location of the plutonium-production reactor and the re-processing facility at Yongbyon, and, as former Secretary of Defense William Perry has written, the United States military has the capability to destroy them quickly and without causing release of radioactive materials. Such an attack would block the prospect of North Korea extracting some half-dozen bombs worth of plutonium within the next year. But it would not eliminate the North Korean nuclear program, much less Pyongyang's ability to respond with devastating force. Even with regard to North Korea's nuclear programs, the Yongbyon facilities are only part of North Korea's potential. There has been no claim that the United States knows the location of either the plutonium that was extracted in 1991-92 or of the couple of bombs for which that plutonium may have supplied the fissile material. Nor is there a claim that the United States has the detailed knowledge required for high-confidence targeting of other elements of the North Korean program – notably its incipient uranium-enrichment facilities – much less its extensive chemical weapons capabilities. But the real problem with pre-emption in the North Korean case is that the North Korean capability to respond and escalate does not (so far) rest on its WMD, but on its massive conventional forces – and there is no chance that, that capability could be eliminated pre-emptively, even by a massive effort. Of course, the problem will only grow worse if North Korea is able to expand its nuclear potential, and at some point, if diplomacy fails, it may be the wiser course to act militarily, accepting the limits on American capability to preempt and relying on deterrence and defense to block or blunt a conventional attack in response. But it is the risks of such a course that have made not just South Korea, but the United States as well, so uneager to press the case for military confrontation.

In a sense, the case for dealing with the Iraqi WMD programs by military force now may be said to be the case for not letting Iraq reach the point Korea is at now. Essentially the argument for eliminating Saddam Hussein's WMD by military force if he will not eliminate it himself under UN monitoring is that, despite the real risks, if the capability is not stopped now, it will be too late – and the world and the region will have to deal with a Saddam regime armed with a powerful WMD capability that can neither be pre-empted nor confidently defended against. But it is significant that the military option being considered against Iraq today is pre-emptive only in the strategic, not the operational, sense. The military option is not to strike at the WMD programs directly but to replace the regime, as the only confident means of eliminating its WMD programs. This is not the product of over-ambition, but of operational reality. Intelligence of a granularity and comprehensiveness necessary for an effective pre-emption limited to the WMD programs themselves is no more available in the Iraqi than the Korean case. Indeed, in the Iraqi case there is not even an equivalent to Yongbyon, that is, a single key facility whose destruction is military feasible and would at a stroke deeply set back the WMD efforts. It is this lack of a military option able to eliminate the WMD that makes a campaign to oust the regime the only military option if UN disarmament efforts fail. Happily, Saddam Hussein has less formidable responsive options than does Kim Jong Il because his military is relatively weak and his ability to strike rapidly at high value targets is much less. The American assessment is that none of his potential responses is anything like as significant as the North Korean potential to wreak immense destruction on South Korea, and that the risks entailed by what he can do can be reduced to acceptable levels – and are in any event better run now that faced later when his WMD programs are far more developed. But Iraq has some potentially very destructive responses, and their potential use is a major complication for military planning – and a major source of the reluctance to many to support an invasion.

In short, the contrasting cases of Iraq and North Korea today may be said to illustrate both the conceptual strength of the administration's doctrine of pre-emption against rogue state WMD, and its limitations in practice. There will, unfortunately perhaps, still be plenty of scope for military operations and capabilities aimed at deterrence and for defense if deterrence fails.

INTERNATIONAL LAW AND THE UNITED NATIONS: THE USE OF MILITARY FORCE

There are innumerable areas in which the roles of international law and the United Nations intersect in ways that are fundamentally important for our ever more interdependent world, including international trade and communications, environmental protection and the conduct of diplomatic relations. But no issue involving this intersection is of more immediate importance, or more controversial and difficult, than the current status of the international rules governing the use of military force.

As we look out on the world around us, those rules seem to be in serious disarray, their application erratic and their interpretation contested. No universally accepted practice currently governs their use. States are seen as making up the rules as they go along, going to war when they should not be, and not taking military action when they should.

Secretary General Kofi Annan put part of the problem in a nutshell when he said to the General Assembly on 23 September last year, six months after the Coalition invasion of Iraq, if 'States reserve the right to act unilaterally, or in ad hoc coalitions' without waiting for agreement in the Security Council, 'this logic represents a fundamental challenge to the principles on which, however imperfectly, world peace and stability have rested for the last fifty-eight years'.

He put the other part of the problem – states not going to war when they should – equally starkly in his Millennium Report to the General Assembly three years earlier: "…if humanitarian intervention is, indeed, an unacceptable assault on sovereignty, how should we respond to a Rwanda, to a Srebrenica – to gross and systematic violations of human rights that affect every precept of our common humanity?" In the United Nations Charter of 1945 the use of force was subjected to the rule of law in a much clearer way than had ever previously been attempted, including in the ill-fated League of Nations Covenant, and the law was backed with a system of collective security much more potentially effective than anything that had gone before. The Charter made absolutely clear in Article 2(4) that all UN member states "shall refrain in their international relations from the threat or use of force against the territorial integrity or political independence of any state, or in any other manner inconsistent with the Purposes of the United Nations". It allowed only two exceptions to the prohibition on the use of force in international law: self-defence under Article 51, and military measures authorised by the Security Council in response to "any threat to the peace, breach of the peace or act of aggression".

But it was one thing to create a new legal order, quite another to make it work as intended. The founders of this new order were not naïve, recognising as Adlai Stevenson said at the time, that "(e)verything depends on the active participation, pacific intentions and good faith of the Big Five." And the mutual hostility among the five permanent members themselves which very soon emerged, to be sustained throughout the Cold War years, certainly did threaten to bring the whole edifice down. For forty-four years, until 1989, states repeatedly used military force against others (by one count 200 times and by another 680 times)-a great many of which occasions could not begin to be explained or justified as self-defence under Article 51, although that fig-leaf was regularly relied upon.

But a paralysed Security Council passed very few Chapter VII resolutions, and there was only one large scale collective military action responding to a breach of the peace (Korea in 1950, during the Soviet Union's misjudged period of absence from the Council). The order which prevailed was essentially a new variation on an old balance of power theme.

Through all this the UN security system somehow managed to stay afloat, playing a reasonably significant role at least in defusing and managing conflict. 'Good offices' diplomacy contributed to the peaceful abatement of some 25 per cent of the post 1945 conflicts. And peacekeeping, a role invented by the Secretariat – involving the verification, monitoring, and supervision of ceasefire and broader peace agreements – proved crucial in reducing the risk of a number of further wars, especially in South Asia and the Middle East. But it is hard to argue that the new international legal order promised by the Charter was, for the duration of the Cold War, under anything but stress. All that changed, dramatically, after the Berlin Wall came down. The removal of a major source of ideological and great power conflict liberated the UN to play the global security role its founders intended, as became immediately apparent with the response to Iraq's invasion of Kuwait in 1991. Expectations were reinforced by UN-organised or authorised military deployments in the former Yugoslavia, Somalia, and Haiti. The average number of resolutions passed in a year went from 15 to 60, or from a resolution a month to a resolution a week. Ninety-three percent (247 of 267) of all Chapter VII resolutions of the Council were passed between 1990 and 2002. Before 1989 the Council applied sanctions twice; since then it has imposed sanctions fifteen times.

Not all this activity was either effective or uncontroversial: too often what happened – not least in Somalia in 1993, Rwanda in 1994 and Bosnia in 1995 – was too little too late, misconceived, poorly resourced, poorly executed, or all of the above. And of course in Kosovo in 1999, in what was arguably a very strong case for intervention, a divided Security Council was bypassed completely. But there was reason to believe that step by step, painful and disappointing as so much of the process was, a new and much more responsive international legal order was falling into place.

But now the wheel has turned again, and maybe even more seriously than in the Cold War years. The decision of the U.S., and its coalition allies, to go to war in Iraq in March 2003 in defiance not only of one or more threatened vetoes, but of the clear and overwhelming majority of the members of the Security Council, was a watershed of a wholly different, and more disconcerting kind. Three different kinds of challenges to the international legal order are involved, all of them serious.

First, to the extent that the invasion of Iraq was based on a claim of anticipatory self-defence more far-reaching than any previously asserted, Article 51 has been stretched beyond endurance. Secondly, to the extent that the invasion was based on claims of threats to international peace and security sufficient under Chapter VII to justify Security Council authorization, but with those claims poorly argued and the Council eventually bypassed, the credibility of the whole Charter system has again been frontally challenged. And thirdly, to the extent that the invasion was based on Saddam Hussein's record of tyranny over his own people – but again poorly and inconsistently argued, and with the Council bypassed – we have seen close to being choked at birth what many were hoping was an emerging new norm justifying intervention on the basis of the principle of "responsibility to protect".

Article 51 and Anticipatory Self Defence. It has long been accepted, both as a matter of customary international law predating Article 51 and international practice since, that notwithstanding the language of the article referring only to the right arising "if an armed attack occurs", the right of self-defence extends beyond an actual attack to an imminently threatened one. Provided there is credible evidence of such an imminent threat, and the threatened state has no obvious alternative recourse available, there is no problem – and never has been – with that state, without first seeking Security Council approval, using military force 'preemptively'. If an army is mobilising, its capability to cause damage clear, and its hostile intentions unequivocal, nobody has ever seriously suggested that you have to wait to be fired upon. In this sense, what has been described generically as 'anticipatory self-defence' has always been legal.

The problem arises with another kind of anticipatory self-defence: when the threat of attack is claimed to be real, but there is no credible reason to believe it is imminent. It should be said immediately that the issue here is not with the principle of military action against non-imminent threats as such. It is perfectly possible to imagine real threats which are not imminent – including the nightmare scenario combining rogue states, WMD and terrorists.

The problem boils down to whether or not there is credible evidence of the reality of the threat in question (taking into account, as always, both capability and specific intent); whether the military attack response is the only reasonable one in all the circumstances; and – crucially – who makes the decision.

The question is not whether preventive military action can ever be taken: it is entirely within the scope of the Security Council's powers under Chapter VII to authorise force if it is satisfied a case has been made (and the Council and others these days are quite properly giving increased attention, in relation to both WMD proliferation and terrorism, to circumstances in which such cases might be made). The question is whether military action in response to non-imminent threats can ever be taken unilaterally.

This is the question on which the U.S. has led with its chin, and generated a storm of continuing international controversy in the lead up to the 2003 Iraq war, in particular with the release in September 2002 of the National Security Strategy, arguing for a broadening of "concept of imminent threat to the capabilities and objectives of today's adversaries" and stating that "there is a compelling case for taking anticipatory action to defend ourselves, even if uncertainty remains as to the time and place of the enemy's attack".

The biggest problem with extending the scope of unilateral self-defence action under Article 51 in the way contemplated by the Bush administration is that it utterly fails to acknowledge that what is sauce for the goose is sauce for the gander, legitimising the prospect of preventive strikes in any number of volatile regions, starting with the Middle East, South and East Asia. To undermine so comprehensively the norm of non-intervention on which any system of global order must be painstakingly built is to invite a slide into anarchy. We would be living in a world where the unilateral use of force would be the rule, not the exception.

External Threats. When a state poses a threat to other states, or individuals outside its borders, the UN Charter fully empowers the Security Council to take any coercive action at all, including ultimately military action, that it deems "necessary to maintain or restore international peace and security". It doesn't matter whether the threat involves a "threat to the peace, breach of the peace or act of aggression"; whether it is occurring now, or in the imminent future or in the distant future; or whether it is constituted by an act or an omission; or whether it is constituted by the state's own actions or by non-state actors it harbours or supports.

Nor does it matter whether the threat is constituted by an actual or potential act of violence, or simply a challenge to the Council's authority. If the Security Council decides that a state is not acting in compliance with previous resolutions and for that reason alone, by putting the credibility of the Council's decisions at risk it is posing a 'threat to the peace' – whatever other kind of threat that state may or may not constitute – the Council is fully entitled to make that judgement and act accordingly.

Usually the only question – a huge one politically, but not legally-is how the unquestioned authority of the Council should be exercised, when the Charter offers no detailed criteria, when States see their interests so differently and when some States exercise so much more influence than others. There is growing acceptance that, as the Secretary-General said last September, that there may need to be 'early authorisation of coercive measures to address certain types of threats – for instance, terrorist groups armed with weapons of mass destruction'.

Internal Threats. While the UN Charter is as clear as it possibly could be on the question of external threats, it is much less clear about the right of collective action against a state when the only threat involved is to those within it: the issue of so-called humanitarian intervention. Article 2.7 expressly prohibits intervention "in matters which are essentially within the jurisdiction of any state", but this is in tension with language elsewhere acknowledging individual human rights, and with a mass of law and practice over the last few decades which have set real conceptual limits claims of untrammeled state sovereignty, not least the Genocide Convention.

What is clear is that the Security Council can always authorise Chapter VII military action against a state if it is prepared to declare that the situation, however apparently internal in character, does in fact amount to a 'threat to international peace and security'

– as it did for example in Somalia, and eventually Bosnia, in the early 1990s. For all practical purposes, threats to international peace and security are what the Security Council says they are. But more often than not, even in conscience shocking situations like Rwanda in 1994, it has declined to initiate or authorise any enforcement action at all. And that has led to a willingness, in cases where necessity seemed to demand, to bypass the Council, as in Kosovo in 1999, in ways that – if repeated – can't help but diminish its authority.

The need to actually mean it when we say 'never again' after each Cambodia, or Rwanda, or Srebrenica is in constant tension with desire of sovereign states not to see a diminution of their sovereign authority. The tenacity of that attachment can be seen to this day in the reluctance that has been evident in the Security Council to take on and hold to account Sudan for its contribution to the horrors continuing to unfold.

It was this to try to resolve this tension between the claims of state sovereignty and individual rights that the Canadian Government sponsored the International Commission on Intervention and State Sovereignty (ICISS), which I co-chaired with the Secretary-General's Special Adviser on Africa, Mohamed Sahnoun, and which produced its report, The Responsibility to Protect in December 2001.

The most groundbreaking contribution of the report was the its characterization of the central issue not as the 'right' of anybody to intervene, but rather the responsibility of the international community to act to protect a State's peoples when the State itself abdicated that responsibility, either through ill-will or incapacity. The ICISS Commission spelt it out in the form of two critical principles. The primary responsibility for the protection of a state's own people must lie with the state itself. But where a population is suffering serious harm, as a result of internal war, insurgency, repression or state failure, and the state in question is unwilling or unable to halt or avert it, the principle of non-intervention should lead to a larger principle, that of the international responsibility to protect. We had no doubt that the proper authority to authorise action in these circumstances was the Security Council, but had to face the problem that the Council has not always acted as it should in the face of conscience shocking violations of humanity. Our bottom line was that the task was not to find alternatives to the Security Council, but to make the Security Council work better. And that led us specifically to formulate a set of criteria for military action, which we argued strongly should be accepted at least informally as guidelines by the Security Council-and hopefully could ultimately become so embedded in practice that they assumed the status of customary international law. The 'responsibility to protect' principles were quietly gaining momentum in the academic and political debate, albeit rather submerged by the preoccupations with terrorism and WMD that emerged after 911. But they have been rather thrown off course by the emergence of the argument in relation to last year's invasion of Iraq – as other rationales in terms of bombs and terrorists dropped away – that it was Saddam's murderous tyrannising of his own people that made him a suitable case for humanitarian intervention treatment. The argument was a very strong one a decade and more ago, when Saddam was massacring Kurds in the late 80s and southern Shiites in the early 90s – as the world in both cases looked steadfastly the other way – but it had much less application in recent years, when no such catastrophe was occurring or imminent and, awful as it was, the Iraqi regime's behaviour was not much worse than a score or two of others.

It had all the appearance of a convenient rationalisation rather than genuine motivation, and certainly looked that way to those concerned, for good reasons or bad, about the potential overreach of the humanitarian intervention principle. Was Robert Mugabe to be the next case for military treatment, the ostensible rationale for the enterprise being not his current onslaught on democracy and human rights, but the slaughters in Matabeleland in the 1980s? The net result of all this was that an emerging international norm of real potential utility was once again struggling for acceptance.

INTERNATIONAL LAW AND PRE-EMPTIVE WAR

A strategy of addressing an emerging threat with a range of options including force was envisioned by the UN Charter. While traditional international law emphasized respect for state sovereignty by placing greater restrictions on the use of force, the literal language of the UN Charter has a more liberal standard when force is used under the auspices of the Security Council. For cases where force is used outside of the Security Council framework, it is not definitively clear whether under the UN Charter a state retains a traditional right of self-defense, including a right of anticipatory self-defense against an imminent threat, or if that right is curtailed to not include anticipatory self-defense. Some commentators argue that the UN Charter itself is no longer a valid source of international law, in which case a right of anticipatory self-defense would exist regardless and traditionally be limited to cases in which there is a threat of imminent attack.

Given the UN Charter's authorization of pre-emptive acts by the Security Council, ultimately the real division over pre-emption is not necessarily over pre-emption itself but over the multilateral framework under which it is carried out, who holds decision-making authority, and the extent to which those arrangements are codified and therefore rendered more stable and predictable. If the original concept of the Security Council was that the ad hoc coalition which won World War II would remain intact to stamp out future Hitlers before they reached a critical level of strength, historical changes such as the Cold War may have altered the course of that plan.

The right and obligation of a governing authority to use force to defend its citizens against an aggressor predates by centuries modern nation-states and modern international law. Christian just war theory, upon which the modern laws of armed conflict are based, recognized such a duty as early as the 4th Century. Since their emergence in the 16th Century, modern nation-states have been believed to hold such a right. While aggression is traditionally considered unlawful, and self-defense lawful, more problematic is the question of whether a first-strike could ever be considered a defensive act rather than an act of aggression. The right of anticipatory self-defense assumes that an aggressor is poised to strike, and that one acts defensively in anticipation of the attack rather than waiting for the attack to occur. Traditionally, it was deemed theoretically possible that even a first-strike could be deemed defensive in nature, and lawful, if it was to forestall an attack that was imminent.

The most widely accepted modern standard for anticipatory self-defense was articulated by U.S. Secretary of State Daniel Webster in diplomatic correspondence with his British counterpart over the *Caroline* incident (often mischaracterized as the *Caroline* "case") and consisted of two prongs. One was that the need to use force in anticipatory self-defense must first rise to the level of being a necessity, and one that is instant, overwhelming, and leaving no choice of means and no moment for deliberation. The other requirement was that the action taken must be proportionate to the threat and not be excessive.

Debate continues over the impact of the UN Charter on this area of international law. The UN Charter has a general prohibition against the use of force, but authorizes the Security Council to use force even in the absence of an act of aggression by the target, and permits unilateral and non-UN multilateral acts of self-defense under certain constraints.

With respect to the Security Council, the literal language of the UN Charter, in Articles 39, 41, and 42, envisions the use of a range of options, such as economic sanctions and varying degrees of force (e.g., blockades as well as all-out war) in response to acts of aggression, breaches of the peace, and threats to the peace. As a result, under the Charter force may be used against even a mere threat when authorized by the Security Council.

For unilateral acts and the multilateral use of force outside of the UN framework, Article 51 of the UN Charter refers to an inherent right of self-defense against armed attack, permitting defensive actions until the Security Council addresses the matter, and requires that such a defensive use of force be reported to the Security Council. The literal language of Article 51 seems to roll back the traditional right of self-defense, requiring that an armed attack have occurred before self-defense can be exercised, and implying that unilateral self-defense is an interim measure until the Security Council addresses the situation. Some commentators argue, however, that by referring to an "inherent" right of self-defense the UN Charter simply retains pre-existing international law regarding self-defense, including anticipatory self-defense. While it is not necessarily clear what role he plays in the matter, it appears that Secretary General Koffi Annan might hold the latter view, referring to states "retain[ing]" the inherent right of self-defense under the Charter.

To the extent the UN Charter can be deemed a relevant source of international law then some right of self-defense remains, which very well may include a right of anticipatory self-defense. At the same time, in international law, if a consistent pattern of state practice demonstrates a departure from preexisting norms, it can be argued that international law has changed. Some commentators suggest that state practice has indicated that with respect to the use of force the UN Charter no longer is a part of international law. If that is the case, then presumably international law would revert to the standard of anticipatory self-defense articulated by Webster.

The bottom line, then, is that with respect to anticipatory force exercised without Security Council authorization, either the UN Charter is essentially defunct with respect to the laws of armed conflict and the Webster standard continues, or the UN Charter is not defunct but retains the Webster standard, or that the Webster standard is displaced by a stricter standard requiring an armed attack to have occurred before one may invoke a right of self-defense. The prevailing view probably is that, one way or another, anticipatory self-defense is permissible but traditionally has required the existence of an imminent threat.

Another aspect of the UN framework, emphasized during the Cuban missile crisis, is that the UN Charter does permit regional security arrangements as long as they are consistent with the purposes and principles of the United Nations. However, the literal language of Article 53 requires that enforcement actions taken under regional arrangements not be initiated without Security Council authorization.

With respect to pre-emption, the National Security Strategy (NSS) issued by U.S. President George W. Bush itself does not necessarily significantly challenge prevailing international law. It rests upon a standard doctrine of anticipatory self-defense, and explores the question of when an attack is imminent. On its face it does not seek to overturn the rule, but to explore how the rule and its underlying purpose could be applied in particular situations not existing in the past.

One could argue that the rule does not actually require an attack to be imminent to act, but rather permits defensive measures to be taken before one passes a point in time when it is too late to prevent catastrophe.

The NSS focuses on several major considerations, one being that the imminence of a terrorist attack is much harder to detect, another being the fact that innocents are often targeted, and the third being the devastating impact of weapons of mass destruction (WMD.) While the text in the NSS relating to pre-emption does not necessarily limit its scope to WMD, it comes in a section dedicated to WMD.

Some commentators have suggested that WMD, and WMD proliferation, might be carved out as a special category under anticipatory self-defense. They argue that the right implied by anticipatory self-defense to act against a threat before it is "too late" may require setting a threshold in the context of WMD at some earlier point in the proliferation process, with that earlier point serving as the equivalent of the imminence of a threat. Such a point, it is argued, could represent the presence of a danger justifying a "defensive" first-strike, perhaps when accompanied by other factors such as a history of aggression, ties to terrorism, or certain criminal activities by the target regime.

Even if an exception were limited to WMD, or rogue state WMD, however, there still would remain the problem of setting a new and potentially destabilizing precedent, with the U.S. pre-emption policy serving as a basis for other countries initiating or threatening conflicts they might not otherwise have been emboldened to undertake.

Concerns over precedent highlight the fact that international law does in fact mean something, and serves more than simply a cosmetic role providing a rhetorical backdrop for actions taken for entirely different reasons. Whether in a local domestic context or the international arena, law and security go hand-in-hand to the extent that assumptions about reliable rules limit and guide conduct, if only by making more predictable its consequences. Countries do seem to care about what kind of reaction a particular course of conduct will bring. In two major wars, Korea and Gulf War I, the United States in hindsight was accused of having overlooked hints by the aggressors of their intentions, failing to respond strongly enough to the hints. International law can help serve to warn state actors what other states would think of particular courses of action, by clearly articulating norms of conduct and by drawing up more clearly defined parameters for joint action in response to unlawful or otherwise dangerous situations.

The Bush administration therefore faces an important challenge to articulate its own policies clearly and carefully, determine the extent to which the United States is willing to help contribute to the establishment of clear international norms, and explain whether and in what manner an international framework for decision-making will be honoured. Concerns expressed by allies over the shaping of pre-emption do not necessarily evidence an unwillingness to adapt shared understandings of law and security to changing circumstances. Rather, they reflect a fundamental appreciation for the prospect of a stable, effective and sustainable global security system in which the sole superpower ideally provides leadership that is clearly articulated, predictable, reasonable and promotes respect for the law.

The National Security Strategy calls for accurate, honest, and timely threat-assessments and coordination with allies, wisdom reinforced by the Iraq war. One of the biggest lessons from the Iraq conflict might not centre around what to call it (*i.e.*, pre-emption or something else) but rather the weaknesses inherent in relying on potentially flawed intelligence and the difficulties that could be posed in the future if a U.S. administration once again seeks to convince the citizenry and the world community to trust undisclosed information, or disclosed allegations resting on similar intelligence-gathering. Another lesson is that even the United States needs help dealing with a large and complicated problem, whether it is before, during, or after a conflict addressing what the Bush administration deems a grave and gathering threat.

In the past, Bush has been somewhat reserved with respect to his own presentation of a pre-emption doctrine, and his decision to lead a multilateral coalition against Saddam Hussein was presented with a tapestry of arguments among which were references to Security Council resolutions, the ongoing situation since the previous Gulf War, Saddam's ties to terrorists, and humanitarian concerns. Secretary of State Colin Powell also has adopted a multifaceted and internationalist approach, and recently articulated a view of pre-emption that was closely akin to traditional anticipatory self-defense, referring to taking action when "see[ing] ... a danger coming at you ...." Vice President Dick Cheney until recently adopted a more aggressive posture reminiscent of a Cold War ideology — "us good, them bad" — and the United States needing an unfettered capacity to take action anywhere at any time. Publicly, Cheney's focus seems to have shifted away from open support for pre-emption to the engagement of terrorists in an ongoing series of hostilities, the need to appraise the future of the system of global security, and the importance of democracy.

Important questions that must be answered include whether the world is safer with or without a strengthening of international law and carefully crafted international institutions restricting the use of force, and whether the United States is willing to provide the leadership it has demonstrated in the past in these areas.

At the same time, an examination of the global system of sovereign states might not be complete without a consideration of the rightful purpose of sovereignty itself, taken together with the more broad-based views of security expressed by the National Security Strategy, and Bush's decision to draw greater attention to the need to create a safer and more just world by promoting freedom and democracy.

Sovereignty was never appropriately meant to sanctify the frontiers of tyrants and prevent outside intervention against their crimes, but truly *is* meant to serve the cause of peace. The theoretical basis for having nation-states in the first place was the idea that power would be concentrated in the hands of the sovereign, rather than private armies, local warlords, and armed bands, and that sovereigns themselves would be limited with respect to the instances in which they would attack each other, with the overall effect of reducing the incidence of war and violence and thereby protecting innocent lives. This system has been challenged by the nexus of modern technology with the reemergence of warlords and private armies, but it also has been challenged wherever sovereignty rests on oppression rather than democratic legitimacy.

Security and the diverse realities impacting it encompass a growing range of concerns. The National Security Strategy with its consideration of the importance of development and trade relationships, the president's renewed focus on democratization, and an appraisal of the forces of globalization and the connection between terrorism and poverty all point to a new direction in security that is not simply based on force but most definitely is based on prevention. The key, however, will be to not simply be preventive, but to be proactive. To not simply put out fires and react to events, but to invest in human potential and human freedom, to promote respect for human life and the dignity of the human person, and to sign on for the long haul to create a world that is more free, more just, and therefore decidedly more secure.

Addendum

Since the drafting of this article, President George W. Bush delivered his London address of Nov. 19, 2003, in which he refrained from openly rearticulating a policy of pre-emption but did, in his second "pillar," voice the need for free nations to be willing as a last resort to use force to restrain "aggression and evil." While force employed in response to "aggression" could fall into the category of defense against an actual attack, using force to restrain "evil" seems a somewhat more nebulous concept, and Bush did not elaborate as to timing and circumstance. By referring to "free nations" in the plural, Bush did seem to continue a theme of multilateral action.

Efforts at multilateralism would be consistent with his first pillar, the need for international organizations to be effective at meeting today's challenges, with effectiveness measured by results and not just procedure. Bush recognized that global problems such as terrorism do require a global response. He pointed to the need for the United Nations to adequately address threats while also citing an American commitment to NATO, the need for security cooperation between the United States and the European Union, his multilateral approach to North Korea, and the importance of the International Atomic Energy Agency adequately addressing concerns over Iranian nuclear technology.

The question of "where to go from here" would seem to centre around working to build greater effectiveness for international institutions and frameworks for multilateral action, but the third pillar, the president's call for democratization, especially in the Middle East, also is noteworthy. The United States appears to be expressing contrition for past policies of building ties with regimes of less than stellar democratic credentials, and even more importantly to be focusing on policy directions which are not simply pre-emptive or preventive, but actually proactive. Just as at the conclusion of World War II the United States learned from the mistakes of the Treaty of Versailles, it appears that the United States once again is endeavouring to learn from past mistakes by focusing on longer-term goals, addressing the sources of instability and aggression, and aspiring to unite values with practical action by investing in human potential and cultivating the foundations of true peace. As Pope John Paul II cautioned in Coventry in 1982, peace is more than just the absence of war, and must be built thoughtfully and patiently over time. A sincere and farsighted approach to that principle, grounded in freedom, justice, and the rule of law, would appear to be the rightful mission of a United States that assumes a position of global partnership with other free nations.

8

Military Authority Diplomacy in South Asia

ASEAN has sought to restrain Chinese power by enmeshing it in regional institutions. Whereas ASEAN is attractive China to tame the aggressive realpolitik that has characterised Chinese foreign relations, Beijing views the same institutions as a way to extend its regional influence and has sought to exclude the US.

In planning for the first EAC summit, which was held in Malaysia, China tried to exclude India, Australia and New Zealand, but was overruled by Japan and ASEAN members. As China's regional influence grows, most ASEAN members are working to push against or balance Chinese power. While deepening trade and diplomatic co-operation with Beijing, many members, US allies such as Thailand and the Philippines, key 'swing states' such as Singapore, and emerging regional powers such as Indonesia, have also increased security ties with Washington.

The question is why the US has changed its policy in the region from a benign power to one almost squarely focusing on hard power balance issues including terrorism as the overall obsession. For Southeast Asia, long under the United States' political and economic influence, times are rapidly moving in a new direction. A decade ago about three-quarters of US investment in East Asia went to Southeast Asia. That figure has now fallen to 10 percent. Approximately 80 percent of US investment in East Asia now goes to China.

The United States remnants the region's single biggest destination for exports, and will be for some years to come. This is probably why the White House is on the defensive in terms of coming to grasp with the regional and multilateral setting in East and Southeast Asia. As one observer remarks: ''Relations between Southeast Asia and the United States are perhaps best described as 'a policy without a strategy''. Asian leaders are organizing and building new regional institutions precisely to avoid the sort of power politics that America is practicing. Progress has been tenuous but real, and most regional leaders are cautiously optimistic about Asia's future. As long as this remains true, American emphasis on balance-of-power politics will continue to meet with only limited success. Indeed, this approach is likely to be under-mined by regional players, who are more interested in participating in economic integration and building regional communities than in divisive balancing behaviour. Most troubling for the United States, it will also cede its leadership role in Asia and limit Washington's ability to influence the future shape of regional institutions in the region.

China's ultimate strategic purpose remains a subject of debate and speculation among analysts. Southeast Asia, in this respect, is the sole region adjacent to China in which Chinese influence can most easily expand. A benign interpretation would see China as simply cultivating the sort of stable, peaceful, and prosperous regional environment that is required for its own successful modernization. A more sceptical view sees China playing a long-term game designed to curtail American influence and weave a close-knit economic and security community with China at the centre.

Beijing is in fact using nationalism and the 'glories of the Chinese civilisation' to instil a sense of unity among Chinese nationals domestically and among the Chinese Diaspora in Southeast Asia. Although Beijing may acknowledge that rampant nationalism could pose a danger to its own internal stability, it has astutely harnessed it to build a new Asian pride and identity, which it hopes might help establish a new Asian system of politics, economics, security and culture within the 'ASEAN+3' framework.

The PRC ardently hopes this could be transformed ultimately into an East Asian Community under its leadership (Teo 2005). To realize its peaceful rise, China is using a sophisticated blend of trade, confidence building measures, and development assistance to establish itself as an important regional-cum-global leader.

Of course the appeal of Confucianism offers Beijing a definite comparative advantage in its soft supremacy approach. Moreover, the relationship China enjoys with the Chinese Diaspora in the region, who dominate the economic and, in some countries like Thailand, increasingly the political scene, is another advantage. The immediate implications of such an approach are that it would be naive to believe that China is not interested in exerting a dominant influence over its regional hinterland; commercial and financial muscle will eventually be the levers of choice, perhaps spearheaded by a strong regional currency. As much as the Chinese may be more ethnically exclusive than Americans and some Europeans, they are every bit as eager to see Chinese culture and traditions adopted by others - as a mark of civilization. As more and more Chinese tourists visit the region and even begin to dominate the tourist trade, the service sector response will be to tailor to Chinese taste and custom. This will inevitably result in a revival of Chinese culture and language in local communities once believed to have assimilated. Already one of the fastest growing Chinese language media groups is based in Malaysia, where Chinese language education has an unbroken history of more than a century. Up to the present, businesses have catered to a culture that projects modernity and sophistication in a Western guise - this could change and have an impact on U.S. and European influence.

The use of culture as a tool of diplomacy highlights the sense of theatre that China skilfully deploys to exaggerate kin, ethnicity and national bonds between the Motherland and the Diaspora. It also reflects an increased appreciation by the Chinese government of the importance of norms and soft power in diplomacy. Chinese print media, television, music, food, and popular culture are spreading around the region as never before. So, too, are Chinese tourists fanning out across the region, often filling the void left by American tourists staying home after 9/11, the Bali bombing, and tsunami; 800,000 Chinese toured both Thailand and Singapore in 2004.

In this way it is safe to say that ethnic Chinese business communities scattered in Southeast Asia have facilitated 'the rearticulation of mainland China into the global economy' not least through their reciprocal involvement in more than 100,000 joint ventures in China. It is also arguable that the Chinese Diaspora has been used not 'just as a financial resource in China to fund revolutions in the past and economic reforms in the present; they have been an important symbolic resource in the construction of Chinese nationalism'.

The combination of geo-political and geo-economic strategies and cultural expansion begs an answer to the question: 'what are the implications of China's policy of soft power for US influence in the region'? Elizabeth Economy notes the important point that, China's rise to date appears to be less about the 'inevitable conflict of rising power' theory, popular in some circles, than about creeping power transition.

Chinese thinkers, themselves, have recognized that the international community is concerned by the potential implications of China's rise and have taken pains to ensure that it will be perceived as non-threatening. This is well illustrated by Li Junru, Vice-President of the Central Party School at the Chinese Communist Party (CCP), who explicitly outlined the benefits to China's neighbours, stating, 'China's rise will not damage the interests of other Asian countries. That is because as China rises, it provides a huge market for its neighbours. At the same time, the achievements of China's development will allow it to support the progress of others in the region' (2005: 3-4). In order to understand the motives and objectives of Chinese pragmatism, it is important to put both bilateral and multilateral diplomatic initiatives and foreign policy into the overall trade and security context and understand the internal and external constraints for a Chinese expansive strategy in Southeast Asia. The region as a whole maintains a trade surplus with China of US$8 billion annually, largely from its enormous exports of raw materials and precision machinery. China also agreed to an 'Early Harvest Package' that is perceived by ASEAN as 'largely a concession' to provide benefits through tariff reductions on 573 products including agricultural and manufactured goods. Individual Chinese entrepreneurs are also now expanding China's economic reach throughout Laos and Myanmar.

In some areas, locals now use only the Yuan and speak Chinese. The forays of Chinese companies fit in with a broader strategic push by Beijing to establish closer economic cooperation with and among Asian countries. Unofficial reports by ASEAN officials claim that the foreign policy aim is part of a broader thrust by China to deploy multilateralism against what it sees as US unilateralist hegemony in the region and the world. 'This is a long-term game that China is playing,' says a senior ASEAN official. 'They want a situation in Southeast Asia that automatically takes into account China's interests. The whole objective of the policy is to avoid strategic encirclement by the U.S.'.

Critical voices note that ASEAN's trade with Japan of $136 billion and that of the United States of more than $136 billion in 2004 exceeds trade with China. At the same time, in both Indonesia and Malaysia, people complain that jobs are being lost to China. Not least because Chinese textile exports since January 2005 have increased, thus implying down-ward competition for Cambodia and Vietnam.

A growing mainland Chinese economic presence could also fuel latent resentment against the sizable ethnic Chinese economic elites in the region. In fact, almost no research has so far been done to investigate the impact of China's FDI on labour markets, environment and social issues and the question is whether China is exporting its own poor labour practices.

Factors inhibiting Chinese private investment and tourism are sensitive to the treatment of Chinese minorities in Southeast Asia and in particular in the Philippines and Indonesia. The Indonesian racial riots in the aftermath of the financial crisis in 1998 which targeted ethnic Chinese created long-term damage to the 'bamboo network'. There are also cultural impediments when it comes to expansion as noted by a senior ASEAN official: 'Unlike Americans, Chinese don't embrace foreigners - you cannot 'become Chinese''.

China's approach has been subtle, using soft power and economic diplomacy to build a benign multilateral framework in the shape of a free-trade agreement with ASEAN. 'China has shown a great deal of sensitivity,' says Singapore Prime Minister Goh Chok Tong. 'China realizes that it is a huge elephant, and even if it treads softly, it can still shake the ground.' One observer notes that 'China is seen by some to be slowly filling the vacuum left behind by the United States in the political, economic and security spheres in the region. This implies that 'U.S. Influence in Asia under Bush is Waning' (Agence France Presse, August 29, 2004.) and being replaced by China.

Beijing has also enthused the dynamics of regional cooperation in many other ways. One example is China's enthusiasm for developing the ASEAN-China dialogue into a vibrant web of multilevel and multi-sector cooperation. The 1997 financial crisis was the main catalyst for the creation of a full-fledged diplomatic mechanism spanning summit, ministerial, and senior official levels. As Cheng-Chwee notes, the mechanism has stretched into various semi-state and civil society organizations that include research departments, media outlets, youth organizations, and the business sector. Also cooperation in agriculture, transport infra arrangement, as well as energy has been included.

Over time, these ties have interwoven into a web of interdependence between China and ASEAN. The PRC has also taken the initiative in pushing for the creation of the Network of East Asia Think-Tanks (NEAT) (2005: 115). These moves are not merely tactical but part of PRCs overall goal to utilize the ASEAN-plus-three as the main vehicle of East Asian cooperation and the creation of the hybrid East Asian Community. Although there are other factors at play, China has played a decisive role in pushing in that direction. 'China's enthusiasm for East Asian cooperation is clearly driven by its aspiration to shape the direction of the existing regional institutions'.

Diplomatically, China's goals and vision in Southeast Asia are clear as it rivals the US and Japan worldwide and regionally. Moreover it may be again considering ASEAN as its own Monroe sphere, as it was during the 400 years of the Chinese tributary system under the Ming-Qing Emperors. Southeast Asian countries appear to be accepting sub-ordination as they seek to profit from the rising China.

AID, DIPLOMACY AND SOFT AUTHORITY

In early April, Premier Wen Jiabao conducted a four nation Asia-Pacific diplomatic tour that dealt with subjects of concern to China-Southeast Asian relations and included a two day visit to Cambodia (April 7-8). The tour also involved a visit to Australia marked by accords on Australian uranium exports to China; a visit to Fiji, where Wen attended the China-Pacific Island Countries Economic Development and Cooperation Forum, and advanced a range of policies promoting development of island countries; and a stop in New Zealand marked by legal, cultural, and educational accords. China concluded 60 bilateral accords during the trip. Wen sought in particular to establish a schedule for completion of the negotiations on China's proposed free trade agreements with Australia and New Zealand, which complement China's accord with Southeast Asian countries, the China-ASEAN Free Trade Agreement.

Earlier media reports disclosed that Wen also planned to visit Thailand on this tour but that visit was postponed because of the political demonstrations that ultimately resulted in the April 4 resignation of Prime Minister Thaksin Shinawatra. Thaksin developed close relations with China since assuming power in 2001. Official Chinese media avoided taking sides in reporting Thaksin's resignation, his assessment of his years as prime minister, and the charges made by opposition forces.

In Cambodia, Premier Wen and Cambodian Prime Minister Hun Sen witnessed the signing of 10 agreements including those dealing with a low-interest Chinese loan, grant aid, and the donation of 30 firetrucks by the Chinese government. Wen also attended a groundbreaking ceremony for a Chinese-funded office complex for Hun Sen and his deputies. The Cambodian leader predicted that "Cambodia will benefit greatly from this visit," and added that China is Cambodia's "most trustworthy friend." The Chinese government in the last decade provided grant aid, agreed to write off past debts, and granted tariff-free status for some 400 Cambodian items. Investments by Chinese companies were said by unofficial media reports to be worth $240 million in 2005, and were mainly in the garment industry, Cambodia's main foreign exchange earner.

The lengthy joint communiqué marking the end of the visit recounted Cambodia's appreciation of Chinese support and assistance, and China's appreciation of Cambodia's support for closer Chinese relations with ASEAN and Cambodia's opposition to Taiwan. There was no mention of their common interest in deflecting international criticism of their respective human rights practices, nor did the communiqué refer to their positions on long delayed international efforts seeking to bring to justice surviving members of the notorious Khmer Rouge regime that was closely aligned with China as it carried out policies resulting in mass deaths in Cambodia in the 1970s.

The devastating earthquake in Java, Indonesia in May saw a coordinated effort in the international community to provide humanitarian aid to the survivors and the Indonesian government. As international assistance efforts gathered pace, the Chinese government was quick to respond with a highly publicized contribution of $2 million in cash aid. It also pledged to send a 44-person team of medical and earthquake experts to Java.

The Chinese effort to highlight its contribution and seize media attention seemed reminiscent of the Chinese response to the tsunami that hit Indonesia, southern Thailand, and other parts of southern Asia in December 2004. Although Beijing at that time was relatively quick to react, its efforts were only a relatively small part of the international humanitarian and military assistance to the areas struck by the natural disaster. This time around, Japan led the efforts, with a pledge of $10 million. It sent in two medical teams. The U.S., in addition to $2.5 million worth of aid, also sent doctors and nurses from a military base in Okinawa. According to USAID, U.S. military personnel were also deployed to Yogyakarta, Indonesia, the city worst hit by the earthquake. On June 1, the U.S. Marine Corps Fleet 3rd Surgical Company set up a field hospital in Bantul District.

Beijing continues to make important strides in improving China's soft power and diplomatic image in Southeast Asia. Recent assessments in an article in the journal *Survival* and a policy brief released by the Carnegie Endowment for International Peace noted the success of Chinese economic development as a driver for countries in Southeast Asia and elsewhere, encouraging them to adopt similar improvements through market-style incentives in an authoritarian political system with features of a planned economy. Cambodia, Laos, and Vietnam were cited among admirers of the development policies and practices of their neighbor to the north. According to the assessments, these countries have adopted the Chinese model of market-based authoritarianism. Beijing's ability to present an alternative political and economic model is said to be a telling indicator of a growing Chinese ideological influence that is countering Western perspectives that insist democratic principles are a requisite for economic prosperity.

Recent polls conducted by *BBC World Service*, a Sydney-based Lowy poll, and the Pew Survey all point to a positive image of Chinese influence. China's charm is primarily focused on trade and a diplomatic agenda that looks at win-win collaboration. In an effort to allay regional fears of China's economic, political, and military clout, Chinese leaders use the guidelines of "do good to our neighbours, treat our neighbours as partners" (*yulin weishan, yilin weiban*) and "maintain friendly relations with our neighbours, make them feel secure, and help to make them rich".

China, the SCO Summit, and ASEAN contribution

Chinese commentary and official statements continue to show common ground in Chinese policies and practices with the two most important Asian regional bodies China works closely with, the Shanghai Cooperation Organization (SCO) and ASEAN. The annual summit and fifth anniversary of the Shanghai Cooperation Organization (SCO) was held in June in Shanghai, where it was first founded. With much pomp and circumstance, the summit marked the highlight of China's diplomacy during the quarter. Chinese President Hu Jintao rolled out the red carpet, welcoming heads of state from the member countries. Throughout the two-day summit, they were joined by leaders from neighbouring countries sitting in as observers, notably Iran, and by senior representatives from ASEAN as well as from the Commonwealth of Independent States. The Chinese hosts ensured seats for each and every regional actor at the working table.

Since its inception five years ago, the SCO has made steady progress in carrying out its mandate for closer regional cooperation on economic and political subjects. As a co-founder, China worked to create an organization where broad cooperation among all countries and regional organizations can be sought. It originally started with functional subjects including the demilitarization of the Chinese borders with Russia and involved Central Asian states, tackling drug trafficking, and boosting regional trade. It grew in prominence for efforts against other transnational subjects, notably terrorism.

For China and the Southeast Asian delegates, there was good reason to invite ASEAN representatives to the 2006 Shanghai meeting. Last year, Philippine President Gloria Arroyo, among others, proposed that Southeast Asia should also look into collaborating with other regional organizations in Asia to combat terrorism, a transnational threat that observes no borders. In response to ASEAN's request, and with the convenience of playing host to this year's summit, China had the ASEAN secretariat as its guest of honour to further discuss joint efforts between the SCO and ASEAN to counter terrorism.

Assessing China's Increase

The U.S. and other international media covered Chinese leaders' visits along the lines of past coverage that emphasized how rapidly China has risen in influence in Southeast Asia and the broader Asia-Pacific region, and how this has undercut U.S. influence in the area, even with close U.S. allies like Australia. Even though Chinese leaders have been at pains to emphasize China's intention to rise "peacefully" and to avoid significant competition with the United States, China's economic growth, burgeoning trade, and adroit diplomacy were depicted by the media as more than a match for U.S. policy and behaviour, as the U.S. leadership was seen as distracted and hampered, its focus on the war in Iraq and the broader war on terrorism. More in-depth assessments by prominent international observers and analytical publications provided greater balance in examining strengths and limitations of China's rise in Southeast Asia, and their implications for U.S. leadership in the region, however.

The American Enterprise Institute and National Defence University published in 2006 the findings of the final conference in a year-long series of seminars and meetings dealing with China in Asia and focusing on China's rise in Southeast Asia and its meaning for the United States. The findings showed that China's economic and military power is increasing, that many Asian countries (especially in Southeast Asia) are accommodating China's increasing influence, and that the U.S. lacks a clear Asia strategy that would be useful in supporting U.S. objectives in the region.

At the same time, the findings showed that while attentive Chinese diplomacy has alleviated regional fears, China's long-term ambitions remain a concern for many countries. A prominent Philippine expert at the meeting was reported to emphasize that his government reacts to China's rise by "hedging," and Manila's alliance relationship with the U.S. is used to balance Chinese influence. A specialist from Thailand explained the balance in Bangkok's relations with China and the U.S. He showed that the level of Thailand's trade with each country is about the same; Thailand runs a trade deficit with China that offends some Thai farmers in particular; and China's policies on Myanmar and Chinese immigration are significant irritants in Thai-Chinese relations. Also this quarter, the academic journal *Asian Security* published what may be the most comprehensive and up-to-date assessment in the fast-growing list of analyses dealing with China's rising influence in Southeast Asia and what it means for U.S. influence. On the one hand, it highlighted evidence that Chinese polices and behaviour have reduced the worries of Southeast Asian governments over Chinese intentions. Southeast Asian government leaders more often refer to China as an opportunity than a challenge, and they express frequent appreciation for Chinese actions seen to benefit Southeast Asia. Chinese trade levels with Southeast Asia have grown rapidly and seem likely to continue to grow strongly, adding to China's importance to the region. On the other hand, the article cautioned that it is easy to exaggerate China's influence while underestimating the continued power and influence of other regional actors, notably the United States. There remain long-term concerns in Southeast Asia over whether a more powerful China may decide to try to more assertively increase its influence or even try to dominate the region. According to the article, a prevailing Southeast Asian view is that it is too early to declare that China has proved itself to be a good neighbor, though it has become a better neighbor whose recent contributions to regional peace and prosperity make Southeast Asian representatives more hopeful for the future. Meanwhile, Southeast Asian governments see a variety of significant obstacles to continued improvement in China-Southeast Asian relations, and welcome the continued prominence in the region of the U.S., Japan, and other powers seen as providing balance to China's rise.

The article noted that even in the area of trade, where China's growing role has been most pronounced, few Southeast Asian countries conduct more than 10 percent of their trade with China. The level of Chinese-Southeast Asian trade, after many years of rapid growth, only now is approaching and/or surpassing the level of Southeast Asian trade with Japan and with the U.S. Meanwhile, growing Southeast Asian trade with China depends heavily on U.S. and European consumers purchasing products from China with components and materials from Southeast Asia. China remains a small investor in Southeast Asia, especially in comparison to the U.S., and a small aid donor to Southeast Asia, especially when compared to Japan.

Chinese military ties with Southeast Asia are very small in comparison with the robust and recently enhanced wide range of U.S. military exercises, exchanges, training, and other activities with a broad range of Southeast Asian counterparts. The asymmetry in Chinese and U.S. influence in this area was graphically illustrated in their respective responses to the tsunami disaster in South and Southeast Asia in December 2004.

Apparently taking a cue from Chinese leaders' visits and attentive diplomacy, Japanese and U.S. leaders have joined with Indian, Russian, and European representatives in showing greater interest in and more frequent visits with counterparts from Southeast Asia. All of these powers, along with Australia and New Zealand and with the exception of the U.S., welcomed the opportunity to participate with Southeast Asian leaders in the East Asian Summit of December 2005, even though doing so was at odds with China's initial efforts to restrict the summit to members of ASEAN Plus Three.

The *Asian Security* analysis found few direct unenthusiastic implications for U.S. interests flowing from China's growing relations with Southeast Asia. The main exception was China's support for Myanmar and for authoritarian governments in Laos, Cambodia, and Vietnam, which is at odds with U.S. efforts to promote democracy abroad. It saw little grounds for the fear of a China-dominated economic regionalism in Southeast Asia; the trading and investment environment is too competitive and China's position too small and dependent on the United States and others to allow it. U.S. alliances and military relations with Southeast Asia seemed secure as Southeast Asian governments generally welcomed the greater U.S. military activism in the region, and China adopted a moderate stance on U.S. military activities in the interest of convincing U.S. leaders of China's commitment to rise "peacefully." China-ASEAN improvements also have reduced the danger of regional conflict and helped U.S. interests in secure sea lanes and regional stability. According to the article, Southeast Asia's growing interest in China ties should not be interpreted as welcoming China's dominance; most ASEAN states welcome closer ties with the U.S., Japan, India, and others as a means to keep the region stable and independent of any one power's dominance.

Meanwhile, the assessment saw several serious obstacles to China forward momentum in relations with Southeast Asia. Economically, Chinese competitiveness in world trade threatens to leave even some advanced Southeast Asian economies behind, or to relegate them to the position of suppliers of raw materials to the fast-growing Chinese economy. This asymmetrical relationship could lead to serious resentment and backlash from nationalistic Southeast Asian governments. China's growing military power and growing energy needs could prompt disputes with Southeast Asian neighbours over disputed territory similar to the disputes raging between China and Japan today. Assertive Chinese actions against Taiwan, even if provoked by pro-independence leaders on the island, would endanger Asian stability and probably lead Southeast Asian leaders to seek closer ties with one another and other powers, notably the U.S. Meanwhile, Chinese leaders clearly resent Japan's efforts to compete for influence in Southeast Asia, and they may not adjust gracefully to intensified involvement in the region, encouraged by the ASEAN members, of India, Australia, Russia, and the U.S.

CHINA'S DIPLOMACY FOR THE 21ST CENTURY

"Doing our own business well first" – this is one of the admonitions left to the Chinese people by Deng Xiaoping, the designer of the improvement and opening up of the contemporary China. It is also the most direct and the simplest expression of "development demand". The half a century history since the founding of New China has proved that if the domestic economic construction and the improvement of the living of the people do not receive enough attention, the foreign policy of peace and independence would often than not remain empty and powerless, without the social base to last. Only when the domestic economy has developed and the political situation and the relations among all nationalities are kept stable, is it possible for diplomatic work to acquire a solid base. The main threat to China's state security comes not from foreign invasion or other wars, but from within, that is, whether or not China itself can maintain a stable, orderly and healthy development.

The "internal weakness" exhibit by Russia in the Kosovo subject has fully testified to this point. The most profound lesson taught by Russia is: first, a country must first of all manage its own affairs well so as to make it hard for potential or realistic enemy or rival to "penetrate" by exploiting the weakness. It is a common sense that flies hover over only rotten eggs. The fundamental destructive factor to the death of a big country lies not in external sources but the inner problems in the deep layers of the society. It is impossible to wipe out a big country. Its decline often starts from within, from the roots, say national separatism or economic stagnation or political turmoil or social disorder, for if a country were thrown into confusion, it would fall apart without being attacked.

The Russian arena over the recent decade has exactly been experiencing every process of "national split—economic stagnation—political upheaval—social disorder". The serious "internal weakness" displayed before the nibbling by NATO is due, essentially, to the "internal war" without the smoke of gunpowder. If asked what we should learn from Russians, it is very simple to answer: it should not be soft toward separatists and, even more important, there should be no internal political strife or social disorder; economic development must not stop and the improvement and institutional improvement should not be interrupted. Stability of a country and growing national strength constitute the corner stone for the security of the country and a major source for having a say externally and exert international influence. "The easiest way to capture a fortress is from within". Without internal security, there would be no defending the state security to speak about, let alone safeguarding it.

It should be stressed here that in spite of the grave negative developments like Kosovo crisis, the relations among big powers have become more dependent upon each other while their relations are growing more complicated and delicate. The globalization process of the economy and science and technology has not been slowing down and the global scientific and technological creation is becoming more active than ever before. The economic growth of most countries is still strong. The world's economic aggregates are still growing. What is the most important is that the comprehensive judgment from all features shows that a worldwide nuclear war or a world war with the involvement of all major countries in confrontation could be prevented for a considerably long period of time to come.

All countries will seize the time to develop their own economies, science and technology and boost their national strength and make great efforts to improve the living of the people and infrastructure facilities. Recall that during the recent 200 years, China has in most part been in a state of being bullied and humiliated or in an intense period of mobilization for "war and revolution". It did not make any real development and construction until only in the recent 20 years. But the short span of 20 years has brought about a tremendous leap forward: the country walked out of the shadow of exhaustion in the motive forces for economic development; the GDP has ranked among the first ten in the world if calculated according to the exchange rate; till today, the Chinese people are continuing to realize the most massive economic growth in human history (a country with a population of 1.2 billion has expanded its economy at an annual rate of 8% within 20 years). To look forward, even in another 20 years, not to say in another 100 years, if China should maintain the speed of the last 20 years and "concentrate its efforts on economic construction", the Chinese people have every reason to expect that the country will reach the level of a middle-developed country in per capita average and secure a place among the top three in the world in total aggregates. By then, China would have a significant say in the international affairs and the new international political and economic order will be most likely to develop toward the direction we expect.

Before talking about a methodical change in the current international relations or about making greater contributions to the external world, the Chinese people must have a sober estimation of themselves. It should be admitted that, after half a century construction, especially the rapid development over the recent 20 years through improvement and opening up, our comprehensive national strength has ascended a new stair and our international status and influence have grown greatly, China remains a developing country, still trailing behind other countries in many areas and still a far cry as compared with developed countries.

This manifests itself not only in the "hardware", such as the per capita GNP, the living standards, development of roads, the modernization of educational facilities and means of information, labour productivity and product quality, and the proportion in the global trade and investment, but also in "software", such as institutional creation, comprehensive quality of services, understanding of the external world by the average people, the attractiveness of the whole country to foreign resources (including materials and intelligence), the general level of theoretical studies and the capability of keeping track with the advanced world levels.

The strength of software includes the strength in political and social development and in theory and also the following factors: (1) the domestic political, social and economic system arrangements that are open, stable, lasting, and absorbing; (2) powerful culture, political and ethical appeal and rallying power; (3) theoretical guidance; (4) strategic insight and diplomatic skills; (5) effective domestic and international management, including the effective mobilization of domestic and international resources (especially non-military resources; (6) the populace of high educational level and strong cultural awareness; (7) high level of living standards. It is a long way to go for China to acquire such strength. Economic and military strength cannot substitute for the powerful political and social base". Historically, the contemporary China has not and will not possibly have what it used to experience in the heydays of Han and Tang dynasties.

Ever since the modern times, it has been in "tight operation" economically, socially and politically. As the changes in the economic structure advance simultaneously with the changes of the whole social and political system, the awareness of opening up grows together with the growth of the awareness of nationalism. The whole country has grown rapidly, but with problems cropping up one after another and a large number of troubles put on the agenda before the problems left from the old system had not be rooted out, such as bankruptcy of enterprises and workers thrown out of jobs, the regional economic and educational disparities, corruption and the so-called "crises in belief, credit and confidence". The problems in themselves have already restricted its power of influencing the world. If no steps are taken to deepen improvement and opening up, no efforts are made to continue the great development, stopping there, rest contented, the prospects of China and the world would not develop toward the direction in our favour. In this sense, the focus of China's diplomacy for a quite a long period of time to come still remains to be on the creation of a neighbouring environment favourable to China's improvement, development and stability and on meeting the major demands of economic construction. Unless major wars break out not to our liking, there would be no reason to change the priority of this demand.

The above essentials show that what is referred to as "development demand" is much richer and much more extensive in content than what we used to construe or disseminate in the past. For instance, economically speaking, the Chinese people have basically realized a "comfortable living". But when measured by fairly comprehensive standards, China needs more profound political democracy and legal construction and needs the synchronization of the development of spiritual civilization (belief, ethics and values) and material civilization, needs more rational and smooth run-in between the stratification of the society and the various interest groups, needs more Chinese people who have broader and more lenient insight on the world, and needs greater development of the strategic thinking and theoretical nature about China's international relations. The term "Development" covers political development, the development of civilization, social development and development of values. Under the precondition of making economic development the central task, the development in all features mentioned above will greatly help China to raise its status and power of influence internationally in the new millennium and that will naturally provide more solid base for China's diplomacy to display its prowess.

MILITARY DIPLOMACY AND CHINA'S SOFT POWER

The majority significant developments in this quarter included China's military activism and greater emphasis on "soft power" diplomacy. Assessment of the high-level China-Southeast Asian interchange shows that while China's influence is rising, Beijing continues to face several constraints and limitations in allaying Southeast Asian governments' concern about its long-term intentions.

On April 13-15, Chinese Defence Minister Gen. Cao Gangchun visited Malaysia, Singapore, and Vietnam to enhance military cooperation between China and Southeast Asia. With more than

70 percent of Chinese imported oil coming through the Malacca Strait, China's national security interests and stakes in Southeast Asia are rising. According to the People's Liberation Army's (PLA) *White Paper on National Defence* in 2004, the defence of sovereignty, territorial integrity, and "maritime rights and interests" were all classified as "national security goals." China may be regarded as a rising continental power, but its vast coastline makes it an important maritime nation as well.

Cao's visit reflected a low-key approach that endeavored to minimize regional concerns about rising Chinese military and other power, and to seek greater common ground with neighbouring countries. Outwardly, Cao's trip to Southeast Asia amounted to little more than observations of the various military camps and establishments in Singapore, Malaysia, and Vietnam. Cao's dialogues with his counterparts were said to include clarifying growing U.S. military involvement in Southeast Asia. There were no formal joint statements subjectd at the conclusion of the Southeast Asian leg of his trip.

This Chinese military activism comes at a time of greater U.S. military involvement in Southeast Asia and is seen by some observers as a sign of a continuing Chinese interest in regional strategic adjustments and realignments, especially with countries that provide military access to the United States. Singapore's close military relationship with the U.S., for example, gives U.S. warships a convenient entrance to the region. Meanwhile, Singapore's training fields in Taiwan (not to mention Lee Hsien Loong's visit to the island in 2004 before he was prime minister) are also a cause of concern for Beijing.

As for the Malacca Strait, the longstanding problem of piracy on the high seas is a looming concern for China. The disruption of China's energy supplies would be a great detriment to its burgeoning economy, and Cao's visit highlighted China's willingness to step up its effort to cooperate with Singapore and Malaysia in patrolling the Malacca Strait. In Vietnam, Cao's visit was said to include consideration of Cam Rahn Bay. The port facilities at Cam Rahn include two well-paved runways, a deep-water port, and a large storage site for petroleum. Due to its close proximity to Hainan Island, Cam Rahn Bay is strategically located to monitor and intercept communications in the southeastern coast of China. China complained for years over the Soviet Union's use of the base against China's interests, and presumably would oppose any U.S.-Vietnam military cooperation that would involve U.S. use of the base.

According to a report subjectd at the Aspen Institute Congressional Conference on U.S.-China Relations in April, China's military modernization – especially the PLA Navy's capabilities to secure "blue water" naval surface fleet – is a trend that will continue unabated and a reality with which countries in the region and the U.S. will have to come to terms. China continues to reassure its neighbours that its rising military and other power will not endanger their interests as Chinese officials remain well aware of the concern among many Southeast Asian governments regarding China's long-term intentions.

Shangri-La Conversation

Despite Cao's visit and other military contacts with Southeast Asia, China once again chose to participate at a minimal level by sending a nonministerial delegation to the annual Shangri-La Dialogue in Singapore in June. As a result, China missed an opportunity for close consultations on maritime security with countries with most important trade routes passing through Southeast Asia and littoral states in the region. The military chiefs at the conference introduced and institutionalized several mechanisms to combat terrorism and piracy on the high seas through the strengthening of multilateral coastguard patrols, enhancing naval surveillance systems and sharing data, and revamping the littoral states' navies. The conference also included a Malaysian proposal for a regional disaster-relief centre to coordinate military and civilian aid in emergencies. The U.S. proposed closer military cooperation between countries in the Asia-Pacific region two years ago. Efforts by involved Southeast Asian states to strengthen naval cooperation are welcomed by the U.S. and defence ministers from other parts of the world as they pledge to provide greater technical and monetary assistance to Southeast Asian navies and militaries. China's conspicuous absence at the conference implied that it may not feel comfortable with military cooperation that so prominently involves the U.S.

INDIA FALLING BEHIND CHINA IN SOUTH ASIAN DIPLOMACY

India has always been a local superpower, being by far the largest country within South Asia, and is, in fact, the only one in the group that borders every other South Asian country except Afghanistan, which shares a border with Pakistan. But India's economic performance was stunted by years of state control of the kind now prevalent in Iran. Over the past 15 years, however, economic growth has been strong, enabling the country to have a much greater diplomatic reach than at any time since the 1950s when India briefly emerged as the leader of those countries that were being de-colonized by the European powers. Given this situation, it ought to have been the case that New Delhi would be preeminent in its own backyard. Instead, over the past two decades, India has lost the status of being the lead player in any South Asian country barring Bhutan, a country with which it still has a treaty relationship. In almost the entire region, China has overtaken India in that intangible quality - influence - especially in Nepal and Sri Lanka, while Beijing's existing alliances with Pakistan and Bangladesh are growing stronger.

This is not due to a lack of quality within India's diplomatic service. Instead, the Indian Foreign Service (IFS) has produced a modern corps of skilled diplomats, many experts in different regions of the world, and eager to do more to advance their country's interests. The wall they face is the ambivalence that has become second nature to the country's top policy makers, both within the political crust as well as the administrative backup. Phrases such as "going all the way" and "going for the kill" are inelegant. Yet they represent a reality that is that sometimes a country has to formulate and then determinedly implement a clear policy to be carried out till success is achieved.

In South Asia, such a quality was recently displayed by President Percy Mahinda Rajapaksa of Sri Lanka. He succeeded in wiping out the terrorist group known as the Liberation Tigers of

Tamil Eelam (LTTE) where, over the past three decades, all his predecessors had failed. Unlike them, President Rajapaksa did not heed (well-meaning but disastrous) advice to slow down his offensive or agree to a cease-fire, the latter being a device that the LTTE used since 1987 to gain time to recover after having lost the initiative in the field. Once the LTTE recovered its strength, the ceasefire would be abandoned. This point was repeatedly made by Rajapaksa to the peacemakers who clustered around him, especially in the final months of the brief, brutal war against the LTTE that began with his coming to office in 2005.

Once India, because of political considerations such as the need to avoid alienating the country's sizable Tamil population, refused to give the Sri Lankan army equipment, Rajapaksa turned to Pakistan and China. Both countries opened their warehouses to him, and so built up immense capital both within Sri Lanka's Sinhala most importantity as well as the country's policy establishment. Rajapaksa showed none of the half-heartedness that has characterized so much of Indian policy and, as a result, emerged a winner. In the case of India, the desire to win brownie points with key international players (by heeding their sometimes incorrect advice) as well as an aversion to risk ensured that much of Indian diplomacy was too watered down to be effective. This is especially the case in its immediate neighbourhood.

This on-again, off-again excellence can be seen in Indian diplomatic policy towards Pakistan especially in regard to the long-term pattern of instituting confidence building measures (CBM) being followed - usually after a mass terror attack - with strong rhetoric and a withdrawal of contact. The reality is that in the case of Pakistan, conventional war may have ceased to be an option. This is because the Pakistan army has itself lost control of many of the jihadis that it has trained, equipped and funded for so long.

Instead of reducing the risk of a terror attack, going after the Pakistan military would inflame a large segment of the Pakistani population thus making them susceptible to recruitment in the ongoing jihad against India. Given that situation, it may have been preferable for Indian policymakers to publicly resort to a conventional war except in the case of a conflict started by Pakistan, an unlikely possibility. The military option would work only if (a) the Pakistan army controls the jihadi networks and (b) is comprehensively defeated in battle. Neither condition exists.

A "No War" declaration by India would remove the Pakistani military establishment's most frequently used excuse to station more than 60 percent of its army along the India border, even as the force is engaged in a life-and-death struggle with the Pakistan Taliban. Instead, even though New Delhi has no intention of going to war, the prospect of one is deliberately kept open especially after terror strikes such as Mumbai 11/26-28. Thus, the benefits of India's "No War" declaration are denied, while the other side is aware that the mock-aggressive posture is a bluff and hence will not change its behaviour as a result of the threat.

A glaring example of how promoting the idea that India would go to war over Pakistani provocations has hurt New Delhi can be seen in the 2002 standoff with Pakistan in the mountains separating the two. Ostensibly to scare the international community into putting pressure on Pakistan to call off its Kashmir jihad, the then-Vajpayee government mobilized two Indian army strike corps on the border, keeping them and their support units on a hair-trigger alert for the greater part of the year. Aware that the Indians were bluffing, the Pakistan government refused to budge from its policy of helping jihadists active in Kashmir. The long Indian army mobilization created a perception of regional instability that affected India's status as a safe investment destination even as it exhausted the elite army units on the front line. Given the information that India would not attack, the 2002 mobilization came at a horrendous cost and no benefit. In a system where posturing comes easily to the higher levels of the Indian policy establishment, Prime Minister Manmohan Singh has thus far resisted jingoism and has made it evident that India would not be stampeded into military action. In the case of Sri Lanka, the policy was to intensify conflict until victory. What is needed is a clear policy that is carried out effectively, not a zig-zag routine that confuses the international community and results in a loss of credibility for India.

Military sales can become an effective instrument of diplomacy, were they deployed by India. Within the region, including in Sri

Lanka and Nepal, the military is a significant component of the policy process, often the crucial player. Because of New Delhi's longstanding policy of not permitting foreign military sales save for exceptional situations, China has been provided an opportunity to fill the gap. Had Bangladesh, Nepal and Sri Lanka been more reliant on Indian equipment and training for their armed forces, New Delhi would have been in a much stronger position to influence policy in those places than it is today. Instead, the "weapons gap" isincreasingly being filled by China.

The mantra of "non-alignment" has in most instances become a cover for lack of action. Even during the period of the Cold War, when India suffered many of the consequences of being seen as a Soviet ally, not a single Soviet soldier was ever stationed in India or trained here, nor did any Indian soldier undertake any sort of mission in the USSR. In contrast, there are regular exchanges of U.S. and Indian soldiers and joint training exercises have become routine. The warming of ties is because there is a natural fit between the two sides. India has a significant pool of trained (and trainable) manpower, while the United States has abundant stocks of equipment that could be transferred to New Delhi rather than mothballed or left under-utilized. This is especially the case with naval vessels, where India is now being made to pay $3 billion for a secondhand Russian aircraft carrier that it is finding it difficult to float and move at the same time.

Progress in U.S.-India military to military relatives has been slow and is still far below its potential in substantial part because of the wariness of the Indian establishment over China's reaction. Compare this with Pakistan which has built up close military ties with both China and the United States, its friendship with one not affecting the other. In the military field, the choice is between going with the United States or going alone, because a military alliance with China is not an option. Beijing sees New Delhi as a potential competitor and has repeatedly shown through its actions its commitment to a strategic policy that inhibits the growth of Indian power. Unfortunately, in this case, Indian ambivalence is now being matched by the United States under the Obama administration, which has downgraded ties with India to a level much below that set under President George W. Bush. It seems inevitable, however, that both countries will, hopefully within the present presidential term, awaken to the need for a partnership that can ensure that Asia does not fall under the sway of any single power.

The persistent Indian ambivalence in policy was visible in Sri Lanka, where India simultaneously called for a cease-fire while backing the unity of the island nation. As a consequence of simultaneously conveying two contradictory messages, neither the Tamil nor the Sinhala zealots have anything other than distaste for India, while the abundant provision of military supplies has led the Sri Lankan military towards becoming as close to Beijing as are their counterparts in Pakistan.

In Nepal, after first helping to get King Gyanendra to abdicate, New Delhi threw its support behind the Maoists, who promptly reacted by threatening to scrap the India-Nepal agreement and replace it with a similar deal with China. After its embrace of the Maoists, which ended only after their tilt to Beijing became manifest (by the end of 2008), no other Nepali party is willing to trust New Delhi and see it as a reliable partner, even the once-friendly Nepali Congress.

Meanwhile, in a show of deft footwork, Chinese diplomats have been active in Kathmandu renewing ties with the non-Maoist parties that today run the government (after the departure of the Maoists), so as to accelerate the growth of PRC influence in Nepal.

Today, there are almost as many radical training camps located within Bangladesh as there in Pakistan, camps whose specific purpose is to replenish the stream of jihadis into India. Yet, unlike in the case of Pakistan, the Indian government is not posturing as if was is likely. A hostile Pakistan, an unfriendly Bangladesh, and Nepal and Sri Lanka heading towards the PRC. These are the wages of a diplomacy that refuses to go for the jugular in the pursuit of objectives, but almost invariably crafts a compromise that gives much less geopolitical benefit. India presents an example of how a most important power that avoids a clear policy line or a better deployment of its assets gives way to the other who is ruthless and willing to complete the marathon rather than slow down and stop before the finish line. Such a policy is the delight of politicians and anathema to statesmen, who understand the need for not just vision, but for will and perseverance.

THEORETICAL SUPPORT OF CHINESE DIPLOMACY

Surly there are some typical resources in terms of which China lays its diplomatic philosophy on the foundation—pluralism. Due to the diversity of resources, not only the practical and objective factors but also the historical and subjective ones should be taken into account. In general, the resources or roots of pluralism as Chinese diplomatic philosophy are in relations with Chinese traditional culture with tolerance, its modernization in the making, nation-state system it faces and particular development routine since 1980s.

Chinese Traditional Culture's Deep Power

It's self-evident that a country's diplomatic features are absolutely influenced by its national culture which not only provides a potential model of the diplomatic practice but also influences the decision-makers who are in charge of national diplomacy. As one country with five thousand years' continuity of statehood and civilization, China's diplomatic philosophy of course should be shaped inescapably by its national traditional cultures. It's very complicated to sort the contents of a culture with a long history, and to examine the influence of each factor of the culture on national diplomatic features, yet it's easy to examine the potential influence of only one factor of the culture on diplomacy. As for China, tolerance as one outstanding factor or feature of Chinese culture has powerful influence on China's foreign affairs.

If tracing back to 2000 B.C., a kingdom called Xia Dynasty ruled one small part of today's China in Yellow River region. After Xia was ended then Shang (also called Yin) Dynasty followed. In that time, Shang kingdom long-drawn-out its territory and created the most primitive Chinese words based on which the recorded history of Chinese civilization was emerged. Shang classified the people living in the world (all under the heaven) into two kinds and five sections, the Chinese (living in Shang, the world centre) and the barbarians which consisted of four ethnics—Yi (in the East), Rong (in the West), Di (in the North) and Man (in the South). When the political legitimacy of the last king of Shang Dynasty was suspected by his people due to his cruelty and inability, one Rong's tribe led by Gi Fa then in the name of the Heaven *(Ban)* called all the people under the heaven to fight against Shang king's ruling. Finally this tribe from western barbarians defeated Shang and built a new dynasty called Zhou, a kingdom that influenced Chinese culture strongly, especially on morality very deeply. It can be concluded that the early Chinese history mirrors one outstanding feature of Chinese culture—openness—not only Chinese living in "world centre" but those Barbarians could govern China, then the feature was consolidated by the following centuries.

For example, as one kingdom located in the China's periphery, Qin was recognized by other Chinese kingdoms as one barbarian-like regime in the Rong district. Yet finally this kingdom unified all parts of China and erected a powerful empire—Qin Dynasty which influenced and shaped Chinese cultures deeply, especially in fields of bureaucratic politics and social systems. Generally saying, the openness and incorporation of Chinese culture is due to the helps of the communication and even marriages among different ethnics. In Chinese history, there are several times in which the minority of Chinese ethnics becomes the ruling people, all of whom inescapably not only accepted the core of Chinese culture but also contributed some typical cultures of their own into Chinese civilization.

In accordance with this constant incorporation of diverse ethnics' cultures, the openness of Chinese culture was kept very well and finally made this culture become one of important and famous cultures in the world. Clearly, this honesty directly leads to emergence of tolerance which doesn't permit those extreme and fundamentalist ideologies to grow and boom in China. For this reason, it's hard to find the persecution within different religions as well as the authority's terrible persecution on religious groups in China. The terrible conflicts between two most influential religions, Buddhism and Daoism, never happened. In reality, some Buddhists were Daoists at the same time. In one famous Chinese classic master, Journey to the West, recorded one interesting story in which the Buddha had helped the Yu Emperor, one God of Daoism, to defeat one monkey monster, that is, the Buddha and Yu Emperor are friends.

Then how was this tolerance functioned in ancient China's foreign affairs? This question could be answered by the example of tributary system which had been run for almost fifteen hundred years in East Asia.

The China-centred tributary system was the overriding international system in which although China was the dominant power, those neighbouring countries as China's vassals could keep their domestic systems well and would not be interfered by China if they could showed their respects for China by visiting Chinese emperor's court regularly. Only those that were invaded by foreigners or suffered from serious civil conflicts would be intervened by Chinese officials or militaries in order to restore their domestic orders and regional stability. In a sum, Chinese influence on its neighbouring vassals' inner affairs not by political and military approaches but simply by Chinese cultural charm.

At present, after a terrible so-called immense Cultural Revolution (1966-1976) which damaged traditional culture badly, and after a new round westernization since 1979 which faded the influence of Marxist ideologies on public daily lives, the renaissance of Chinese traditional culture in the beginning of the 21 century seems become a tendency that is firstly emerged in civil society and gradually supported by Chinese government. In terms of the restoration of traditional culture, Chinese diplomacy will be partly shaped by those ideas including tolerance.

China's Modern Statehood is in the Creation

As a state on the road to modernization, China must defend its sovereign independence, and the idea of pluralism just can legitimize the sovereign independence. Strictly speaking, China started modernization in each facet in 1912 when the Republic of China (ROC) was built in Nanjing city. Perhaps the idea of modernity was emerged in China in the late of 19 century when a Westernization movement for China's richness and strength was taken place by top-down approach and on the one hand, a vacillating political democratization and de-feudalization was also happened before the building of ROC. However, the most influential enlightenment movement was the "May 4" which deeply impressed Chinese common people by the idea of democracy and the spirit of science or rationality.

Unfortunately, this enlightenment group was broken off by Japan's invasion of China in period of 1931-1945. Then, after three years' terrible civil war (1946-1949) between Kuo Min tang (KMT) and Chinese Communist Party (CCP), the People's Republic of China (PRC) was built in 1949, and since this year, a new enlightenment movement started, based not on liberalism such as electoral democracy and capitalist economy but on Marxism. When leaders started the reform and openness policy in 1979, Chinese government never forsakes the political slogan—Four Modernizations (in fields of industry, agriculture, national defence and science & technology).

Up to now, China is still addressing to two tasks—nation-building and state-building. For a very long time, Chinese as a nation is not a traditional idea for Chinese people. In Chinese traditional culture, to be a Chinese was not a difficult thing if one got ready to accept Chinese culture and Chinese identity, although the person was a barbarian or had very different blood from that of most of other Chinese people. "Before the nineteenth century, when China was still an empire, nationalism did not exist. The Chinese political elite begin to embrace modern nationalist doctrines for China's defence and regeneration only after China's disastrous defeat by British troops in the 1840-1842 Opium War, which led not only to the eventual disintegration of the Chinese empire but also to the loss of national sovereignty to imperialist powers". There are many different ethnics in ancient China, yet after the building of ROC, all these ethnics were grouped into one nation—Chinese *(Zhonghua Minzu).* Within about 100 years (1912-2009), Chinese as a integrated modern nation is still in problem. Some ethnics living in Northwest and Southwest China don't have the strong Chinese identity. The policy towards almost all minority ethnics is actually undermining the Chinese identity and consolidating those minority ethnics' identity, though this policy is somehow necessary for some reasons. Simultaneously, China's political reform is still not foreseeable in recent years, which means democratic transition is not finished although to some degree it has begun with two typical processes—so-called "inner party's democratization" and "grassroots democratization". In economic field, a capitalist market's construction was started in 1980s and accelerated in 1990s after Deng Xiaoping visited South China in Spring of 1992, and most importantly, China as one big economy has entered the World Trade Organization (WTO) in 2001. However, an integrated national economic market is still a myth rather than a reality by virtue of the imbalance of regional development and the unclear role of government in economic field.

Meanwhile, citizenship authorized by the Constitution always cannot be safeguarded for the immatureness of rule of law. Social justice in some cases cannot be defended and restored well when some citizens are bullied by some others. Citizenship is abased by the societal stratification especially in 21 century when political corruption and the combination of officials and capitalists become more and more serious social problems. Additionally, because of Taiwan's separation from Mainland, Chinese territory is not unified and some people of Tibetan and Uygur at the same time request for their independence. Clearly, a territory-divided country is hard to be recognized as a nation- or modern state. The state-building is also still in the making.

Westphalia System and result of the Cold War in East Asia

In East Asia, after the collapse of China-centric tributary system in the late of 19 century, the international relations were suffered from the unrest situation. After the end of the World War II, the Cold War followed. After the Cold War was finished, potential regional conflicts were still there. It can be said so far as to now, Westphalia system is the dominant international system in East and Northeast Asia where each country doesn't have the power and legitimacy to dominate other countries and keep regional stability by hegemonic approaches. All of them have to protect national interests and prevent sovereign independence by self-helps, except for Japan and South Korea which can resort to allies with US to defend their security. China's potential conflicts with its neighbouring countries such as Indonesia, the Philippines, Vietnam, Japan and North Korea are only under the surface and seem very difficult to be solved. Although the Taiwan Cross Strait relations look alleviated after Ma Ying-jeou came to power in Taiwan, no one can makes sure that this good relations between two sides can be kept perpetually. National security of China is not better than we imagine and China's defence power has to be enhanced partly for these potential conflicts.

Additionally, the aftermath of the Cold War isn't disappeared in East and Northeast Asia because of the US military presence in Japan and South Korea and the existence of so-called North Korea's nuclear issue. It were surprised that US-led military and supporting allies with Japan and South Korea don't collapse but ironically are strengthened after the end of the Cold War in 1990s. It's well known these allies were resulted from the Cold War and their roles were to prevent Japan and

South Korea from being attacked and invaded by their imaginary enemies—China, Soviet Union and North Korea. After the end of the Cold War, NATO in Europe gradually changed its roles from preventing Europe from Soviet's invasion to functionalist responsibility for European security. But both the aim and role of these two allies in East and Northeast Asia are not changed at all. By virtue of the presence of Westphalia-like system and influential aftermath of the Cold War in East and Northeast Asia, to defend national security is a key task for China's government. Self-help is available and not obsolete for China even in the age of economic interdependence and globalization. Under this condition, it's very significant for China to adhere sovereign independence and non-intervention.

China is to Some Degree an Exceptional State

This conception is rooted in typical Chinese history and complicated reality. Historically, CCP in its early time had considered China as a very typical country whose revolution for democracy ought not to be similar to that of Russia. For CCP, Chinese revolution could be successful as long as it was relied upon a road of "cities should be enclosed by countryside and power should be seized by weapons", which is thoroughly different from Lenin's road in Russia. After People's Republic as a socialist country was built, Chinese government smartly used nationalism as one of dominant ideologies to start social mobilization and as one useful ideological weapon to fight against Soviet Union's Chauvinism in 1960s-1970s and against western liberalism in 1980s-1990s.

As regards of practice of Chinese foreign policy, especially after 1979, China's government initiated the reform and openness policy aiming at building socialism with Chinese characteristic, a very particular socialism differed from any others in the world. From the mid-1990s, China started to build market economy in the name of socialism, although for many scholars, the market economy should only depend on capitalism. Moreover, in accordance with long human being's stories, the rising of any power in the world always was accompanied with regional or global conflicts, yet Chinese government argued that China will select a way of peaceful rising or peaceful development, fighting against hegemonim.

When Washington Consensus was scolded when Asian monetary crisis was broken out in 1998, Joshua Cooper Ramo published his famous reporter on Chinese typical experience which was concluded by him to be one term—Beijing Consensus. Although this idea was debated hotly in academic cycle but Chinese government kept silent. Exactly to say, Beijing Consensus was not accepted by Chinese government since this term or idea indicates China could be a model for other developing countries on the road to modernization. For Chinese government, China is an exceptional country whose road of rising cannot be copied by others. In general, the particular continuity of Chinese civilization in last five thousand years, the success of typical road to revolution for neo-democracy in 1920s-1950s, and the recent rising relied on an exceptional approach that only Chinese uses in the world encourage the Chinese and its government to consider China as an particular country.

9

Constitution Apply to Rights of Military

The rights of military members and civilians on a military installation can vary significantly from your basic Bill of Rights protections. In some respects, the military is legally obligated to provide additional protections to military members suspected of criminal wrongdoing. But in other respects, even basic rights against unreasonable searches and seizures are virtually non-existent. I'll examine many of the basic rules and rights in a military context.

Searches

Anyone (civilian or military) entering a military installation should assume their vehicle and person will be searched. The law permits random inspections of all compartments of a vehicle upon entering a base. Furthermore, unlike in the civilian system where there has to be probable cause to pull you over in the first place, everyone entering an installation will be required to speak with the gate guard. It's typical that, at this point, the guard identifies their probable cause for additional search of the vehicle or your person (i.e. probable cause for DUI). Keep in mind that military police have a very specific interest in protecting the installation from terrorist and domestic threats. If you're uncomfortable with a search that's being performed at the gate or upon a traffic stop, be clear that you are not consenting to a search — but expect that the search will either continue or you'll be escorted off the installation.

Military members do not have the same rights against police searches of their home without a warrant as civilians. Specifically, military members who are housed in dorms, barracks, or deployed housing are subject to inspection. Commanders have wide latitude to order that barracks/dorm rooms be inspected to ensure unit readiness and good order and discipline. The right to order "inspections" may not be used as subterfuge to search a specific individual's room that is suspected of criminal conduct. It's also important to note that a military member inside their barrack/ dorm room is not protected from warrantless arrest (called apprehension in the military). Military police, or command representatives may enter a room to execute their duty to apprehend or issue other lawful orders to a military member (i.e. report to the commander's office).

Military offices, computers and emails are subject to virtually no protections. For instance, a commander is generally fully within their rights to enter your office, search drawers and your computer hard drive without your permission. Keep in mind these searches may take place after hours and without your knowledge. Furthermore, you should assume that even personal computers or devices that are left in your office are subject to be searched without a warrant.

Military members that reside in on-base housing have significantly greater protections from intrusion from the government. Once junior military members are released from their obligation to live in barracks/dorms, they are given an option to rent on-base housing. Command has virtually no ability to order inspections without a warrant being issued in on-base housing. Civilians inside the home cannot be arrested without an arrest warrant or their willing departure from the premises. Military members, however, may be ordered to report to their commander's office or the military investigator's office, even without a warrant.

Your on-base home is not entirely free from the risk of unwelcome inspection. Since the government is essentially your landlord, they may have rules and regulations that permit quarterly or yearly inspections to ensure the property is being properly kept. Furthermore, command may have the right to enter the premises to conduct "health and welfare" checks similar to the warrantless searches on the civilian side by agencies such as the Department of Child & Family Services.

Military members that reside off base have the constitutional protections against unreasonable and warrantless searches and seizures as any other civilian. The only real exception being that a military member may still be ordered to report to a commander's office or law enforcement office without an arrest warrant being issued.

The key with any search on or off a military installation is to be clear that you are not consenting to a search. After making clear that you do not consent, remain silent while they perform their duty. Do not answer questions like, "What are you hiding?"

Counsel & Remain Silent

The military offers significantly greater protections from self-incrimination and the right to counsel than in the civilian system. Article 31 of the UCMJ (Uniform Code of Military Justice), goes significantly beyond the normal Miranda protections. Miranda warnings are only required if a person is in custody by police, but in the military, Article 31 rights must be read at any time. If any military member suspects that another military member may incriminate himself or herself in the course of a conversation, an Article 31 warning is required. Article 31 permits an individual to remain silent. It also permits the right to request legal representation, and informs that such legal representation will be provided for free for any military member that requests it.

It is absolutely critical to assert your rights when you are warned. One of the downsides of your rights being read at the immediate onset of a conversation is that it may seem like it isn't a very serious issue. There may also be a strong impression that your command expects you to speak and that your silence will be used against you. Most commanders are very sensitive to your constitutional rights and will not use your silence or assertion of right to counsel against you in any way.

Law Enforcement Tricks

Just as civilian law enforcement has many tricks they may use to gather evidence against you, so too do military law enforcement agents. Here are a few of the favorites: Driving you to the "police" station. Often investigators will have a senior member of the chain of command drive you to your interrogation. This creates the impression that you are not free to leave and that you are being ordered to cooperate. This is a step to assert control.

Small talk. Prior to the interrogation beginning, agents love to small talk, making you think they're your friends. They can small talk before reading rights since it isn't about something potentially incriminating. Over the years, I have watched hundreds of interviews, and it never ceases to amaze me how well this technique works. They are not your friends. They are not trying to help you, or get you out of trouble, no matter what they tell you. They have a job to do, and your confession is another notch on their belt. Appeal to Integrity & Core Values. Once the interrogation really begins, the agents will focus in on your weakness – your strong sense of integrity and values. Military members have the words "integrity", "honesty", "core values", and similar trigger words beat into them from day one at boot camp. These concepts are critical to a strong military force, but in the interrogation room, it is used as a tool to manipulate suspects. "Does is seem like you are using integrity by not telling us what happened?" "Your commander will look at whether you used integrity and honesty when he decides what to do." These types of questions and comments almost always get the agents the confession they are looking for.

Lies & More Lies. Law enforcement agents are permitted to lie to suspects during interrogations. This trick is permitted equally on the military and civilian side. Be very cautious about believing the elaborate details of the agent's investigation when they are trying to get your confession. They will tell you your friends have turned you in, and that they've collected evidence against you, even though it's all a lie.

MILITARY INTERVENTIONS IN POLITICS

A Cross-national Comparison

Military interventions in politics are very common both in democratic or totalitarian regimes. Although the involvement of the military in determining who gets what, when, and how is too apparent, the issue has not been studied well enough. Students of politics and public administration, up to now, focused generally on individual cases or with regional perspectives while studying military interventions.

The main role of the military as a bureaucratic organization is to defend the country against external threats. The military bureaucracies are expected to carry out defense policies formulated by legislative and executive branches. However, in developing countries, the military has had some other functions like contributing to development (Heper, 1973), and protecting the regime from internal and external sources, etc. The distinctive characteristic of military bureaucracy from civilian bureaucracy with more hierarchic, authoritative, and a legitimate source of coercion make it easy for them to influence political institutions.

The national guard function of the military makes it very powerful, and sometimes unquestionable. For example, in Turkey, criticizing the military can easily be recognized as a crime assuming that as an assault of Turkish Military Identity. Even in developed countries, although the military is restricted to national defense and obedient to the civil authority, it still has significant influence on the governmental policies. Halperin (1975) notes that even in the USA, the military poses a unique set of problems for presidents. Another author (Fourney, 1977) states that no individual can have a significant effect on military budget. The military has almost complete discretion in their specialization or professional area, and this is accepted as normal in a certain extent even in developed countries.

Some authors (Mayer & Burnett, 1977) argue that the military is a major institutional interest group in the industrial world deserving of particular attention, especially in third world countries. What does the military do as an interest group? In this context, the military establishes some institutions or groups. For example, veterans send informal messages to the related offices/officers or agencies etc, to influence their policies.

Military interventions in the form of a coup or military regimes are the most extreme forms of the military having an impact on the policy process. We can define a coup as an irregular transfer of the state's chief executive by the regular armed forces or internal security forces through the use or threat of the use of force (Jenkins and Kposowa, 1992). By means of military interventions, the military wants to control the policy process largely. Hence, the military uses either legislative or executive power or in some cases judiciary power. With military interventions, the military not only changes the executive or legislative powers of government but also tries to exert strict control over other interest groups or society.

THEORIES ON MILITARY INTERVENTIONS

Explaining military interventions is not an easy task, because they are results of a complex mix of historical, political, economic, personal, military, social, ethnic, and cultural factors. Although some authors argue that military interventions are random phenomena unrelated to the structural characteristics of societies and international settings (McGovan and others, 1984), many structural theories see the causal relations to explain military interventions in politics. Different approaches can be brought together in several categories: (1) socio-economic development, (2) political development, (3) the centrality of military, (4) conflict, and (5) regional differences.

Socio-Economic Development

One of the most common arguments relates the propensity of military intervention with socio-economic development. Finer (1988) argues that the density of military interventions is more likely to decrease with increased socio-economic development status. Nations with high socio-economic situations have higher urbanization, industrialization and literacy level, and so have increased mass participation into the social activities (Putnam, 1967). Socio-economic development creates awareness of political events and capacities for political actions. In other words, it increases the number of potential political actors and diffuses increased political resources to these actors who would be willing and able to sustain civilian institutions. On the other hand, the industrialization diminishes the propensity for military interventions since the increased socio-economic complexity puts public administration beyond the skills of armed forces.

Gorman (1967) states that military interventions generally take place in countries of lower income status. According to economic dependency arguments, economically out-dependent countries that are not self-sufficient have more coups where there is sometimes very violent internal competition for very limited internal sources. Likewise, Jenkins and Kposowa (1990) argue that foreign debt problems contribute to coup.

Political Development

The other set of variables that explains military interventions, although related but distinct from social and economic development in a certain extent, can be grouped under the heading of political development. Strong civilian governmental and political institutions, democratic values, and so forth can be indicators of political development level.

THE CENTRALITY OF MILITARY

For the centrality of the military approach, the greater the resources and the cohesion of the military, the greater the likelihood of interventions are (Mayer and Burnett, 1977). One view emphasize the sectoral interests of the military, treating the military as a potentially parasitic institution which, given its centrality to the state's claim on legitimate violence, is prone to use this to dominate politically, and especially if civilian institutions are weak (Jenkins and Kposowa, 1992).

The stronger the military's resources, either as a percent of state resource or relative to the national economy, the weaker the institution of civil society and thereby the greater the probability of military interventions. Several studies have found that larger armies and those with greater claims to the government revenues have been more coups prone. A second view argues that a centralized chain of command, military discipline, and extensive communication make military officers a cohesive group, capable of organizing effective seizure (Finer, 1988).

MYANMAR'S MILITARY USES POLITICAL FORCE TO BLOCK CONSTITUTIONAL CHANGES

Myanmar's military flexed its muscle on Thursday, blocking moves to rescind its veto power in Parliament and refusing to ease a rule that helps prevent Daw Aung San Suu Kyi, the opposition leader and Nobel laureate, from eventually becoming president. The votes in Parliament, although not unexpected, were a reassertion of military power in Myanmar, which was ruled for five decades by the armed forces but has been experimenting in recent years with a more open and democratic system.

Under the Constitution, which was written by a junta, the military controls a quarter of the seats in Parliament, enough to block any amendments to the charter. One vote on Thursday rejected a proposal to allow the Constitution to be amended with 70 percent of votes in Parliament instead of the 75 percent required now, which would have effectively removed the military's veto.

Lawmakers also struck down a motion to amend a clause in the Constitution that bars anyone whose spouse or children have "allegiance to a foreign power" from becoming president or vice president. Ms. Aung San Suu Kyi's husband, who died in 1999, was a British citizen, and so are their two sons. She would have remained ineligible even if the vote had passed, however, because the proposal would have removed only the clause relating to a candidate's spouse.

The votes on Thursday do not preclude Ms. Aung San Suu Kyi's party, the National League for Democracy, from winning an election scheduled for this year. The Nobel laureate remains popular in the country, and her name — as well as that of her father, Aung San, the country's independence hero — remains the most recognizable in the land. Members of her party said after the vote that their campaign to elect Ms. Aung San Suu Kyi as president was not over.

"We expected we would lose this vote," said U Win Htein, a member of the party's central executive committee. "We will continue campaigning within Parliament and outside the Parliament. At the very least, we will be showing people we are trying to amend a Constitution that they don't want." Ms. Aung

San Suu Kyi, who holds a parliamentary seat, took part in Thursday's votes.

Analysts believe that her party could have significant bargaining power in the days after the election, which is expected in late October or November. Parliament selects the president and vice presidents after the election, setting the stage for political haggling between the opposition and the military establishment. Critics say Myanmar's military has been out of sync with the democratization of the country. Military commanders have begun offensives against a number of armed ethnic forces, even as peace talks have continued. Those talks now seem unlikely to produce a national cease-fire that the government of President Thein Sein has been seeking.

On Wednesday, a military representative in Parliament defended the army's prominent role in the country in a speech accompanied by a slide show of tanks and heavy artillery. "It is necessary to keep the Myanmar military in the legislative and administrative sectors in order to protect and stand by the country in its time of need," news outlets in Myanmar quoted the lawmaker, Tin Soe, as saying.

The reassertion of military power has given rise to pessimism among those who had hoped for a swifter emergence of civilian control over the country. "Judging from the votes today, Daw Aung San Suu Kyi should rethink whether she should contest the elections at all," a political commentator, U Yan Myo Thein, said Thursday. "There's no hope that she will become president."

MYANMAR MILITARY RETAINS VETO AFTER CONSTITUTION CHANGE VOTE FAILS

A move to amend Myanmar's constitution to remove the military's legislative veto on key decisions fell short of the required 75 percent support in parliament on Thursday, preserving the armed forces' powerful political role in the Asian nation. The result was no surprise given that a quarter of the seats in the house are, by law, held by the military, which ruled Myanmar for half a century until 2011. The proposal aimed to trim the share of house votes needed to amend the constitution to 70 percent.

Another vote on a clause that effectively bars Nobel laureate Aung San Suu Kyi from becoming president also failed. The motion voted on would have only partially amended that article, however, meaning the 70-year-old democracy icon would still have been ineligible had it been passed. Suu Kyi, whose National League for Democracy (NLD) won the last free election by a landslide in 1990 - a result ignored by the junta - cannot become president because her two children are British citizens, as was her late husband.

The NLD suffered persecution under the former junta and says the military's ability to shoot down changes to the constitution puts a limit on democratic reforms in Myanmar, where a general election is expected in November. Critics see it as an enshrined safeguard to protect the armed forces' sizeable economic and political interests.

Suu Kyi said the outcome was of no surprise and it was "obvious" the military would not support amendments. The vote, she said, showed the electorate which forces in politics were for or against progress in Myanmar.

Bibliography

Ajey Lele: *Strategic Technologies for the Military : Breaking New Frontiers*, Sage, Delhi, 2009.

Arend, A.: *International Law and the Use of Force*, London, Routledge, 1993.

Ashton, S.R.: *British Policy Towards the Indian States, 1905-1939*, London, Curzon, 1982.

Barua, Pradeep: *Gentlemen of the Raj: The Indian Army Officer Corps, 1817–1949*, 2003.

Bassiouni, M. Cherif: *International Criminal Law*. New York: Oxford University Press, 2008

Bouchet-Saulnier, Francoise, Laura Brav: *The Practical Guide to Humanitarian Law*, Lanham, MD: Rowman & Littlefield Publishers, Inc., 2007.

Chesterman, Simon: *Just War or Just Peace: Humanitarian Intervention and International Law*. New York: Oxford University Press, 2003.

Credi, A.: *Molecular Devices and Machines: a Journey into the Nano World*, Weinheim, Wiley-VCH, 2003.

Damrosch, L.F.: *Law and Force in the New International Order*, Boulder, Westview Press, 1991.

Dixit, A.K. : *Military Wars and Rescue Techniques*, Cyber Tech Pub, Delhi, 2010.

Dixit, Prabla: *Communalism: A Struggle for Power*, New Delhi, Orient Longman, 1981.

Duffy, Helen: *The 'War on Terror' and the Framework of International Law*. Cambridge, UK: Cambridge University Press, 2005.

Erickson, Richard: *Legitimate Use Of Force Against State Sponsored Terrorism*. US Air War College, 1989.

Friedman, G.: *The Future of War: Power, Technology and Western Military*, N.Y., Random House, 1996.

Gray, Christine: *International Law and the Use of Force*. Second edition. New York: Oxford University Press, 2004.

Gupta, Asha: *Military Rule and Democratization : Changing Perspectives*, Deep & Deep, Delhi, 2003.

Guy, Alan J.; Boyden, Peter B.: *Soldiers of the Raj, The Indian Army 1600–1947*. National Army Museum Chelsea, 1997.

Heathcote, T. A.: *The Indian Army – The Garrison of British Imperial India, 1822–1922*. David & Charles. Newton Abbot, Devon. 1974.

Holsti, K.: *The State, War, and the State of War*, Cambridge, Cambridge Univ. Press, 1996.

Huntington, S.P.: *The Soldier and the State*, N.Y., Vintage Books, 1964.

Jackson, Major Donovan: *India's Army*. Sampson Low. London, 1940.

Juvale, R.P. : *Military Strategy and Diplomacy*, Cyber Tech Publications, Delhi, 2010.

Lele, Ajey: *Strategic Technologies for the Military : Breaking New Frontiers*, Sage, Delhi, 2009.

Mary, W.: *Military Space Force: the Cultural Dimensions of Authority*, Cambridge, Belknap Press, 1985.

Nayyar, A.K. : *National Security : Military Aspects*, Rupa, Delhi, 2003.

Noorani, A.G. : *Indian Political Trials : 1775-1947*, New Delhi, Oxford University Press, 2005.

Posen, B.R.: *The Sources of Military Doctrine*, Ithaca, 1984, Cornell Univ. Press.

Prahlad, K.: *Governance and Public Administration for Poverty Reduction*, Salvador, Brazil, 1997.

Reydams, Luc: *Universal Jurisdiction: International and Municipal Legal Perspectives*. New York: Oxford University Press, 2005.

Rudolph, Heimanson: *Dictionary of Military*, N.Y.: Oceana Publications, 1967.

Schabas, William A.: *An Introduction to the International Criminal Court*. Cambridge: Cambridge University Press, 2007.

Suresh Goel: *International Encyclopaedia of Military, Security and Intelligence Agencies*, MD Publications, Delhi, 2009.

Victor G. : *Law as a Political Instrument*, New York, Random House, 1955.

Walker, Clive: *The Prevention of Terrorism in British Law*. New York: Manchester University Press & St. Martin's Press, 1992.

Weeks, John: *World War II Small Arms*, New York: Galahad Books (1979).

Ziring, L.: *An Introduction to Asian Politics*, N.J., Prentice-Hall, 1977.

Index

❑❑❑